Critical Acclaim for
FODOR'S AFFORDABLES

"The Fodor's series puts a premium on showing its readers a good time."

—Philadelphia Inquirer

"Concentrates on life's basics...without skimping on literary luxuries."

—New York Daily News

"Good helpmates for the cost-conscious traveler."

—Detroit Free Press

"These books succeed admirably; easy to follow and use, full of cost related information, practical advice and recommendations...maps are clear and easy to use."

—Travel Books Worldwide

"The books can help you fill the gap between deprivation and ostentation when you travel."

—Dawson Sentinel

Fodor's Affordable Paris

FIRST New EDITION

Portions of this book appear in *Fodor's Paris*

Fodor's Travel Publications, Inc.
New York • Toronto • London • Sydney • Auckland

ISBN 0–679–02605–3

First Edition

Fodor's Affordable Paris

Editor: Suzanne De Galan
Editorial Contributors: Bob Blake, Alice Brinton, David Downie, Sandra A. Gustafson, Corinne LaBalme, Valerie Martone, Sheila Mooney, Robert Noah, Marcy Pritchard, Alexandra Siegel
Creative Director: Fabrizio La Rocca
Cartographer: David Lindroth
Illustrator: Karl Tanner
Cover Photograph: Michael Howell/Photonica

Design: Vignelli Associates

Special Sales

Fodor's Travel Publications are available at special discounts for bulk purchases for sales promotions or premiums. Special editions, including personalized covers, excerpts of existing guides, and corporate imprints, can be created in large quantities for special needs. For more information, contact your local bookseller or write to Special Markets, Fodor's Travel Publications, 201 East 50th Street, New York, NY 10022. Inquiries from Canada should be directed to your local Canadian bookseller or sent to Random House of Canada, Ltd., Marketing Dept., 1265 Aerowood Drive, Mississauga, Ontario L4W 1B9. Inquiries from the United Kingdom should be sent to Fodor's Travel Publications, 20 Vauxhall Bridge Rd., London SW1V 2SA.

MANUFACTURED IN THE UNITED STATES OF AMERICA
10 9 8 7 6 5 4 3 2 1

Contents

Maps and Plans

How This Guide Will Save You Money

The Affordables are aimed at people like you and me—people with discriminating tastes and limited budgets. This is a new series that combines essential budget travel information with quality writing, authoritative hotel and restaurant reviews, detailed exploring tours, and wonderful maps. The idea behind these guides is that you, the budget traveler, have the same curiosity, good taste, and high expectations as those who travel first class, and you need information with the same depth and detail as readers of Fodor's gold guides. But as a budget traveler you also need to know about low-cost activities, meals, and lodging, and especially how to get around by train or bus.

Some of you, of course, will spend a bit more on a hotel with full service and amenities but will eat simply; others will be willing to go the hostel route in order to splurge on meals; yet others will save by sticking to public transportation and picnic lunches in order to do some serious shopping. We've tried to include enough options so that each of you can spend your money in the way you most enjoy spending it.

These are not guides for the hotdog-on-the-run-its-okay-to-sleep-on-a-park-bench crowd, but for those of you who insist on at least two good, healthy meals a day and a safe, comfortable place to put your head at night. The hotels we recommend offer good value, and there are no dives, thank you—only clean, friendly places with an acceptable level of comfort, convenience, and charm. There's also a wide range of inexpensive and moderately priced dining options. Equally important, the Affordables organize all travel according to convenient train and bus routes, and include point-to-point directions that get you to each town and attraction. We even locate train routes on maps—a feature you won't find in any other budget guide.

Fodor's has made every effort to provide you with accurate, up-to-date information, but time always brings change, and consequently the publisher cannot accept responsibility for errors. Hours and admission fees in particular may change, so, when it matters to you, we encourage you to call ahead. We also encourage you to write and share your travel experiences with us—pleasant and unpleasant. When a hotel or restaurant fails to live up to its billing, please let us know, and we'll investigate the complaint and revise our entries when the facts warrant it. Send your letters to The Editor, Fodor's Affordables, 201 East 50th Street, New York, NY 10022.

Have a great trip!

Michael Spring
Editorial Director

Fodor's Choice
for Budget Travelers

No two people will agree on what makes a perfect vacation, but it's fun and helpful to know what others think. We hope you'll have a chance to experience some of Fodor's Choices yourself while visiting the City of Light. For detailed information about each entry, refer to the appropriate chapters within this guidebook.

Views

The back of St-Gervais-St-Protais church from the Seine (angle of the Quai de l'Hôtel de Ville and rue des Barres)

Ile de la Cité from the Pont des Arts

The towering twin columns of place de la Nation from the Cours de Vincennes

Paris spread out beneath the Sacré-Coeur at Montmartre

Notre Dame from the Square Jean XXIII

Walks

Along the banks of the Seine between place de la Concorde and the Ile St-Louis

Along the Canal St-Martin in east Paris

Around the banks of the Lac Inférieur in the Bois de Boulogne

From the Arc de Triomphe to the Louvre, via the Champs-Elysées, place de la Concorde, and the Tuileries Gardens

Monuments

Arc de Triomphe

Eiffel Tower

Louvre's glass pyramid(s)

The bronze column on place Vendôme

Museums

Musée d'Orsay

Musée Rodin

Musée Marmottan

Musée des Monuments Français

The Louvre, with plenty of time on your hands

Churches

Notre Dame Cathedral

St-Germain-des-Prés

Sainte-Chapelle

St-Eustache

Dôme Church at the Invalides

Restaurants

Le Grizzli (under 250F)

Le Petit Bourbon (under 250F)

Mìravile (under 250F)

Pharamond (under 250F)

Aux Fins Gourmets (under 175F)

Le Petit Plat (under 175F)

Baracane (under 100F)

Le Petit St-Benoît (under 100F)

Hotels

Elysa Luxembourg (under 750F)

Marronniers (under 750F)

Place des Vosges (under 500F)

Grands Ecoles (under 500F)

Argenson (under 500F)

Castex (under 300F)

Shopping

Rue d' Alésia (discount clothing shops)

Trocadéro–Victor Hugo area (secondhand shops)

Réeiproque (resale clothing)

Rue Lepic, rue de Buci, and rue Mouffetard (street markets)

Poilâne bakery

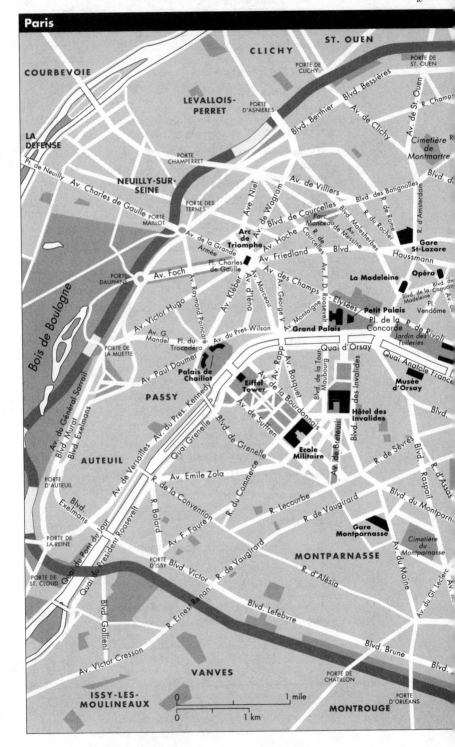

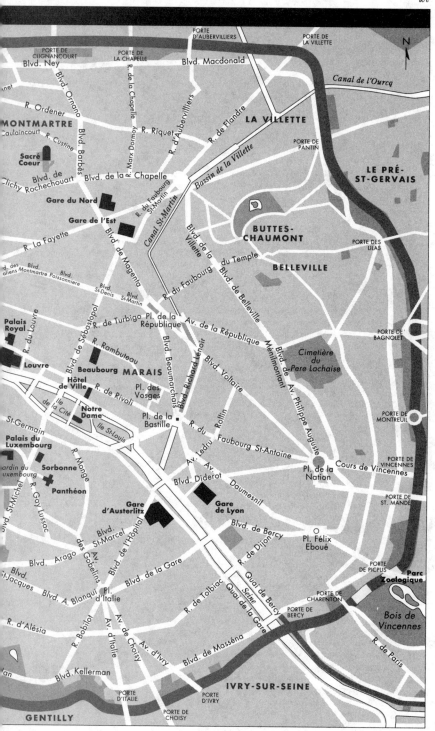

Paris Arrondissements

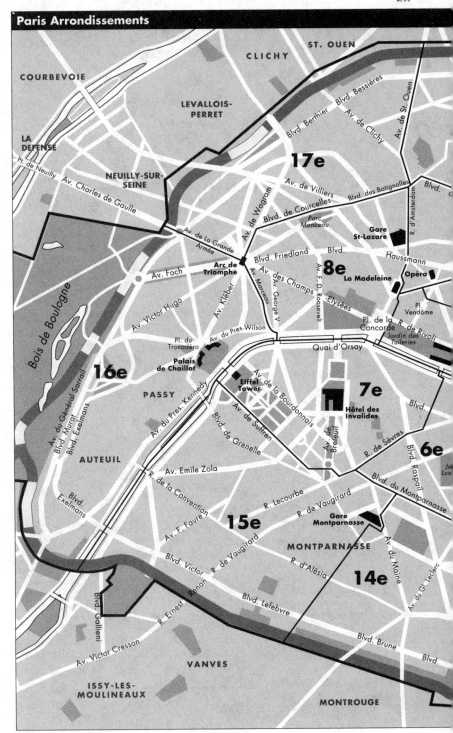

ST. OUEN

CLICHY

COURBEVOIE

LEVALLOIS-
PERRET

Blvd. Berthier

Blvd. Bessières

Av. de St. Ouen

Av. de Clichy

LA
DEFENSE

Pl. de Neuilly

Av. Charles de Gaulle

NEUILLY-SUR-
SEINE

17e

Av. de Villiers

Blvd. des Batignolles

Blvd.

R. d'Amsterdam

Av. de Wagram

Blvd. de Courcelles

Parc
Monceau

Gare
St-Lazare

Blvd.

Av. de la Grande
Armée

Arc de
Triomphe

Blvd. Friedland

8e

La Madeleine

Haussmann

Opéra

Av. Foch

Av. Kléber

Av. des Champs

Av. George V

Av. F. D. Roosevelt

-Elysées

Pl.
Vendôme

Av. Victor Hugo

Av. Moreau

Bois de Boulogne

Pl. de la
Concorde

Jardin des
Tuileries

Pl. du
Trocadéro

Av. du Pres.-Wilson

Quai d'Orsay

R. de Rivoli

Palais
de Chaillot

16e

PASSY

Eiffel
Tower

Av. de la Bourdonnais

7e

Blvd.

Av. du Général Sarrail

Blvd. Murat

Blvd. Exelmans

Av. du Pres. Kennedy

Blvd. de Grenelle

Av. de Suffren

Hôtel des
Invalides

Av. de
Breteuil

R. de Sèvres

6e

AUTEUIL

R. Av. Emile Zola

R. de la Convention

R. Lecourbe

R. de Vaugirard

Blvd. du Montparnasse

Ja
Lux

Blvd.
Exelmans

Av. F. Faure

15e

R. de Vaugirard

Gare
Montparnasse

MONTPARNASSE

Av. du Maine

Blvd. Galieni

Blvd. Victor

R. de Vaugirard

R. d'Alésia

14e

Av. du Gl. Leclerc

R. Ernest Renan

Blvd. Lefebvre

Av. Victor Cresson

Blvd. Brune

Blvd

VANVES

ISSY-LES-
MOULINEAUX

MONTROUGE

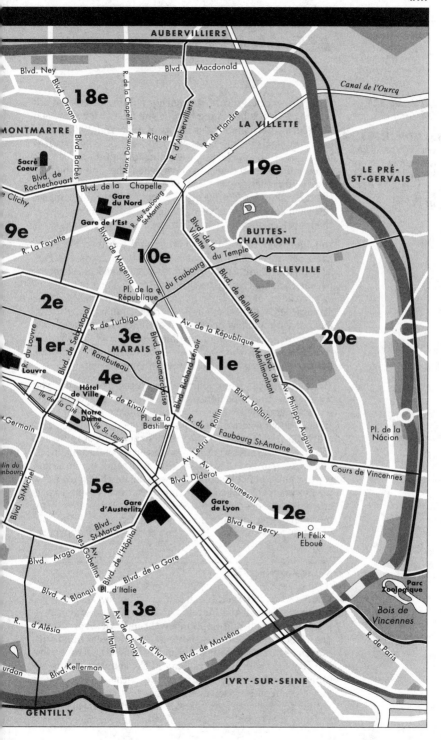

Making Your Vacation Affordable

By Sandra A. Gustafson

Sandra A. Gustafson is the author of Cheap Sleeps in Paris and Cheap Eats in Paris.

With the exchange rate stubbornly holding at around 5.3 francs to $1, it's becoming harder and harder for seasoned travelers to remember the Paris of 1985 and 1986, when gourmet meals by famous chefs were $40, ritzy hotel suites less than $100, and designer clothing going for half of U.S. prices. The great bargain days when the dollar bought nearly 10 francs are gone, and probably forever. And even though a sluggish French economy and a general European recession have reigned in spiraling costs, Paris is still one of the most expensive cities in Europe.

But haute couture, luxury hotels, and three-star restaurants are only one side of Paris. There is another—the Paris of medieval church concerts; tiny, raftered hotel rooms perched among city spires; cozy bistro lunches. It's a walker's paradise of tree-lined boulevards, narrow cobblestone streets, leafy parks, open-air markets, imposing edifices, and enticing window displays. It's a feast for the eyes and a lifetime of memories, and it belongs to any traveler who can replace a lack of wherewithal with a little homework, some advance planning—and a soupçon of imagination.

To get the most from your trip to Paris, know what you want from the experience, what you can and cannot do without, and the trade-offs you're willing to make in order to hold down costs. If dining at gastronomic meccas are a must, perhaps you can make up the expense by staying at a relatively charmless hotel in an outer arrondissement. If you're determined to bring home some French perfume and copper pots, plan on replacing two-star lunches with a few picnics and café snacks. Remember that everything that is cheap is not necessarily a good value. If you spend a little more than you anticipated on something, don't let it ruin your trip. It's not a vacation if you can't relax and have fun, too.

Money-saving Tips

- **Choose when to travel.** If you can, travel in low season—between November and March—or in the shoulder season—April, May, and mid-September through October. Prices are lower, reservations easier to get, and streets filled with Parisians instead of tourists. August, when the French flee the city for their annual holiday in the countryside, is another time when you may save money. Although some shops and restaurants close, many hotels remain open and are willing to negotiate lower rates. (It's vital to call ahead, as a number of hotels also close at this time.) Since many people begin their vacations on Friday or Saturday, airfares are usually more expensive on weekends, so try to travel mid-week.

- **Investigate package tours.** These can offer significant savings over booking each element of your trip separately. If a fully escorted tour does not appeal, study the many airline and hotel packages that are available (*see* Tours and Packages in Chapter 1).

- **Study discounted airfares.** Cheaper flights are available through many avenues, including discount travel clubs, charters, consolidators, and companies that allow you to fly as an air courier (*see* Cutting Flight Costs in Chapter 1).

- **Avoid the single supplement fee.** Solo travelers looking to reduce their expenses can join the **Travel Companion Exchange** (Box 833, Amityville, NY 11701, tel. 516/454–0880), a well-established organization that helps singles find traveling companions, largely by means of a newsletter. An introductory, six-month membership costs $36 if you're looking for a same-sex match, $66 for an opposite-sex match. A sample copy of the newsletter, with a full explanation of services, is available for $4. If you're traveling alone on a group tour, note that **Globus Gateway** is one of only a few tour operators that attempts to match singles willing to share (*see* Tours and Packages in Chapter 1).

- **Be creative about accommodations.** Although Paris offers an abundance of inexpensive hotels, they are not your only budgetwise option. Other possibilities include hostels, university rooms, and *chambres d'Hôte* (bed-and-breakfasts). If you are lucky enough to be in Paris longer than a week, you may be able to cut costs by staying in an apartment, although this is generally a moderately priced—not budget—alternative. Of course, the cheapest lodging is the one you get through a home exchange, when you trade your stateside home for one in Paris (*see* Where to Stay on a Budget, Chapter 2).

- **Go camping!** There are actually facilities in the Bois de Boulogne. Next to a home exchange, there's no cheaper way to stay in Paris (*see* Where to Stay on a Budget, Chapter 2).

- **Take one of the hotel's cheaper rooms.** The least expensive units will be those in the back of the hotel without a private w.c. or shower. Any room with a private shower will cost less than one with a bathtub. However, keep in mind that hotels often charge you to use the shower or bath down the hall. If there are three or more in your party, it may be cheaper to share a room with bath than pay extra for everyone to use the shower. Make inquiries in advance (*see* Where to Stay on a Budget, Chapter 2).

- **Save on breakfast.** Unless it is obligatory to eat where you're lodging, skip the hotel's breakfast and have your brioche and café au lait at the counter of the nearest bar. You must inform your hotel when reserving that you will not be eating breakfast there, and see to it that the cost is deducted per person, per day, from the room rate.

- **Don't make phone calls from your hotel.** Purchase a *télécarte* and go to a public phone if you need to make local calls. For long-distance calls, hook up with an AT&T, MCI, or Sprint program that allows you either to dial direct, billing the call to a credit card, or to make a collect call (*see* Telephones in Chapter 1).

- **Save on money exchange.** Inquire at your hotel or at a tourist bureau about banks that specialize in changing money. Whatever you do, don't cash your traveler's checks at shops, hotels, or tourist attractions (*see* Currency Exchange in Chapter 1).

- **Look for museum discounts.** Many offer reduced rates on Sundays, and some on Wednesdays. Senior citizens and students have reduced admission anytime upon presentation of proof of age or a student ID (*see* Student and Youth Travel and Hints for Older Travelers in Chapter 1). If you plan a lot of museum-hopping, buy a **Museum Pass**. A one-, three-, or five-day pass allows access to 65 museums and monuments in Paris, including the Louvre. Besides saving money, the pass enables you to sidestep long ticket lines (*see* Exploring Paris, Chapter 3).

- **Look for other discounts.** Not all discounts are advertised, so make it a rule of thumb to ask before paying. Watch for weekend rates, promotional deals, and student and age-related discounts (*see* Student and Youth Travel and Hints for Older Travelers in Chapter 1). Movies are cut-rate for Monday shows. Half-price theater tickets for same-day performances can be bought at the booth near the Madeleine Church. Church concerts are often free, as are some of the son-et-lumière performances—sound-and-light extravaganzas staged outdoors at tourist venues in summer (*see* The Arts and Nightlife, Chapter 6).

- **Buy a métro pass.** Buy métro tickets in groups of 10 (a *carnet*) or take advantage of a money-saving pass. A *coupon jaune, carte orange, Formule 1*, and *Paris Visite* are good for unlimited travel over certain blocks of time. Tickets are also good on Paris buses (*see* Getting Around Paris in Chapter 1).

- **Save money at restaurants.** Eat and drink a block or two from major tourist sites and main boulevards. Always check the restaurant menu posted outside for prices. Prixfixe menus are usually considerably less expensive than à la carte. Expensive restaurants often offer a cheaper lunch menu, and you may find you can indulge in a couple of three-star meals by going at midday. Wherever you dine, order the house wine (*vin de la maison*) and stick with tap water (*l'eau ordinaire*) (*see* Where to Eat on a Budget, Chapter 5).

- **Explore other dining options.** Seek out bistros and wine bars (*bistros à vin*) rather than full-blown restaurants. At the former, hearty peasant fare such as casseroles and stews cost less and are more filling than more refined cuisine. At the latter, sandwiches, platters of cold cuts, and wines by the glass are available at reasonable prices. To really save, visit Paris's food shops and markets and put together a gourmet picnic feast for a fraction of what it would cost in a restaurant. You can buy everything you need from one shop (most likely a charcuterie) or stop at a number of specialty stores such as *boulangeries, pâtisseries, fromageries,* and open-air markets (*see* Where to Eat on a Budget, Chapter 5).

- **Shop wisely.** Keep an eye out for the annual sales (*soldes*), usually held in July and January. Markdowns are sometimes meager, but bargains lurk. Look for storefronts announcing *troc* or *dépot-vente*—resale shops. Also check out those advertising *broconte,* which usually means secondhand furniture and trinkets. Discount clothing is available at various locations but mainly in the 14th arrondissement, along the rue d'Alésia. Apply for the *détaxe* if you have spent at least 2,000 francs in a single store. This offers a refund of 13%–18.6%, which is mailed to you or credited to your credit card (*see* Shopping for Bargains, Chapter 4).

- **Avoid expensive pharmacies.** Before leaving home, stock up on the basics: film, batteries, shampoo, toothpaste, etc. All of these are more expensive in Paris. If you do run short, go to one of the many branches of the discount department stores **Monoprix** or **Prisunic** (*see* Shopping for Bargains, Chapter 4).

Paris for Free (or Cheap)

- For a view you will never forget, climb to the top of the Eiffel Tower, Notre Dame, the Arc de Triomphe, or Sacré Coeur. If you don't want to walk up endless flights of stairs, take an elevator to the 9th floor at La Samaritaine Department Store. In the summer, ride the ferris wheel in the Tuileries for an equally spectacular view.

- Spend a relaxed Parisian afternoon in one of the city's many parks and squares. Here you can read a book, sit in the sun, watch children play, and pick up the rhythm of day-to-day life in the city. Top choices are the Jardin du Luxembourg, Parc Monceau, the Jardin d'Acclimitation—the latter with its children's park and zoo—and the Place des Vosges, the oldest and one of the most beautiful squares in Paris.

- Have a sublime ice cream at the most famous maker in Paris, Berthillon, on Ile St-Louis. The faithful line up rain or shine for one of the 50 intense flavors of ice cream and sorbet served forth Wednesday through Sunday from September through July (*see* Exploring the Marais and Ile St-Louis in Chapter 3).

- For the price of a Métro ticket, take a relaxing tour over the steep streets of Montmartre on the Montmartrebus (*see* Exploring Montmartre in Chapter 3).

- Visit a museum when prices are discounted, usually on Sunday or Wednesday. For extensive museum-going, purchase a Museum Pass (*see* Money-saving Tips, *above*).

- Attend a free church concert or musical program in the park. Check the weekly *Pariscope—Une Semaine de Paris* for details.

- Visit more than 100,000 permanent Parisians at the Père Lachaise cemetery. A map to the graves of the famous and infamous is available at the entrance for a small fee (*see* On the Fringe in Chapter 3).

- Stand at the Palais de Chaillot and look across to the Eiffel Tower as the sun sets or at night, when the fountains are lit (*see* Exploring from Orsay to Trocadéro in Chapter 3).

- Join the thousands of Parisians who have taken up "le jogging" in earnest. Choice routes include the 2.5-km path around the Champ de Mars, with the Eiffel Tower at one end and Ecole Militaire at the other, the first two flights of stairs at the Eiffel Tower (8 francs), the Luxembourg Gardens (1.6-km path), Parc Monceau (1-km route), and the Tuileries (1.6-km circuit).

- See the city simply by riding the métro as it travels aboveground at various points along certain routes, revealing excellent views of many of the city's fabled sights (*see* Off the Beaten Track in Chapter 3). Alternatively, several city buses take in incomparable vistas on their way from point A to point B.

- Window-shop along some of the most beautiful streets in the world, including the avenue Montaigne, the place des Victoires, place Vendôme and the rue de la Paix, rue du Faubourg St-Honoré, avenue George V, avenue Marceau, and rue François ler (*see* Shopping for Bargains, Chapter 4).

- Join half of Paris on a Saturday or Sunday morning at the flea market, where even if you never buy a thing, you'll find the people-watching terrific. As for the shopping itself, note that although bargains are possible, rare finds are almost unheard-of these days (*see* Shopping for Bargains, Chapter 4).

- For a river's-eye view of Paris, take one of the bateaux-mouches that travel the Seine. Daytime cost is only 30 francs if you don't have a meal, and there's no better introduction to the city (*see* Guided Tours in Chapter 1).

- Thrill seekers can rent a bicycle and try their luck keeping body and soul together in death-defying traffic. A more peaceful ride can be had in the Bois de Boulogne and the Bois de Vincennes (*see* Getting Around by Bike in Chapter 1).

- Take your camera to one of Paris's open-air markets or shopping streets. Plan to spend at least an hour or two and pick up the fixings for a picnic afterward (*see* Shopping for Bargains, Chapter 4).

- Although café drinks and beverages are expensive, you can stretch your $3 espresso or beer into an hour or two of contemplative idleness. Don't worry about the waiter or anyone else expecting you to leave: In Paris, sitting in a café is an inalienable right, and a front-row seat on humanity's passing parade. Find time to do this at least once in your visit.

- Walk! Wander the tiny streets of the Marais, follow the Champs-Elysée from the Arc de Triomphe to the place de la Concorde, prowl the hilly slopes of Montmartre, poke among the bookstalls along the Seine—this is the best way to get to know the timeless delights of Paris.

1 Affordable Paris: The Basics

Before You Go

Government Tourist Offices

Contact the French Government Tourist Office for free information.

In the United States 610 5th Ave., New York, NY 10020, tel. 212/315–0888 or 212/757–1125; 645 N. Michigan Ave., Chicago, IL 60611, tel. 312/337–6301; 2305 Cedar Springs Rd., Dallas, TX 75201, tel. 214/720–4010; 9401 Wilshire Blvd., Beverly Hills, CA 90212, tel. 213/271–6665; 1 Hallidie Plaza, Suite 250, San Francisco, CA 94102, tel. 415/986–4174.

In Canada 1981 McGill College Ave., Suite 490, Montreal, Quebec H3A 2W9, tel. 514/288–4264; 1 Dundas St. W, Suite 2405, Box 8, Toronto, Ontario M5G 1Z3, tel. 416/593–4723.

In the United Kingdom 178 Piccadilly, London W1V 0AL, tel. 071/629–1272.

Tours and Packages

Should you buy your travel arrangements packaged or do it yourself? There are advantages either way. Buying packaged arrangements saves you money, particularly if you can find a program that includes exactly the features you want. You also get a pretty good idea of what your trip will cost from the outset. Generally, two types of packaged travel arrangements are available. **Escorted tours** are most often via motorcoach, with a tour director in charge. Your baggage is handled, your time rigorously scheduled, and most meals planned. Escorted tours are therefore the most hassle-free way to see a destination, as well as generally the least expensive. **Independent packages** allow plenty of flexibility. They generally include airline travel and hotels, with certain options available, such as sightseeing, car rental, and excursions. Independent packages are usually more expensive than escorted tours, but your time is your own.

While you can book directly through tour operators, you will pay no more to go through a travel agent, who will be able to tell you about tours and packages from a number of operators. Whatever program you choose, be sure to find out exactly what is included: taxes, tips, transfers, meals, baggage handling, ground transportation, entertainment, excursions, sports or recreation (and rental equipment if necessary). Ask about the level of hotel used, its location, the size of its rooms, the kind of beds, and its facilities and amenities, such as pool, room service, or programs for children. Find out the operator's cancellation penalties. Nearly everyone charges them, and the only way to avoid them is to buy trip-cancellation insurance (*see* Insurance, *below*). Also ask about the single supplement, a surcharge assessed to solo travelers. Some operators do not make you pay it if you agree to be matched up with a roommate of the same sex, even if one is not found by departure time.

Fully Escorted Tours Escorted tours are usually sold in three categories: deluxe, first-class, and tourist or budget class. The most important differences are the price, of course, and the level of accommodations. Some operators specialize in one category, while others offer a range. Programs that include Paris generally spend two nights and only one full day in Paris; most are first-class, among them **American Express Vacations** (300 Pinnacle Way, Norcross, GA 30093, tel. 800/241–1700), **Globus-Gateway** (95-25 Queens Blvd., Rego Park, NY 11374, tel. 800/221–0090 or 718/268–7000), **Olson-Travelworld** (Box 10066, Manhattan Beach, CA 90226, tel. 800/421–5785 or 310/546–8400), and **Trafalgar Tours** (21 E. 26th St., New York, NY 10010, tel. 800/854–0103 or 212/689–8977).

Most itineraries are jam-packed with sightseeing, so you see a lot in a short amount of time. To judge just how fast-paced the tour is, review the itinerary carefully. If you are in a different hotel each night, you will be getting up early each day to head out, travel to your next destination, do some sightseeing, have dinner, and go to bed; then you'll start all over again. If you want some free time, make sure it's mentioned in the tour brochure; if you want to be escorted to every meal, confirm that any tour you consider does that. Also, when comparing programs, be sure to find out if the motorcoach is air-conditioned and has a rest room on board.

Independent Packages Independent packages, which travel agents call FITs (for foreign independent travel), are offered by airlines, tour operators who may also do escorted programs, and any number of other companies from large, established firms to small, new entrepreneurs. Their programs come in a wide range of prices based on levels of luxury and options—in addition to hotel and airfare, sightseeing, car rental, transfers, admission to local attractions, and other extras. The **French Experience** (370 Lexington Ave., New York, NY 10017, tel. 212/986–1115), has a wide selection of Paris programs. Airline packages, typically including hotel, round-trip airfare, and limited sightseeing, are available through **Air France** (tel. 800/237–2747), **American Airlines Fly AAway Vacations** (tel. 800/321–2121), **Continental Airlines' Grand Destinations** (tel. 800/634–5555), and **Delta Dream Vacations** (tel. 800/328–6877). **Globus-Gateway** and **Trafalgar Tours** (*see above*) offer Paris and London–Paris programs with accommodations, airfare, and some sightseeing.

When to Go

The major tourist season in France stretches from Easter to mid-September. Prices are highest then, except in August, when for a sultry four weeks Parisians retreat en masse to the country and the beach. Although many hotels are closed at this time, those that remain open often offer discounts. Lowest prices will naturally be in the off-season, from November through March, when the weather is dreary but most hotels, restaurants, and shops are open (with some closings around Christmas). You may also find lower prices in the shoulder seasons; that is, April–May and mid-September–October.

Climate What follow are the average daily maximum and minimum temperatures for Paris.

Jan.	43F	6C	May	68F	20C	Sept.	70F	21C
	34	1		49	10		53	12
Feb.	45F	7C	June	73F	23C	Oct.	60F	16C
	34	1		55	13		46	8
Mar.	54F	12C	July	76F	25C	Nov.	50F	10C
	39	4		58	14		40	5
Apr.	60F	16C	Aug.	75F	24C	Dec.	44F	7C
	43	6		58	14		36	2

Information Sources For current weather conditions for cities in the United States and abroad, plus the local time and helpful travel tips, call the **Weather Channel Connection** (tel. 900/WEATHER; 95¢ per minute) from a touch-tone phone.

National Holidays (1994) With 11 national holidays (*jours fériés*) and five weeks of paid vacation, the French have their share of repose. Major holidays, when you should be prepared for stores, banks, and museums to shut their doors, include the following:

January 1 (New Year's Day); April 3 (Easter Monday); May 1 (Labor Day); May 8 (VE Day); May 12 (Ascension); May 23 (Pentecost Monday); July 14 (Bastille Day); August 15 (Assumption); November 1 (All Saints); November 11 (Armistice); December 25 (Christmas).

Festivals and Seasonal Events

Top seasonal events in Paris include the French Open Tennis Championships in May, the Festival du Marais in June through July, July's Bastille Day, the Festival Estival musical event in the summer, and the September Autumn Festival.

Mar. **Salon du Livre,** the international book exposition, is held annually at the Grand Palais at the end of the month.

Late Mar.–Apr. The **Prix du Président de la République** takes place at the Auteuil Racecourse.

Apr.–late Oct. The **Son et Lumière des Invalides** is a sound and light show in the courtyard of the Hôtel des Invalides; there are separate English and French versions.

May–late Sept. **Grandes Eaux Musicales** is a fountain display at the Château de Versailles. Sundays only.

Mid-May **International Marathon of Paris** leaves from the place de la Concorde and ends at the Château de Vincennes.

Late May– early June **Festival de Jazz de Boulogne-Billancourt** attracts big names and varied styles of jazz in the suburbs of Boulogne-Billancourt. Some jazz movies, too.

Late May– early June **French Open Tennis Championships** take place at Roland-Garros Stadium.

Mid-June–mid-July **Festival du Marais** features everything from music to dance to theater in the churches and historic mansions of the Marais. (Tickets: 44 rue François-Miron, 4e, tel. 48–87–60–08.)

Mid-June **Grand Steeplechase de Paris** is a popular horse race at Auteuil Racecourse. The **Course des Garçons de Café** is an entertaining race through the streets of Paris by waiters bearing full trays of drinks. It begins and ends at the Hôtel de Ville.

June 21 **Fête de la Musique de Paris** celebrates the summer solstice with parades, street theater, and live bands throughout the city.

Late June   **Grand Prix de Paris,** a major test for three-year-old horses, is held at Longchamp Racecourse.

July 14   **Bastille Day** celebrates the storming of the Bastille prison in 1789. This national holiday is commemorated throughout France. In Paris, there's a military parade along the Champs-Elysées in the morning and fireworks at night above Trocadéro.

Mid-July–   **Festival Estival of Paris** features classical music concerts in
late Sept.   churches, museums, and concert halls throughout the city. (Tickets: 20 rue Geoffroy-l'Asnier, 4e, tel. 48–04–98–01.)

Late July   **Tour de France,** the world's leading bicycle race, finishes on the Champs-Elysées.

Mid-Sept.–   **Festival d'Automne,** with concerts, plays, dance, and exhibi-
end Dec.   tions throughout Paris. (Tickets: 156 rue de Rivoli, 1er, tel. 42–96–96–94.)

Early Oct.   **Prix de l'Arc de Triomphe,** one of Europe's top horse races, takes place at Longchamp Racecourse. The **Fêtes des Vendanges,** held the first Saturday of the month, marks the grape harvest in the Montmartre Vineyard, at the corner of rue des Saules and rue St-Vincent.

Mid-Oct.–Early   **Festival de Jazz de Paris** is a two-week celebration that includes
Nov.   lots of big-name jazz artists. (Tel. 47–83–33–58 for information.)

Oct.–Nov.   **Festival d'Art Sacré** features concerts and exhibitions held in churches throughout the city. (Tel. 42–77–92–26 for information.)

Nov. 11   **Armistice Day** ceremonies at the Arc de Triomphe include a military parade down the Champs-Elysées.

Dec.   **Christmas** in Paris is highlighted by illuminations throughout the city, particularly on the Champs-Elysées, avenue Montaigne, and boulevard Haussmann.

What to Pack

Clothing   Pack light: Baggage carts are scarce at airports, and luggage restrictions on international flights are tight. What you pack depends more on the time of year than on any particular dress code. It can rain a fair amount in Paris, even in the summer, so consider bringing a raincoat and umbrella. Otherwise, pack as you would for a major American city: formal clothes for formal restaurants and nightclubs, casual clothes elsewhere. Jeans are as popular in Paris as anywhere and are perfectly acceptable for sightseeing and informal dining. However, a jeans-and-sneakers outfit will raise eyebrows at the theater, at expensive restaurants, and when visiting French families. Note that men and women wearing shorts will not be allowed in many churches and cathedrals.

Wear sturdy walking shoes for sightseeing: Paris is full of cobblestone streets, and many historic buildings are surrounded by gravel paths. To protect yourself against purse snatchers and pickpockets, take a handbag with long straps that you can sling across your body, bandolier-style, with a zippered compartment for your money and passport—French law requires that you carry identification at all times.

Miscellaneous If you have a health problem that requires you to take a prescription drug, pack enough to last the duration of the trip or have your doctor write a prescription using the drug's generic name, as brand names vary widely from country to country. If you're staying in budget hotels, take along small bars of soap. And don't forget to pack a list of the addresses of offices that supply refunds for lost or stolen traveler's checks.

Luggage Regulations Free baggage allowances on an airline depend on the airline, the route, and the class of your ticket. In general, on domestic flights and on international flights between the United States and foreign destinations, you are entitled to check two bags—neither exceeding 62 inches, or 158 centimeters (length + width + height), or weighing more than 70 pounds (32 kilograms). A third piece may be brought aboard as a carryon; its total dimensions are generally limited to less than 45 inches (114 centimeters), so it will fit easily under the seat in front of you or in the overhead compartment. There are variations, so ask in advance. The single rule, a Federal Aviation Administration safety regulation that pertains to carry-on baggage on U.S. airlines, requires only that carryons be properly stowed and allows the airline to limit allowances and tailor them to different aircraft and operational conditions. Charges for excess, oversize, or overweight pieces vary, so inquire before you pack.

If you are flying between two foreign destinations, note that baggage allowances may be determined not by the piece method but by the weight method, which generally allows 88 pounds (40 kilograms) of luggage in first class, 66 pounds (30 kilograms) in business class, and 44 pounds (20 kilograms) in economy. If your flight between two cities abroad *connects* with your transatlantic or transpacific flight, the piece method still applies.

Safeguarding Your Luggage Before leaving home, itemize your bags' contents and their worth; this list will help you estimate the extent of your loss if your bags go astray. To minimize that risk, tag them inside and out with your name, address, and phone number. (If you use your home address, cover it so that potential thieves can't see it.) At check-in, make sure that the tag attached by baggage handlers bears the correct three-letter code for your destination. If your bags do not arrive with you, or if you detect damage, do not leave the airport until you've filed a written report with the airline.

Electricity The electrical current in Paris is 220 volts, 50 cycles alternating current (AC); the United States runs on 110-volt, 60-cycle AC current. Unlike wall outlets in the United States, which accept plugs with two flat prongs, outlets in France take plugs with two round prongs.

Adapters, Converters, Transformers To plug in U.S.-made appliances abroad, you'll need an adapter plug. To reduce the voltage entering the appliance from 220 to 110 volts, you'll also need a converter, unless it is a dual-voltage appliance, made for travel. There are converters for high-wattage appliances (such as hair dryers), low-wattage items (such as electric toothbrushes and razors), and combination models. Hotels sometimes have outlets marked "For Shavers Only" near the sink; these are 110-volt outlets for low-wattage appliances; don't use them for a high-wattage appliance. If you're traveling with a laptop computer, especially an older one, you may need a transformer—a type of converter used with electronic-circuitry products. Newer laptop computers are auto-sensing, operating equally well on 110 and 220 volts (so you need only the appropriate adapter plug).

Taking Money Abroad

Traveler's Checks The most widely recognized are **American Express, Barclay's, Thomas Cook,** and those issued by major banks such as **Citibank** and **Bank of America.** American Express also issues *Traveler's Cheques for Two,* which can be signed and used by you or your traveling companion. Some checks are free; usually the issuing company or the bank at which you make your purchase charges 1% of the checks' face value as a fee. Be sure to buy a few checks in small denominations to cash toward the end of your trip, when you don't want to be left with more foreign currency than you can spend. Always record the numbers of checks as you spend them, and keep this list separate from the checks.

Currency Exchange Banks and bank-operated exchange booths at airports and railroad stations are usually the best places to change money. Hotels, stores, and privately run exchange firms typically offer less favorable rates.

Before your trip, pay attention to how the dollar is doing vis-à-vis French currency. If the dollar is losing strength, try to pay as many travel bills as possible in advance, especially the big ones. If it is getting stronger, pay for costly items overseas, and use your credit card whenever possible—you'll come out ahead, whether the exchange rate at which your purchase is calculated is the one in effect the day the vendor's bank abroad processes the charge, or the one prevailing on the day the charge company's service center processes it at home.

To avoid lines at airport currency-exchange booths, arrive in France with a small amount of the local currency already in your pocket—a so-called tip pack. **Thomas Cook Currency Services** (630 5th Ave., New York, NY 10111, tel. 212/757–6915) supplies foreign currency by mail.

Getting Money from Home

Cash Machines Automated-teller machines (ATMs) are proliferating; many are tied to international networks such as **Cirrus** and **Plus.** You can use your bank card at ATMs away from home to withdraw money from your account and get cash advances on a credit-card account (provided your card has been programmed with a personal identification number, or PIN). Check in advance on limits on withdrawals and cash advances within specified periods. Ask whether your bank-card or credit-card PIN number will need to be reprogrammed for use in the area you'll be visiting—a possibility if the number has more than four digits. Remember that you pay interest on cash advances from the time you get your money from ATMs just as you do from tellers. And note that, although transaction fees for ATM withdrawals abroad will probably be higher than fees for withdrawals at home, Cirrus and Plus exchange rates tend to be good.

Plan ahead. Though ATMs in Paris work pretty much the same way as in the United States, not all have English prompts. Learn the French equivalents for key words, such as *withdraw, how much?, amount, transaction, okay,* and *clear* before you go. Also obtain ATM locations and the names of affiliated cash-machine networks before departure. For specific foreign Cirrus locations, call 800/4–CIRRUS; for foreign Plus locations, consult the Plus directory at your local bank.

American Express Cardholder Services
The company's **Express Cash** system lets you withdraw cash and/or traveler's checks from a worldwide network of 57,000 American Express dispensers and participating bank ATMs. You must *enroll first* (call 800/CASH–NOW for a form and allow two weeks for processing). Withdrawals are charged not to your card but to a designated bank account. You can withdraw up to $1,000 per seven-day period on the basic card, more if your card is gold or platinum. There is a 2% fee (minimum $2.50, maximum $10) for each cash transaction, and a 1% fee for traveler's checks (except for the platinum card), which are available only from American Express dispensers. At AmEx offices, cardholders can also cash personal checks for up to $1,000 in any seven-day period (21 days abroad); of this $200 can be in cash, more if available, with the balance paid in traveler's checks, for which all but platinum cardholders pay a 1% fee. Higher limits apply to the gold and platinum cards.

Wiring Money
You don't have to be a cardholder to send or receive an **American Express MoneyGram** for up to $10,000. To send one, go to an American Express MoneyGram agent, pay up to $1,000 with a credit card and anything over that in cash, and phone a transaction reference number to your intended recipient, who need only present identification and the reference number to the nearest MoneyGram agent to pick up the cash. There are MoneyGram agents in more than 60 countries (call 800/543–4080 for locations). Fees range from 5% to 10%, depending on the amount and how you pay. You can't use American Express, which is really a convenience card—only Discover, Master-Card, and Visa credit cards.

You can also use **Western Union.** To wire money, take either cash or a check to the nearest office. (Or you can order money sent by phone, using a credit card.) Fees are roughly 5%–10%. Money sent from the United States or Canada will be available for pick up at agent locations in Paris within minutes. (Note that once the money is in the system it can be picked up at *any* location. You don't have to miss your train waiting for it to arrive in City A, because if there's an agent in City B, where you're headed, you can pick it up there, too.) There are approximately 20,000 agents worldwide (call 800/325–6000 for locations).

French Currency

The unit of currency in France is the franc, which is divided into 100 centimes. The bills are 500, 200, 100, and 50 francs. Coins are 20, 10, 5, 2, and 1 francs and 50, 20, 10, and 5 centimes. At press time (mid-1993), the exchange rate was 5.3 francs to the dollar and 8.5 francs to the pound.

What It Will Cost

France's economy was in the doldrums in 1993; as a result, prices at many restaurants and shops remained steady and in some cases actually dropped. Although Paris remains one of the most expensive cities in the world, it's still a place where people live as well as work (unlike, say, central London); Parisians, who shop and lunch locally, are not prepared to pay extravagant rates, and visitors who avoid the obvious tourist traps will not have to pay those rates, either.

Prices tend to reflect the standing of an area in the eyes of Parisians; much-sought-after residential arrondissements such as the 7th, 16th, and 17th—of limited tourist interest—are far more expensive than the student-oriented, much-visited Latin Quarter. The tourist area where value for money is most difficult to find is the 8th arrondissement, on and around the Champs-Elysées. Places where you can be virtually certain to shop, eat, and stay without overpaying include the streets surrounding Montmartre (not the Butte, or hilltop, itself); the St-Michel/Sorbonne area on the Left Bank; the mazelike streets around the Halles and Marais in central Paris; and Bastille and eastern Paris.

Taxes All taxes must be included in affixed prices in France. Restaurant and hotel prices must by law include taxes and service charges: If these appear as additional items on your bill, you should complain. VAT (value added tax, known in France as TVA), at a standard rate of 18.6%, is included in the price of many goods, but foreigners are often entitled to a refund (*see* Shopping for Bargains, Chapter 4).

Sample Costs These prices are meant only as a general guide, and may have changed somewhat since press time. A budget hotel room will start at about $60 a night. A dinner for one at an inexpensive restaurant, including wine and coffee, will be about $20; a prix-fixe lunch at a modest bistro should be half that. A cup of coffee at a bar is about $.80; at a café table, it's about $2. Mineral water is about $2.50 at a café; an aperitif or glass of wine, $4. A single Métro ticket is about $1.30; a book of 10 tickets, $8. A short taxi ride will cost about $4; a round-trip train from Paris to Versailles is $6. It costs about $8 to see a movie in Paris; admission to the Louvre is about $6.

Passports and Visas

If your passport is lost or stolen abroad, report it immediately to the nearest embassy or consulate and to the local police. If you can provide the consular officer with the information contained in the passport, he or she will usually be able to issue you a new passport. For this reason, it is a good idea to keep a copy of the data page of your passport in a separate place, or to leave the passport number, date, and place of issuance with a relative or friend at home.

U.S. Citizens All U.S. citizens, even infants, need a valid passport to enter France for stays of up to 90 days. You can pick up new and renewal application forms at any of the 13 U.S. Passport Agency offices and at some post offices and courthouses. Although passports are usually mailed within two weeks of your application's receipt, it's best to allow three weeks for delivery in low season, five weeks or more from April through summer. Call the Department of State Office of Passport Services' information line (1425 K St. NW, Washington, DC 20522, tel. 202/647–0518) for details.

Canadian Citizens Canadian citizens need a valid passport to enter France. Application forms are available at 23 regional passport offices as well as post offices and travel agencies. Whether applying for a first or subsequent passport, you must apply in person. Children under 16 may be included on a parent's passport but must have their own passport to travel alone. Passports are valid for five years and are usually mailed within two weeks of an application's receipt. For more information in English or French, call the passport office (tel. 514/283–2152).

U.K. Citizens Citizens of the United Kingdom need a valid passport to enter France. Applications for new and renewal passports are available from main post offices as well as at the six passport offices, located in Belfast, Glasgow, Liverpool, London, Newport, and Peterborough. You may apply in person at all passport offices, or by mail to all except the London office. Children under 16 may travel on a parent's passport when accompanying them. All passports are valid for 10 years. Allow a month for processing.

A British Visitor's Passport is valid for holidays and some business trips of up to three months to France. It can include both partners of a married couple. A British visitor's passport is valid for one year and will be issued on the same day that you apply. You must apply in person at a main post office.

Customs and Duties

On Arrival If you're coming from a European Community (EC) country, you may import duty free: (1) 300 cigarettes or 150 cigarillos or 75 cigars or 400 grams of tobacco; (2) 5 liters of table wine and, in addition, (a) 1.5 liters of alcohol over 22% volume (most spirits) or (b) 3 liters of alcohol under 22% volume (fortified or sparkling wine) or (c) 3 more liters of table wine; (3) 90 milliliters of perfume and 375 milliliters of toilet water; and (4) other goods to the value of 2,000 francs (400 francs for those under 15).

If you're coming from anywhere else, you may import duty free: (1) 200 cigarettes or 100 cigarillos or 50 cigars or 250 grams of tobacco (twice that if you live outside Europe); (2) 2 liters of wine and, in addition, (a) 1 liter of alcohol over 22% volume (most spirits) or (b) 2 liters of alcohol under 22% volume (fortified or sparkling wine) or (c) 2 more liters of table wine; (3) 60 milliliters of perfume and 250 milliliters of toilet water; and (4) other goods to the value of 2,400 francs (620 francs for those under 15).

Any amount of French or foreign currency may be brought into France, but foreign currencies converted into francs may be reconverted into a foreign currency only up to the equivalent of 5,000 francs.

Returning Home Provided you've been out of the country for at least 48 hours
U.S. Customs and haven't already used the exemption, or any part of it, in the past 30 days, you may bring home $400 worth of foreign goods duty free. So can each member of your family, regardless of age; and your exemptions may be pooled, so one of you can bring in more if another brings in less. A flat 10% duty applies to the next $1,000 of goods; above $1,400, the rate varies with the merchandise. (If the 48-hour or 30-day limits apply, your duty free allowance drops to $25, which may not be pooled.) Please note that these are the *general* rules, applicable to most countries, including France.

Travelers 21 or older may bring back 1 liter of alcohol duty free, provided the beverage laws of the state through which they re-enter the United States allow it. In addition, 100 non-Cuban cigars and 200 cigarettes are allowed, regardless of your age. Antiques and works of art more than 100 years old are duty-free.

Gifts valued at less than $50 may be mailed duty free to stateside friends and relatives, with a limit of one package per day per addressee (do not send alcohol or tobacco products, nor perfume valued at more than $5). These gifts do not count as part of your exemption, unless you bring them home with you. Mark the package "Unsolicited Gift" and include the nature of the gift and its retail value.

For a copy of "Know Before You Go," a free brochure detailing what you may and may not bring back to the United States, rates of duty, and other pointers, contact the **U.S. Customs Service** (Box 7407, Washington, DC 20044, tel. 202/927–6724).

Canadian Customs Once per calendar year, when you've been out of Canada for at least seven days, you may bring in $300 worth of goods duty-free. If you've been away less than seven days but more than 48 hours, the duty-free exemption drops to $100 but can be claimed any number of times (as can a $20 duty-free exemption for absences of 24 hours or more). You cannot combine the yearly and 48-hour exemptions, use the $300 exemption only partially (to save the balance for a later trip), or pool exemptions with family members. Goods claimed under the $300 exemption may follow you by mail; those claimed under the lesser exemptions must accompany you on your return.

Alcohol and tobacco products may be included in the yearly and 48-hour exemptions but not in the 24-hour exemption. If you meet the age requirements of the province through which you reenter Canada, you may bring in, duty free, 1.14 liters (40 imperial ounces) of wine or liquor *or* two dozen 12-ounce cans or bottles of beer or ale. If you are 16 or older, you may bring in, duty free, 200 cigarettes, 50 cigars or cigarillos, and 400 tobacco sticks or 400 grams of manufactured tobacco. Alcohol and tobacco must accompany you on your return.

Gifts may be mailed to Canada duty free. These do not count as part of your exemption. Each gift may be worth up to $60—label the package "Unsolicited Gift—Value under $60." There are no limits on the number of gifts that may be sent per day or per addressee, but you can't mail alcohol or tobacco.

For more information, including details of duties on items that exceed your duty-free limit, ask the Revenue Canada Customs and Excise Department (Connaught Bldg., MacKenzie Ave., Ottawa, Ont., K1A OL5, tel. 613/957–0275) for a copy of the free brochure "I Declare/Je Déclare."

U.K. Customs If your journey was wholly within EC countries, you no longer need to pass through customs when you return to the United Kingdom. According to EC guidelines, you may bring in 800 cigarettes, 400 cigarillos, 200 cigars, and 1 kilogram of smoking tobacco, plus 10 liters of spirits, 20 liters of fortified wine, 90 liters of wine, and 110 liters of beer. If you exceed these limits, you may be required to prove that the goods are for your personal use or are gifts.

For further information or a copy of "A Guide for Travellers," which details standard customs procedures as well as what you may bring into the United Kingdom from abroad, contact HM Customs and Excise (New King's Beam House, 22 Upper Ground, London SE1 9PJ, tel. 071/620–1313).

Traveling with Cameras and Camcorders

About Film and Cameras Pack some lens tissue and an extra battery for your built-in light meter, and invest in an inexpensive skylight filter, to both protect your lens and provide some definition in hazy shots. Store film in a cool, dry place—never in the car's glove compartment or on the shelf under the rear window.

Films above ISO 400 are more sensitive to damage from airport security X-rays than others; very high speed films, ISO 1,000 and above, are exceedingly vulnerable. To protect your film, don't put it in checked luggage; carry it with you in a plastic bag and ask for a hand inspection. Such requests are honored at American airports and up to the inspector abroad. Don't depend on a lead-lined bag to protect film in checked luggage— the airline may very well turn up the dosage of radiation to see what you've got in there. Airport metal detectors do not harm film, although you'll set off the alarm if you walk through one with a roll in your pocket. Call the Kodak Information Center (tel. 800/242–2424) for details.

About Camcorders Invest in a skylight filter to protect the lens, and check the lithium battery that lights up the LCD (liquid crystal display) modes. As for the rechargeable nickel-cadmium batteries that are the camera's power source, take along an extra pair, so while you're using your camcorder you'll have one battery ready and another recharging. Most newer camcorders are equipped with the battery (which generally slides or clicks onto the camera body) and, to recharge it, with what's known as a universal or worldwide AC adapter charger (or multivoltage converter) that can be used whether the voltage is 110 or 220. All that's needed is the appropriate plug.

About Videotape Unlike still-camera film, videotape is not damaged by X-rays. However, it may well be harmed by the magnetic field of a walk-through metal detector. Airport security personnel may want you to turn the camcorder on to prove that that's what it is, so make sure the battery is charged when you get to the airport.

Staying Healthy

Finding a Doctor The **International Association for Medical Assistance to Travellers** (IAMAT, 417 Center St., Lewiston, NY 14092, tel. 716/ 754–4883; 40 Regal Rd., Guelph, Ontario N1K 1B5; 57 Voirets, 1212 Grand-Lancy, Geneva, Switzerland) publishes a worldwide directory of English-speaking physicians whose qualifications meet IAMAT standards and who have agreed to treat members for a set fee. Membership is free.

Assistance Companies Pretrip medical referrals, emergency evacuation or repatriation, 24-hour telephone hot lines for medical consultation, dispatch of medical personnel, relay of medical records, up-front cash for emergencies, and other personal and legal assistance are among the services provided by several membership organizations specializing in medical assistance to travelers.

Among them are **International SOS Assistance** (Box 11568, Philadelphia, PA 19116, tel. 215/244–1500 or 800/523–8930; Box 466, Pl. Bonaventure, Montréal, Qué. H5A 1C1, tel. 514/874–7674 or 800/363–0263), **Near Services** (450 Prairie Ave., Suite 101, Calumet City, IL 60409, tel. 708/868–6700 or 800/654–6700), and **Travel Assistance International** (1133 15th St. NW, Suite 400, Washington, DC 20005, tel. 202/331–1609 or 800/821–2828), part of Europ Assistance Worldwide Services, Inc. Because these companies will also sell you death-and-dismemberment, trip-cancellation, and other insurance coverage, there is some overlap with the travel-insurance policies discussed below, which may include the services of an assistance company among the insurance options or reimburse travelers for such services without providing them.

Insurance

For U.S. Residents Most tour operators, travel agents, and insurance agents sell specialized health-and-accident, flight, trip-cancellation, and luggage insurance as well as comprehensive policies with some or all of these features. But before you make any purchase, review your existing health and homeowner policies to find out whether they cover expenses incurred while traveling.

Health-and-Accident Insurance Supplemental health-and-accident insurance for travelers is usually a part of comprehensive policies. Specific policy provisions vary, but they tend to address three general areas, beginning with reimbursement for medical expenses caused by illness or an accident during a trip. Such policies may reimburse anywhere from $1,000 to $150,000 worth of medical expenses; dental benefits may also be included. A second common feature is the personal-accident, or death-and-dismemberment, provision, which pays a lump sum to your beneficiaries if you die or to you if you lose one or both limbs or your eyesight. This is similar to the flight insurance described below, although it is not necessarily limited to accidents involving airplanes or even other "common carriers" (buses, trains, and ships) and can be in effect 24 hours a day. The lump sum awarded can range from $15,000 to $500,000. A third area generally addressed by these policies is medical assistance (referrals, evacuation, or repatriation and other services). Some policies reimburse travelers for the cost of such services; others may automatically enroll you as a member of a particular medical-assistance company.

Flight Insurance This insurance, often bought as a last-minute impulse at the airport, pays a lump sum to a beneficiary when a plane crashes and the insured dies (and sometimes to a surviving passenger who loses eyesight or a limb); thus it supplements the airlines' own coverage as described in the limits-of-liability paragraphs on your ticket (up to $75,000 on international flights, $20,000 on domestic ones—and that is generally subject to litigation). Charging an airline ticket to a major credit card often automatically signs you up for flight insurance; in this case, the coverage may also embrace travel by bus, train, and ship.

Baggage Insurance In the event of loss, damage, or theft on international flights, airlines limit their liability to $20 per kilogram for checked baggage (roughly about $640 per 70-pound bag) and $400 per passenger for unchecked baggage. On domestic flights, the ceiling is $1,250 per passenger. Excess-valuation insurance can be bought directly from the airline at check-in but leaves your bags vulnerable on the ground.

Trip Insurance There are two sides to this coin. **Trip-cancellation-and-interruption insurance** protects you in the event you are unable to undertake or finish your trip. **Default** or **bankruptcy insurance** protects you against a supplier's failure to deliver. Consider the former if your airline ticket, cruise, or package tour does not allow changes or cancellations. The amount of coverage to buy should equal the cost of your trip should you, a traveling companion, or a family member get sick, forcing you to stay home, plus the nondiscounted one-way airline ticket you would need to buy if you had to return home early. Read the fine print carefully; pay attention to sections defining "family member" and "preexisting medical conditions." A characteristic quirk of default policies is that they often do not cover default by travel agencies or default by a tour operator, airline, or cruise line if you bought your tour and the coverage directly from the firm in question. To reduce your need for default insurance, give preference to tours packaged by members of the United States Tour Operators Association (USTOA), which maintains a fund to reimburse clients in the event of member defaults. Even better, pay for travel arrangements with a major credit card, so that you can refuse to pay the bill if services have not been rendered—and let the card company fight your battles.

Comprehensive Companies supplying comprehensive policies with some or all
Policies of the above features include **Access America, Inc.,** underwritten by BCS Insurance Company (Box 11188, Richmond, VA 23230, tel. 800/284–8300); **Carefree Travel Insurance,** underwritten by The Hartford (Box 310, 120 Mineola Blvd., Mineola, NY 11501, tel. 516/294–0220 or 800/323–3149); **Tele-Trip** (Mutual of Omaha Plaza, Box 31762, Omaha, NE 68131, tel. 800/228–9792), a subsidiary of Mutual of Omaha; **The Travelers Companies** (1 Tower Sq., Hartford, CT 06183, tel. 203/277–0111 or 800/243–3174); **Travel Guard International,** underwritten by Transamerica Occidental Life Companies (1145 Clark St., Stevens Point, WI 54481, tel. 715/345–0505 or 800/782–5151); and **Wallach and Company, Inc.** (107 W. Federal St., Box 480, Middleburg, VA 22117, tel. 703/687–3166 or 800/237–6615), underwritten by Lloyds, London. These companies may also offer the above types of insurance separately.

U.K. Residents Most tour operators, travel agents, and insurance agents sell specialized policies covering accident, medical expenses, personal liability, trip cancellation, and loss or theft of personal property. Some policies include coverage for delayed departure and legal expenses, winter-sports accidents, or motoring abroad. You can also purchase an annual travel-insurance policy valid for every trip you make during the year in which it's purchased (usually only trips of less than 90 days). Before you leave, make sure you will be covered if you have a preexisting medical condition or are pregnant; your insurers may not pay for routine or continuing treatment, or may require a note from your doctor certifying your fitness to travel.

For advice by phone or a free booklet, "Holiday Insurance," that sets out what to expect from a holiday-insurance policy and gives price guidelines, contact the **Association of British Insurers** (51 Gresham St., London EC2V 7HQ, tel. 071/600–3333; 30 Gordon St., Glasgow G1 3PU, tel. 041/226–3905; Scot-

tish Provincial Bldg., Donegall Sq. W, Belfast BT1 6JE, tel.
0232/249176; call for other locations).

Car Rentals

There's no reason to rent a car if you plan to stay in the Paris
area. Traffic is almost always heavy, parking is impossible, and
unpleasant confrontations with Parisian drivers will not contribute to a favorable impression of the city. Moreover, gas is
quite expensive in Paris; prices vary, but expect to pay between 5 and 6 francs per liter. On the other hand, taxis are a
relatively good deal, and public transportation is generally fast
and efficient; RER trains go directly to Versailles and Euro
Disney, and other trains depart frequently for Fontainebleau
and Giverny. For more information on other transportation options, *see* Getting Around Paris, *below*.

All major car-rental companies are represented in Paris, including **Avis** (tel. 800/331–1212, 800/879–2847 in Canada); **Budget** (tel. 800/527–0700); **Dollar** (tel. 800/800–4000); **Hertz** (tel.
800/654–3131, 800/263-0600 in Canada); **National** (tel. 800/227–
7368), known internationally as InterRent and Europcar (tel.
800/227–7368); and **Thrifty** (tel. 800/367–2277). Rates range
from $40 per day for an economy car to $80 for a mid-size car
with automatic transmission, weekly unlimited-mileage rates
range from $200 to $430. This does not include VAT tax, which
in France is among the highest in Europe, 18.6%.

Requirements Your own driver's license is acceptable. An International Driver's Permit, available from the American or Canadian Automo-
bile Association, is a good idea.

Extra Charges Picking up the car in one city or country and leaving it in another may entail drop-off charges or one-way service fees, which
can be substantial. The cost of a collision or loss-damage waiver
(*see below*) can be high, also. Automatic transmissions and air-
conditioning are not universally available abroad; ask for them
when you book if you want them, and check the cost before you
commit yourself to the rental.

Cutting Costs If you know you will want a car for more than a day or two, you
can save by planning ahead. Major international companies
have programs that discount their standard rates by 15%–30%
if you make the reservation before departure (anywhere from
two to 14 days), rent for a minimum number of days (typically
three or four), and prepay the rental. Ask about these advance-
purchase schemes when you call for information. More economical rentals are those that come as part of fly/drive or other
packages, even those as bare-bones as the rental plus an airline
ticket (*see* Tours and Packages, *above*).

Budget companies with offices in town may cost less than major
companies with an airport outlet; but you could waste time trying to locate it in return for only a small savings. If you're arriving and departing from different airports, look for a one-way
car rental with no return fees.

Other sources of savings are the several companies that operate as wholesalers—companies that do not own their own fleets
but rent in bulk from those that do and offer advantageous
rates to their customers. Rentals through such companies must
be arranged and paid for before you leave the United States.
Among them are **Auto Europe** (Box 1097, Camden, ME 04843,

tel. 207/236–8235 or 800/223–5555, 800/458–9503 in Canada), **Connex International** (23 N. Division St., Peekskill, NY 10566, tel. 914/739–0066, 800/333–3949, 800/843–5416 in Canada), **Europe by Car** (mailing address, 1 Rockefeller Plaza, New York, NY 10020; walk-in address, 14 W. 49th St, New York, NY 10020, tel. 212/581–3040 or 212/245–1713; 9000 Sunset Blvd., Los Angeles, CA 90069, tel. 213/252–9401 or 800/223–1516 in CA), **Kemwel** (106 Calvert St., Harrison, NY 10528, tel. 914/835–5555 or 800/678–0678), and **Foremost Euro-Car** (5430 Van Nuys Blvd., Suite 306, Van Nuys, CA 91401, tel. 818/786–1960 or 800/272–3299). Always ask whether the prices are guaranteed in U.S. dollars or foreign currency and if unlimited mileage is available. Find out about any required deposits, cancellation penalties, and drop-off charges, and confirm the cost of the collison damage waiver (CDW). One last tip: Remember to fill the tank when you turn in the vehicle, to avoid being charged for refueling at what you'll swear is the most expensive pump in town.

Insurance and Collision Damage Waiver The standard rental contract includes liability coverage (for damage to public property, injury to pedestrians, etc.) and coverage for the car against fire, theft (not included in certain countries), and collision damage with a deductible—most commonly $2,000–$3,000, occasionally more. In the case of an accident, you are responsible for the deductible amount unless you've purchased the CDW, which costs an average $12 a day, although this varies depending on what you've rented, where, and from whom.

Because this adds up quickly, you may be inclined to say "no thanks"—and that's certainly your option, although the rental agent may not tell you so. Planning ahead will help you make the right decision. By all means, find out if your own insurance covers damage to a rental car while traveling (not simply a car to drive when yours is in for repairs). And check whether charging car rentals to any of your credit cards will get you a CDW at no charge. Note before you decline that deductibles are occasionally high enough that totaling a car would make you responsible for its full value.

Rail Passes

If you're traveling outside Paris, you may want to invest in a rail pass or a combination air-and-rail, rail-and-car, or air-rail-car pass. All must be purchased before leaving for France, and are sold by travel agents and by **Rail Europe** (226–230 Westchester Ave., White Plains, NY 10604, tel. 914/682–5172 or 800/848–7245 from the East and 800/848–7245 from the West).

Student and Youth Travel

In keeping with a tradition of subsidizing education, Paris offers a variety of student discounts. Most museums and movie theaters offer students a **tarif réduit** of 20%–50%. An International Student Identity Card (*see below*) entitles you to significant discounts on train and airplane travel, theater, and youth hostels. For a detailed listing of deals for students in Paris, ask for the brochure *Jeunes à Paris* from the main tourist office (127 av. des Champs-Elysées, tel. 47–23–61–72). Also try **Usit Voyages** (12 rue Vivienne, tel. 42–96–15–88), a travel agency specializing in youth travel, for current information. **Accueil**

des Jeunes en France (AJF, 119 rue St-Martin, 4e, tel. 42–77–87–80) provides information on low-cost lodging and can supply you with maps, ISIC cards, reduced-fare train and bus tickets, and meal vouchers for student cafeterias. **Office de Tourisme Universitaire** (OTU, 39 av. G. Bernanos, 5e, tel. 43–36–80–27) has reduced-fare plane and train tickets. Starving students with valid Student ID can purchase meal tickets at university restaurants for around 25 francs. The food won't dazzle gourmets, but it will probably beat the institutional fare you are used to. Contact **CROUS** (30 av. Georges Brenanos, 5e, tel. 40–51–36–00) for more information.

Travel Agencies The foremost U.S. student travel agency is **Council Travel,** a subsidiary of the nonprofit Council on International Educational Exchange. It specializes in low-cost travel arrangements, is the exclusive U.S. agent for several discount cards, and, with its sister CIEE subsidiary, **Council Charter,** is a source of airfare bargains. The Council Charter brochure and CIEE's twice-yearly *Student Travels* magazine, which details its programs, are available at the Council Travel office at CIEE headquarters (205 E. 42nd Street, New York, NY 10017, tel. 212/661–1450) and at 37 branches in college towns nationwide (free in person, $1 by mail). The **Educational Travel Center** (ETC, 438 N. Francis St., Madison, WI 53703, tel. 608/256–5551) also offers low-cost rail passes, domestic and international airline tickets (mostly for flights departing from Chicago), and other budgetwise travel arrangements. Other travel agencies catering to students include **Travel Management International** (TMI, 18 Prescott St., Suite 4, Cambridge, MA 02138, tel. 617/661–8187) and **Travel Cuts** (187 College St., Toronto, Ont. M5T 1P7, tel. 416/979–2406).

Discount Cards For discounts on transportation and on museum and attractions admissions, buy the **International Student Identity Card** (ISIC) if you're a bona fide student, or the **International Youth Card** (IYC) if you're under 26. In the United States the ISIC and IYC cards cost $15 each and include basic travel accident and sickness coverage. Apply to **CIEE** (*see* address, *above*, tel. 212/661–1414; the application is in *Student Travels*). In Canada the cards are available for $15 each from **Travel Cuts** (*see above*). In the United Kingdom they cost £5 and £4 respectively at student unions and student travel companies, including Council Travel's London office (28A Poland St., London W1V 3DB, tel. 071/437–7767).

Hosteling An International Youth Hostel Federation (IYHF) membership card is the key to more than 5,300 hostel locations in 59 countries; the sex-segregated, dormitory-style sleeping quarters, including some for families, go for $7–$20 a night per person. Membership is available in the United States through American Youth Hostels (AYH, 733 15th St. NW, Washington, DC 20005, tel. 202/783–6161), and costs $25 for adults 18–54, $10 for those under 18, $15 for those 55 and over, and $35 for families. Volume 1 of the two-volume *Guide to Budget Accommodation* lists hostels in Europe and the Mediterranean ($13.95, including postage). IYHF membership is available in Canada through the Canadian Hostelling Association (CHA, 1600 James Naismith Dr., Suite 608, Gloucester, Ont. K1B 5N4, tel. 613/748–5638) for $26.75, and in the United Kingdom through the Youth Hostel Association of England and Wales (Trevelyan House, 8 St. Stephen's Hill, St. Albans, Herts. AL1

2DY, tel. 0727/55215) for £9. For more information on student and budget accommodations, *see* Where to Stay on a Budget, Chapter 2.

Traveling with Children

Despite their reputed chilliness, most Parisians regard children warmly. Many restaurants serve children's portions and have high chairs, and larger hotels will provide cribs free to guests with young children. (This is often not the case in *pensions* and smaller hotels.) Paris has plenty of diversions for the young, and almost all museums and movie theaters offer discounted rates to children.

Getting around Paris with a stroller can be a challenge. Not all métro stations have escalators, and many museums will require you to check the stroller at the entry. Buses are a better bet, since they are often not as crowded as the métro and have adequate space for strollers and carriages. You won't have a problem finding items such as diapers (*couches à jeter*) or baby food. Supermarkets carry several major brands of each, and after-hours pharmacies provide the essentials.

Publications *Family Travel Times*, published 10 times a year by **Travel With**
Newsletter **Your Children** (TWYCH, 45 W. 18th St., 7th Floor Tower, New York, NY 10011, tel. 212/206–0688; annual subscription $55), covers destinations, types of vacations, and modes of travel; an airline issue comes out every other year (the last one, February/March 1993, is sold to nonsubscribers for $10). On Wednesday, the staff answers subscribers' questions on specific destinations.

Books *Great Vacations with Your Kids*, by Dorothy Jordan and Marjorie Cohen ($13; Penguin USA, 120 Woodbine St., Bergenfield, NJ 07621, tel. 800/253–6476), and *Traveling with Children—And Enjoying It*, by Arlene K. Butler ($11.95 plus $3 shipping per book; Globe Pequot Press, Box 833, Old Saybrook, CT 06475, tel. 800/243–0495, or 800/962–0973 in CT), both help you plan your trip with children, from toddlers to teens. *Innocents Abroad: Traveling with Kids in Europe*, by Valerie Wolf Deutsch and Laura Sutherland ($15.95 or $4.95 paperback, Penguin USA, *see above*), covers child- and teen-friendly activities, food, and transportation.

Tour Operators **GrandTravel** (6900 Wisconsin Ave., Suite 706, Chevy Chase, MD 20815, tel. 301/986–0790 or 800/247–7651) offers international and domestic tours for grandparents traveling with their grandchildren. The catalogue, as charmingly written and illustrated as a children's book, positively invites armchair traveling with lap-sitters aboard. **Families Welcome!** (21 W. Colony Pl., Suite 140, Durham, NC 27705, tel. 919/489–2555 or 800/326–0724) packages and sells family tours to Europe. **Rascals in Paradise** (650 5th St., Suite 505, San Francisco, CA 94107, tel. 415/978–9800, or 800/872–7225) specializes in programs for families. Another family travel arranger that can even set up short-term rentals is **The French Experience** (370 Lexington Ave., New York, NY 10017, tel. 212/986–3800).

Hotels The **Novotel** chain (international reservations, tel. 800/221–4542) allows up to two children under 15 to stay free in their parents' room, and many properties have playgrounds. **Sofitel** hotels (international reservations, tel. 800/221–4542) offer a free second room for children during July and August and over the Christmas period.

Getting There On international flights, the fare for infants under 2 not occupy-
Airfares ing a seat is generally 10% of the accompanying adult's fare; children ages 2–11 usually pay half to two-thirds of the adult fare.

Baggage In general, infants paying 10% of the adult fare are allowed one carry-on bag, not to exceed 70 pounds or 45 inches (length + width + height). The adult baggage allowance applies for children paying half or more of the adult fare. Check with the airline for particulars, especially regarding flights between two foreign destinations, where allowances for infants may be less generous than those above.

Safety Seats The FAA recommends the use of safety seats aloft and details approved models in the free leaflet **"Child/Infant Safety Seats Recommended for Use in Aircraft"** (available from the Federal Aviation Administration, APA–200, 800 Independence Ave. SW, Washington, DC 20591, tel. 202/267–3479). Airline policy varies. U.S. carriers must allow FAA-approved models, but because these seats are strapped into a regular passenger seat, they may require that parents buy a ticket even for an infant under 2 who would otherwise ride free. Foreign carriers may not allow infant seats, may charge the child's rather than the infant's fare for their use, or may require you to hold your baby during takeoff and landing, thus defeating the seat's purpose.

Facilities Aloft Airlines do provide other facilities and services for children, such as children's meals and freestanding bassinets (to those sitting in seats on the bulkhead, where there's enough legroom to accommodate them). Make your request when reserving. The annual February/March issue of *Family Travel Times* gives details of the children's services of dozens of airlines (*see above*). "Kids and Teens in Flight" (free from the U.S. Department of Transportation, tel. 202/366–2220) offers tips for children flying alone.

Baby-sitting First check with the hotel concierge for recommended child-
Services care arrangements. Local agencies include: **Ababa,** 8 av. du Maine, 15e, tel. 45–49–46–46; **Allô Service Maman,** 21 rue de Brey, 75017 Paris, tel. 42–67–99–37; **Allo Maman Poule,** 4 rue Greffulhe, Levallois, tel. 47–48–01–01; **Baby Sitting Service,** 18 rue Tronchet, 75008 Paris, tel. 46–37–51–24; and **Home Service,** 5 rue Yvon-Villarceau, 75016 Paris, tel. 45–00–82–51. All can provide English-speaking baby-sitters with just a few hours notice. *L'Officiel des Spectacles* lists baby-sitting agencies under "Gardes d' Enfants." Expect to pay between 28 and 35 francs per hour, plus an additional 50-franc agency fee.

Miscellaneous Contact the **CIDJ** (Centre d'Information et de Documentation pour la Jeunesse, 101 quai Branly, 75015 Paris, tel. 45–67–35–85) for information about activities and events for youngsters in Paris.

Hints for Travelers with Disabilities

Though it has a long way to go, Paris ranks above many European cities in its ability to accommodate travelers with mobility impairments. Most sidewalks now have low curbs, and most arrondissements have public rest rooms and telephone boxes that are wheelchair-accessible. Taxi drivers are required by law to assist travelers with disabilities in and out of their vehicles; specially adapted taxis are available by calling 48–37–85–85. In addition, most métro stations are wheelchair-accessible; an RER and métro access guide is available from the Paris Transit Authority (RATP) office (Pl. de la Madeleine, 8e, tel. 40–46–42–17). Ask for the free brochure *Touristes Quand Même* at the main tourist office (127 av. des Champs-Elysées) for detailed information about wheelchair accessibility.

Organizations Several organizations provide travel information for people with disabilities, usually for a membership fee, and some publish newsletters and bulletins. Among them are the **Information Center for Individuals with Disabilities** (Fort Point Pl., 27–43 Wormwood St., Boston, MA 02210, tel. 617/727–5540 or 800/462–5015 in MA between 11 and 4, or leave message; TDD/TTY tel. 617/345–9743); **Mobility International USA** (Box 3551, Eugene, OR 97403, voice and TDD tel. 503/343–1284), the U.S. branch of an international organization based in Britain and present in 30 countries; **MossRehab Hospital Travel Information Service** (1200 W. Tabor Rd., Philadelphia, PA 19141, tel. 215/456–9603, TDD tel. 215/456–9602); the **Society for the Advancement of Travel for the Handicapped** (SATH, 347 5th Ave., Suite 610, New York, NY 10016, tel. 212/447–7284, fax 212/725–8253); the **Travel Industry and Disabled Exchange** (TIDE, 5435 Donna Ave., Tarzana, CA 91356, tel. 818/368–5648); and **Travelin' Talk** (Box 3534, Clarksville, TN 37043, tel. 615/552–6670).

In the United Main sources include the **Royal Association for Disability and**
Kingdom **Rehabilitation** (RADAR, 25 Mortimer St., London W1N 8AB, tel. 071/637–5400), which publishes travel information for the disabled in Britain, and **Mobility International** (228 Borough High St., London SE1 1JX, tel. 071/403–5688), the headquarters of an international membership organization that serves as a clearinghouse of travel information for people with disabilities.

Travel Agencies **Directions Unlimited** (720 N. Bedford Rd., Bedford Hills, NY
and Tour Operators 10507, tel. 914/241–1700), a travel agency, has expertise in tours and cruises for the disabled. **Evergreen Travel Service** (4114 198th St. SW, Suite 13, Lynnwood, WA 98036, tel. 206/776–1184 or 800/435–2288) operates Wings on Wheels Tours for those in wheelchairs, White Cane Tours for the blind, and tours for the deaf, and makes group and independent arrangements for travelers with any disability. **Flying Wheels Travel** (143 W. Bridge St., Box 382, Owatonna, MN 55060, tel. 800/535–6790 or 800/722–9351 in MN), a tour operator and travel agency, arranges international tours, cruises, and independent travel itineraries for people with mobility disabilities. **Nautilus,** at the same address as TIDE (*see above*), packages tours for the disabled internationally.

Publications Several free publications are available from the Consumer Information Center (Pueblo, CO 81009): "New Horizons for the Air Traveler with a Disability," a U.S. Department of Transportation booklet describing changes resulting from the 1986 Air Carrier Access Act and those still to come from the 1990 Americans with Disabilities Act (include Department 608Y in the address), and the Airport Operators Council's *Access Travel: Airports* (Dept. 5804), which describes facilities and services for the disabled at more than 500 airports worldwide.

Twin Peaks Press (Box 129, Vancouver, WA 98666, tel. 206/ 694–2462 or 800/637–2256) publishes the *Directory of Travel Agencies for the Disabled* ($19.95), listing more than 370 agencies worldwide; *Travel for the Disabled* ($19.95), listing some 500 access guides and accessible places worldwide; the *Directory of Accessible Van Rentals* ($9.95) for campers and RV travelers worldwide; and *Wheelchair Vagabond* ($14.95), a collection of personal travel tips. Add $2 per book for shipping.

Hints for Older Travelers

Older travelers to Paris enjoy most of the same discounts offered students. Museums and movie theaters offer a 20%–50% discount for people over 60. Seniors 60 and older are also eligible for the **Carte Vermeil,** which entitles the bearer to discounts on the French domestic airline (Air Inter), rail travel outside Paris, the bus and Métro, and reduced admission prices for films and many cultural events. Cards are available at any rail station in France (cost: 139 francs).

Organizations The **American Association of Retired Persons** (AARP, 601 E St. NW, Washington, DC 20049, tel. 202/434–2277) provides independent travelers the Purchase Privilege Program, which offers discounts on hotels, car rentals, and sightseeing, and the AARP Motoring Plan, provided by Amoco, which furnishes domestic trip-routing information and emergency road-service aid for an annual fee of $39.95 per person or couple ($59.95 for a premium version). AARP also arranges group tours, cruises, and apartment living through AARP Travel Experience from American Express (400 Pinnacle Way, Suite 450, Norcross, GA 30071, tel. 800/927–0111); these can be booked through travel agents, except for the cruises, which must be booked directly (tel. 800/745–4567). AARP membership is open to those 50 and over; annual dues are $8 per person or couple.

Two other membership organizations offer discounts on lodgings, car rentals, and other travel products, along with such nontravel perks as magazines and newsletters. The **National Council of Senior Citizens** (1331 F St. NW, Washington, DC 20004, tel. 202/347–8800) is a nonprofit advocacy group with some 5,000 local clubs across the United States; membership costs $12 per person or couple annually. **Mature Outlook** (6001 N. Clark St., Chicago, IL 60660, tel. 800/336–6330), a Sears Roebuck & Co. subsidiary with 800,000 members, charges $9.95 for an annual membership.

Note: When using any senior-citizen identification card for reduced hotel rates, mention it when booking, not when checking out. At restaurants, show your card before you're seated; discounts may be limited to certain menus, days, or hours. If you are renting a car, ask about promotional rates that might improve on your senior-citizen discount.

Tour Operators **Saga International Holidays** (222 Berkeley St., Boston, MA 02116, tel. 800/343–0273), which specializes in group travel for people over 60, offers a selection of variously priced tours and cruises covering five continents as well as a Road Scholar program of educational tours, mostly to European destinations. If you want to take your grandchildren, look into **GrandTravel** (*see* Traveling with Children, *above*).

Arriving and Departing

From North America by Plane

Flights are either nonstop, direct, or connecting. A **nonstop** flight requires no change of plane and makes no stops. A **direct** flight stops at least once and can involve a change of plane, although the flight number remains the same; if the first leg is late, the second waits. This is not the case with a **connecting** flight, which involves a different plane and a different flight number.

Airlines　The airlines that serve Paris from various major U.S. cities include **Air France** (tel. 800/237–2747, tel. 45–35–61–61 in Paris), **TWA** (tel. 800/892–4141, tel. 47–20–62–11 in Paris), **American Airlines** (tel. 800/433–7300, tel. 42–89–05–22 in Paris), **Delta** (tel. 800/241–4141, tel. 47–68–92–92 in Paris), **United** (tel. 800/538–2929, tel. 48–97–82–82 in Paris), **Continental** (tel. 800/231–0856, tel. 42–99–09–09 in Paris), **Northwest** (tel. 800/225–2525, tel. 42–66–90–00 in Paris) and **USAir** (tel. 800/428–4322, tel. 49–10–29–00 in Paris). Most local reservations offices are closed on Sundays.

Flying Time　From New York: 7 hours. From Chicago: 9½ hours. From Los Angeles: 11 hours.

Cutting Flight Costs　The Sunday travel section of most newspapers is a good source of deals. When booking, particularly through an unfamiliar company, call the Better Business Bureau to find out whether any complaints have been registered against the company, pay with a credit card if you can, and consider trip-cancellation and default insurance (*see* Insurance, *above*).

Promotional Airfares　All the less expensive fares, called promotional or discount fares, are round-trip and involve restrictions. The exact nature of the restrictions depends on the airline, the route, and the season, and on whether travel is domestic or international, but you must usually buy the ticket—commonly called an APEX (advance purchase excursion) when it's for international travel—in advance (seven, 14, or 21 days are usual). You must also respect certain minimum- and maximum-stay requirements (for instance, over a Saturday night or at least seven and no more than 30, 45, or 90 days), and you must be willing to pay penalties for changes. Airlines generally allow some changes for a fee. But the cheaper the fare, the more likely the ticket is nonrefundable; it would take a death in the family for the airline to give you any of your money back if you had to cancel. The cheapest fares are also subject to availability.

Consolidators　Consolidators or bulk-fare operators—also known as bucket shops—buy blocks of seats on scheduled flights that airlines anticipate they won't be able to sell. They pay wholesale prices, add a markup, and resell the seats to travel agents or directly to the public at prices that still undercut the airline's promotional or discount fares. You pay more than on a charter but ordinarily less than for an APEX ticket, and, even when there is not much of a price difference, the ticket usually comes without the advance-purchase restriction. Moreover, although tickets are marked nonrefundable so you can't turn them in to the airline for a full-fare refund, some consolidators sometimes give you your money back. Carefully read the fine print detailing penalties for changes and cancellations. If you doubt the reliability of a company, call the airline once you've made your booking and confirm that you do, indeed, have a reservation on the flight.

The biggest U.S. consolidator, C.L. Thomson Express, sells only to travel agents. Well-established consolidators selling to the public include **UniTravel** (Box 12485, St. Louis, MO 63132, tel. 314/569–0900 or 800/325–2222); **Council Charter** (205 E. 42nd St., New York, NY 10017, tel. 212/661–0311 or 800/800–8222), a division of the Council on International Educational Exchange and a longtime charter operator now functioning more as a consolidator; and **Travac** (989 6th Ave., New York, NY 10018, tel. 212/563–3303 or 800/872–8800).

Charter Flights Charters usually have the lowest fares and the most restrictions. Departures are limited and seldom on time, and you can lose all or most of your money if you cancel. (Generally, the closer to departure you cancel, the more you lose.) The charterer, on the other hand, may legally cancel the flight for any reason up to 10 days before departure; within 10 days of departure, the flight may be canceled only if it becomes physically impossible to operate it. The charterer may also revise the itinerary or increase the price after you have bought the ticket, but if the new arrangement constitutes a "major change," you have the right to a refund. Before buying a charter ticket, read the fine print for the company's refund policy and details on major changes. Money for charter flights is usually paid into a bank escrow account, the name of which should be on the contract. If you don't pay by credit card, make your check payable to the escrow account (unless you're dealing with a travel agent, in which case, his or her check should be payable to the escrow account). The Department of Transportation's Consumer Affairs Office (I–25, Washington, DC 20590, tel. 202/366–2220) can answer questions on charters and send you its "Plane Talk: Public Charter Flights" information sheet.

Charter operators may offer flights alone or with ground arrangements that constitute a charter package. Well-established charter operators include **Council Charter** (205 E. 42nd St., New York, NY 10017, tel. 212/661–0311 or 800/800–8222), now largely a consolidator, despite its name, and **Travel Charter** (1120 E. Long Lake Rd., Troy, MI 48098, tel. 313/528–3570 or 800/521–5267), with Midwestern departures. **DER Tours** (Box 1606, Des Plains, IL 60017, tel. 800/782–2424), a charterer and consolidator, sells through travel agents.

Discount Travel Travel clubs offer their members unsold space on airplanes, *Clubs* cruise ships, and package tours at nearly the last minute and at well below the original cost. Suppliers thus receive some revenue for their "leftovers," and members get a bargain. Membership generally includes a regular bulletin or access to a toll-free telephone hot line giving details of available trips departing anywhere from three or four days to several months in the future. Packages tend to be more common than flights alone, so if airfares are your only interest, read the literature before joining. Reductions on hotels are also available. Clubs include **Discount Travel International** (114 Forrest Ave., Suite 203, Narberth, PA 19072, tel. 215/668–7184; $45 annually, single or family), **Moment's Notice** (425 Madison Ave., New York, NY 10017, tel. 212/486–0503; $45 annually, single or family), **Travelers Advantage** (CUC Travel Service, 49 Music Sq. W, Nashville, TN 37203, tel. 800/548–1116; $49 annually, single or family), and **Worldwide Discount Travel Club** (1674 Meridian Ave., Miami Beach, FL 33139, tel. 305/534–2082; $50 annually for family, $40 single).

Flying as a Courier A courier is someone who accompanies a shipment between designated points so it can clear customs quickly as personal baggage. Because the courier company actually purchases a seat for the package, which uses the seat's checked-baggage allowance, it can allow you to occupy the paid seat at a vastly reduced rate. You must have a flexible schedule, however, as well as the ability to travel light, because you usually must make do with only carry-on baggage. *The Insiders Guide to Air Courier Bargains,* by Kelly Monaghan, gives more information ($16.95, including postage; Intrepid Traveler, Box 438, New York, NY 10034, tel. 800/356–9315). If you're really serious, you might want to join a membership organization such as the International Association of Air Travel Couriers (Box 1349, Lake Worth, FL 33460, tel. 407/582–8320), which publishes six newsletters and six bulletins yearly listing courier opportunities worldwide. In general, couriers get their assignments from a booking agent, not directly from the courier company. One such agent is **Now Voyager** (74 Varick St., Suite 307, New York, NY 10013, tel. 212/431–1616), which places couriers on flights to various destinations.

Enjoying the Because the air aloft is dry, drink plenty of beverages while on
Flight board; remember that drinking alcohol contributes to jet lag, as do heavy meals. Sleepers usually prefer window seats to curl up against; restless passengers ask to be on the aisle. Bulkhead seats, in the front row of each cabin, have more legroom, but since there's no seat ahead, trays attach awkwardly to the arms of your seat, and you must stow all possessions overhead. Bulkhead seats are usually reserved for the disabled, the elderly, and people traveling with babies.

Smoking Since February 1990, smoking has been banned on all domestic flights of less than six hours' duration; the ban also applies to domestic segments of international flights aboard U.S. and foreign carriers. On U.S. carriers flying to Paris and other destinations abroad, a seat in a no-smoking section must be provided for every passenger who requests one, and the section must be enlarged to accommodate such passengers if necessary as long as they have complied with the airline's deadline for check-in and seat assignment. If smoking bothers you, request a seat far from the smoking section.

Foreign airlines are exempt from these rules but do provide no-smoking sections, and some nations have gone as far as to ban smoking on all domestic flights; other countries may ban smoking on flights of less than a specified duration. The International Civil Aviation Organization has set July 1, 1996, as the date to ban smoking aboard airlines worldwide, but the body has no power to enforce its decisions.

Between the The many public transportation options between the airports
Airports and and central Paris make the trip affordable and convenient.
Downtown Avoid taxis unless you are three or more (often drivers will
Charles de Gaulle only take three passengers anyway). A taxi ride from either
(Roissy) airport to downtown Paris can run as high as 200 francs, with an additional 5 francs per bag. The easiest way to get into Paris is on the **RER-B** line, the suburban express train. A free shut-

tle bus—look for the word *navette*—runs between the two terminal buildings and the train station; it takes about 10 minutes. Trains to central Paris (Les Halles, St-Michel, Luxembourg) leave every 15 minutes. The fare (including métro connection) is 33 francs, and journey time is about 30 minutes. **Buses** run every 20 minutes between Charles de Gaulle airport and the Arc de Triomphe, with a stop at the Air France air terminal at Porte Maillot. The fare is 48 francs, and journey time is about 40 minutes. The **Roissybus,** operated by the Paris Transit Authority, has buses every 15 minutes to rue Scribe at the Opéra; cost is 30 francs.

Orly Airport   The easiest way to get into Paris is on the **RER-C** line, the suburban express train. Again, there's a free shuttle bus from the terminal building to the train station. Trains to Paris leave every 15 minutes. The fare is 42 francs, and journey time is about 25 minutes. A shuttle-train service, **Orlyval,** runs between the Antony RER-B station and Orly airport every 7 minutes. The fare from downtown Paris is 42 francs during peak periods, or 32 francs daily 11 AM–3 PM and after 9 PM, and Sat. noon–Sun. noon. **Buses** run every 12 minutes between Orly airport and the Air France air terminal at Les Invalides on the Left Bank. The fare is 32 francs, and journey time is between 30 and 60 minutes, depending on traffic. The Paris Transit Authority's **Orlybus** leaves every 15 minutes for the Denfert-Rochereau métro station; cost is 23 francs.

From the United Kingdom

By Plane   **Air France** (tel. 081/742–6600) and **British Airways** (tel. 081/897–4000) together offer service from London's Heathrow Airport to Paris every hour to two hours. The cost of round-trip tickets is almost halved if you purchase them 14 days in advance and stay over on a Saturday night. There are three **British Airways** and up to five **Air France** flights daily, except weekends, to Paris from London's most central airport, London City, in the Docklands area.

Other airlines with regular scheduled flights from London to Paris include **British Midland** (tel. 081/754-7321), **TAT European** (tel. 0293–567955), and **Dan Air** (tel. 081/759-1818). Except on Sundays, there are several daily flights (mostly Air France and BA) direct to Paris from Manchester, Bristol, and Birmingham, and up to four from Glasgow, Edinburgh, Aberdeen, Cardiff, Belfast, Newcastle, and Southampton.

The Paris Travel Service (115 Buckingham Palace Rd., London SW1 V9SJ, tel. 071/2337892) operates a good-value weekly Paris Express from Gatwick to Beauvais (a 40-minute flight and a one-hour bus ride into central Paris). Departure is on Friday, and return is the following Monday.

By Car   There are a number of different driving routes to Paris. The Dover–Calais route includes the shortest Channel crossing; the Newhaven–Dieppe route requires a longer Channel crossing but a shorter drive through France.

Dover–Calais   Ticket prices for ferries vary widely depending on the number of passengers in a group, the size of the car, the season and time of day, and the length of your trip. Call one of the ferry service reservation offices for more exact information. **P&O European Ferries** (Channel House, Channel View Rd., Dover, Kent CT17

9TJ, tel. 081/575–8555) has up to 15 sailings a day; the crossing takes about 75 minutes. **Sealink** (Charter House, Park St., Ashford, Kent TN24 8EX, tel. 0233/646801) operates up to 18 sailings a day; the crossing takes about 90 minutes. **Hoverspeed** (Maybrook House, Queens Gardens, Dover, Kent CT17 9UQ, tel. 0304/240241) operates up to 23 crossings a day, and the crossing (by Hovercraft) takes 35 minutes.

Dover–Boulogne **P&O European Ferries** has up to six sailings a day with a crossing time of 100 minutes. Fares are the same as for the Dover–Calais crossing. **Hoverspeed** also operates on this route, with six 40-minute crossings a day. The fares are the same as for the Dover–Calais route.

Ramsgate– **Sally Line** (Argyle Centre, York St., Ramsgate, Kent CT11
Dunkerque 9DS, tel. 0843/595522) has up to five 2½-hour crossings a day.

Newhaven–Dieppe **Sealink** has up to four sailings a day; the crossing takes four hours.

Portsmouth– **P&O European Ferries** has up to three sailings a day, and the
Le Havre crossing takes 5¾ hours by day, 7 by night.

Driving distances from the French ports to Paris are as follows: **from Calais,** 290 kilometers (180 miles); **from Boulogne,** 243 kilometers (151 miles); **from Dieppe,** 193 kilometers (120 miles); **from Dunkerque,** 257 kilometers (160 miles). The fastest routes to Paris from each port are via the N43, A26, and A1 from Calais; via the N1 from Boulogne; via the N15 from Le Havre; via the D915 and N1 from Dieppe; and via the A25 and A1 from Dunkerque.

By Train **British Rail** has four departures a day from London's Victoria Station, all linking with the Dover–Calais/Boulogne ferry services through to Paris. There is also an overnight service using the Newhaven–Dieppe ferry. Journey time is about eight hours. Round-trip fare is around £65 (five-day excursion). Credit card bookings are accepted by phone (tel. 071/834–2345) or in person at a British Rail Travel Centre.

The Channel Tunnel, destined for trains only (with cars taken on board) and which will slash the Paris–London journey time to under four hours, pushed back its scheduled opening date to spring 1994. Fare details were not available at press time.

Train Stations Paris has six international rail stations: **Gare du Nord** (northern France, northern Europe, and England via Calais or Boulogne); **Gare St-Lazare** (Normandy, England via Dieppe); **Gare de l'Est** (Strasbourg, Luxembourg, Basle, and central Europe); **Gare de Lyon** (Lyon, Marseille, the Riviera, Geneva, Italy); and **Gare d'Austerlitz** (Loire Valley, southwest France, Spain). Note that **Gare Montparnasse** has taken over as the main terminus for trains bound for southwest France since the introduction of the new TGV-Atlantique service. For train information from any station, call 45–82–50–50. You can reserve tickets in any Paris station, irrespective of destination. Go to the **Grandes Lignes** counter for travel within France and to the **Billets Internationaux** desk if you're heading out of France.

By Bus **Eurolines** (52 Grosvenor Gardens, London SW1W 0AU, tel. 071/730–0202) operates a nightly service from London's Victoria Coach Station, via the Dover–Calais ferry, to Paris. Departures are at 9 AM, arriving at 6:15 PM; 12 noon, arriving at 9:45

PM; and 9 PM, arriving at 7:15 AM. Fares are £52 round-trip (under-25 youth pass £49), £31 one-way.

Hoverspeed (Maybrook House, Queen's Gardens, Dover, Kent CT17 9UQ, tel. 0304/240241) offers a faster journey time with up to five daily departures from Victoria Coach Station. The fare is £25 one-way, £43 round-trip.

Both the Eurolines and Hoverspeed services are bookable in person at any **National Express** office or at the **Coach Travel Centre,** 13 Regent Street, London SW1 4LR. Credit card reservations can be made by calling 071/824–8657.

Staying in Paris

Important Addresses and Numbers

Tourist Information The main **Paris Tourist Office** (127 av. des Champs-Elysées, 75008 Paris, tel. 47–23–61–72) is open daily 9–8. There are also offices at all main train stations, except Gare St-Lazare. Dial 47–20–88–98 for recorded information in English.

Embassies **U.S. Embassy** (2 av. Gabriel, 8e, tel. 42–96–12–02). **Canadian Embassy** (35 av. Montaigne, 8e, tel. 44–43–32–00). **British Embassy** (35 rue du Fbg. St-Honoré, 8e, tel. 42–66–91–42).

Emergencies **Police** (tel. 17). **Ambulance** (tel. 15 or 45–67–50–50). **Doctor** (tel. 47–07–77–77). **Dentist** (tel. 43–37–51–00).

Hospitals **The American Hospital** (63 blvd. Victor Hugo, Neuilly, tel. 46–41–25–25) has a 24-hour emergency service. **The Hertford British Hospital** (3 rue Barbès, Levallois-Perret, tel. 47–58–13–12) also offers a 24-hour service.

Pharmacies **Dhéry** (Galerie des Champs, 84 av. des Champs-Elysées, 8e, tel. 45–62–02–41) is open 24 hours. **Drugstore Publicis** (corner of blvd. St-Germain and rue de Rennes, 6e) is open daily till 2 AM. **Pharmacie des Arts** (106 blvd. Montparnasse, 14e) is open daily till midnight.

Tour Operators **American Express** (11 rue Scribe, 9e, tel. 47–77–70–00). **Air France** (119 av. des Champs-Elysées, 8e, tel. 42–99–23–64). **Wagons-Lits** (8 rue Auber, 9e, tel. 42–66–90–90).

Money Exchange Exchange offices in most of the main-line Paris rail stations (Austerlitz, Lyon, Est, Nord, St-Lazare) are open daily 7 AM–8 PM. They are convenient but do not offer the best rates. A majority of the banks in central Paris provide exchange facilities at more competitive rates, usually with a fixed commission. You can change money at several locations near the tourist office on the Champs Elysées: **Union de Banques à Paris** (154 Champs Elysées); **Chequepoint** (no commission, open 24 hours, 150 Champs Elysées); and **Banque Niçoise de Credit** (125 Champs Elysées). Note the 24-hour **Change Automatique** (66 Champs Elysées), which accepts $5, $10, and $20 bills. There are also numerous exchange offices around the Louvre.

Telephones

To call Paris from the United States, dial 011–33–1 and then the local eight-digit number.

Local Calls The French telephone system is modern and efficient. A local call costs 73 centimes plus 12 centimes per minute. Call-boxes are plentiful; they're found at post offices and often in cafés.

Most French pay phones are now operated by cards *(télécartes)*, which you can buy from post offices and some *tabacs* (cost is 40 francs for 50 units; 96 francs for 120). In cafés you can still find pay phones that operate with 50-centime, 1-, 2-, and 5-franc coins (1 franc minimum). Lift the receiver, place your coin(s) in the appropriate slots, and dial. Unused coins are returned when you hang up. All French phone numbers have eight digits; a code is required only when calling Paris from outside the city (add 16–1 for Paris) and when calling outside the city from Paris (add 16, then the number). Note that the number system was changed in 1985, so you may come across some seven-figure numbers in Paris and some six-figure ones elsewhere. Add 4 to the start of such Paris numbers, and add the former two-figure area code to the provincial numbers.

International Calls Dial 19 and wait for the tone, then dial the country code (1 for the United States and Canada, 44 for the United Kingdom) and the area code (minus any initial 0) and number. Expect to be overcharged if you make calls from your hotel. Approximate daytime rates, per minute, are 9.36 francs to the United States and Canada; 4.50 francs to the United Kingdom; reduced rates, per minute, are 5.71 francs (2 AM–noon) to the United States and Canada or 7.17 francs (8 PM–2 AM weekdays, noon–2 AM Sun. and public holidays); and 3 francs to the United Kingdom (before 8 AM and after 2 PM).

AT&T's USA Direct program allows callers to take advantage of AT&T rates by connecting directly with the AT&T system. To do so from France dial 19-0011. You can then either dial direct (area code + number), billing the call to a credit card, or make a collect call.

Operators and Information To find a number within France or to request information, dial 12. For international inquiries, dial 19–33 plus the country code.

Mail

Post offices, or PTT, are scattered throughout every arrondissement, and are recognizable by a yellow sign. They are usually open weekdays 8 AM–noon and 2:30–7 PM, Sat. 8 AM–noon. The main office, 52 rue du Louvre, 1er, is open 24 hours.

Rates Airmail letters to the United States and Canada cost 4 francs for 20 grams, 7.30 francs for 30 grams, 7.60 francs for 40 grams, and 7.90 francs for 50 grams. Letters to the United Kingdom cost 2.50 francs for up to 20 grams, as they do within France. Postcards cost 2.30 francs within France and to Canada, the United States, the United Kingdom, and EC countries; 3.70 francs if sent to North America by airmail. Stamps can be bought in post offices and cafés sporting a red TABAC sign.

Receiving Mail If you're uncertain where you'll be staying, have mail sent to **American Express** (if you're a card member), or to **Poste Restante** at any post office.

Getting Around Paris

Paris is relatively small as capital cities go, and most of its prize monuments and museums are within easy walking distance of one another. Walking also lets you participate in the French national sport of people-watching, and gives you an appetite (and an excuse) for that next memorable meal. The most convenient form of public transportation is the métro, with stops every few hundred yards. Buses are a slower alternative, though you do see more of the city. Taxis are relatively inexpensive and convenient, but not always easy to hail. Private car travel within Paris is best avoided; parking is extremely difficult.

Maps of the métro/RER network are available free from any métro station and in many hotels. They are also posted on every platform, as are maps of the bus network. Bus routes are also marked at bus stops and on buses. To help you find your way around Paris, we suggest you buy a *Plan de Paris par arrondissement* (about 20 frs), a city guide with separate maps of each district, including the whereabouts of métro stations and an index of street names. They're on sale in newsstands, bookstores, stationers, and drugstores.

By Métro Métro stations are recognizable either by a large yellow M within a circle or by the distinctive curly green Art Nouveau railings and archway bearing the full title (Métropolitain). The métro is the most efficient way to get around Paris and is so clearly marked at all points that it's easy to find your way around without having to ask directions.

There are 13 métro lines crisscrossing Paris and the suburbs, and you are seldom more than 500 yards from the nearest station. It is essential to know the name of the last station on the line you take, as this name appears on all signs. A connection (you can make as many as you like on one ticket) is called a *correspondance*. At junction stations, illuminated orange signs bearing the name of the line terminus appear over the correct corridors for each *correspondance*. Illuminated blue signs marked *sortie* indicate the station exit.

The métro service starts at 5:30 AM and continues until 1:15 AM, when the last train on each line reaches its terminus. Some lines and stations in the less salubrious parts of Paris are a bit risky at night; in particular Lines 2 and 13. But in general, the métro is relatively safe throughout, provided you don't walk around with your wallet hanging out of your back pocket or (especially women) travel alone late at night. The biggest nuisances you're likely to come across will be the wine-swigging *clochards* (tramps) blurting out drunken songs as they bed down on platform benches.

The métro network connects at several points in Paris with the **RER** network. RER trains, which race across Paris from suburb to suburb, are a sort of supersonic métro and can be great time-savers.

All métro tickets and passes are valid for RER *and* bus travel within Paris. Métro tickets cost 6.50 francs each, though a carnet (10 tickets for 39 francs) is better value. If you're staying for a week or more and plan to use the métro frequently, the best deal is the weekly *(coupon jaune)* or monthly *(carte orange)* ticket, sold according to zone. Zones 1 and 2 cover the entire métro network; tickets cost 59 francs a week or 208 francs a

Paris Métro

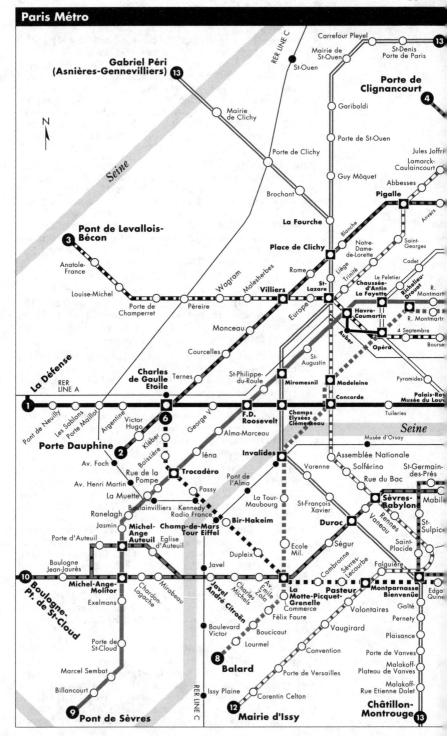

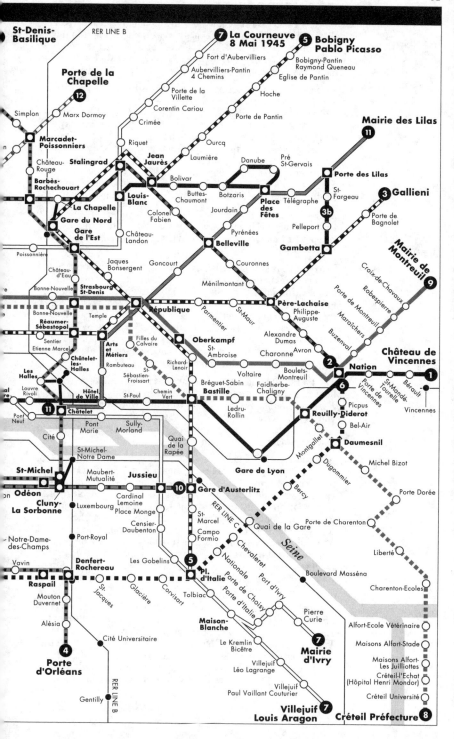

month. If you plan to take suburban trains to visit places in the Ile-de-France, we suggest you consider a four-zone (Versailles, St-Germain-en-Laye; 109 francs a week) or six-zone (Rambouillet, Fontainebleau; 142 francs a week) ticket. For these weekly/monthly tickets, you will need a pass (available from rail and major métro stations) and two passport-size photographs.

Alternatively, there are one-day (*Formule 1*) and two-, three-, and five-day (*Paris Visite*) unlimited travel tickets for the métro, bus, and RER. Their advantage is that, unlike the *coupon jaune*, which is good from Monday morning to Sunday evening, *Formule 1* and *Paris Visite* passes are valid starting any day of the week and also give you discounts on a limited number of museums and tourist attractions. The price is 36 (one-day), 65 (two-day), 90 (three-day), and 145 (five-day) francs for Paris only; 85, 150, 200, and 275 francs, respectively, for suburbs including Versailles, St-Germain-en-Laye, and Euro Disney.

Access to métro and RER platforms is through an automatic ticket barrier. Slide your ticket in and pick it up as it pops out. Keep your ticket during your journey; you'll need it to leave the RER system.

By Bus Travel by bus is a convenient, though slower, way to get around the city. Paris buses are green single-deckers; route number and destination are marked in front and with major stopping-places along the sides. Most routes operate from 6 AM to 8:30 PM; some continue to midnight. Ten night buses operate hourly (1:30–5:30 AM) between Châtelet and various nearby suburbs; they can be stopped by hailing them at any point on their route. The brown bus shelters, topped by red and yellow circular signs, contain timetables and route maps.

The bus accepts métro tickets, or you can buy a single ticket on board. You need to show (but not punch) weekly, monthly, and *Paris-Visite/Formule 1* tickets to the driver as you get on. If you have individual yellow tickets, you should state your destination and be prepared to punch one or more tickets in the red and gray machines on board the bus.

By Taxi Although a taxi ride is more expensive than a bus or the métro, fares are pretty reasonable. Daytime rates (7 AM till 7 PM) within Paris are around 2.80 francs per kilometer, and nighttime rates are around 4.50 francs. There is a basic hire charge of 11 francs for all rides, and a 5-franc supplement per piece of luggage. Rates outside the city limits are about 40% higher. Waiting time is charged at roughly 100 francs per hour. You are best off asking your hotel or restaurant to ring for a taxi, or going to the nearest taxi station (you can find one every couple of blocks); cabs with their signs lit can be hailed, but are annoyingly difficult to spot. Note that taxis seldom take more than three people at a time. Tip the driver about 10%.

By Bike You can hire bikes in the Bois de Boulogne (Jardin d'Acclimatation), Bois de Vincennes, some RER stations, and from the Bateaux-Mouches embarkation point by place de l'Alma. Or try **Paris-Vélo** (2 rue du Fer à Moulin, 5e, tel. 43–37–59–22). Rental rates vary from about 90 to 140 francs per day, 160 to 220 francs per weekend, and 420 to 500 francs per week, depending on the type of bike. There is about a 1,000-franc deposit for rental.

Guided Tours

Orientation Tours Bus tours of Paris offer a good introduction to the city, but they tend to be expensive. The two largest operators are **Cityrama** (4 pl. des Pyramides, 1er, tel. 42–60–30–14) and **Paris Vision** (214 rue de Rivoli, 1er, tel. 42–60–31–25). Their tours start from the place des Pyramides, across from the Louvre end of the Tuileries Gardens. Tours are generally in double-decker buses with either a live or tape-recorded commentary (English, of course, is available) and last three hours. Expect to pay about 150 francs.

The **RATP** (Paris Transport Authority, tel. 40–46–42–17) has many guide-accompanied excursions in and around Paris. Inquire at its Tourist Service on the place de la Madeleine, 8e (to the right of the church as you face it) or at the office at 53 bis quai des Grands-Augustins, 6e. Both are open daily 9–5.

Bike Tours **Paris by Cycle** (99 rue de la Jonquiere, 17e, tel. 42–63–36–63) organizes daily bike tours around Paris and its environs (Versailles, Chantilly, and Fontainebleau) for about 180 francs (an additional 95 francs for bike rental).

Boat Trips Boat trips along the Seine, usually lasting about an hour, are a must for the first-time visitor. Many boats have powerful floodlights to illuminate riverbank buildings; on some, you can also lunch or wine and dine—book ahead. The following services operate regularly throughout the day and in the evening.

Bateaux-Mouches has departures from Pont de l'Alma (Right Bank), 8e, tel. 42–25–96–10. Boats depart 10–noon, 2–7, and 8:30–10:30. The price is 30 francs (40 francs after 8 PM; 15 francs children under 14). Lunch is served on the 1 PM boat and costs 300 francs (150 francs children under 14). Dinner on the 8:30 service costs 500 francs (reservations required; no children). Wine and service are included in the lunch and dinner prices.

Bateaux Parisiens–Tour Eiffel has departures from Pont d'Iéna (Left Bank), 7e, tel. 44–11–33–44. Boats depart at 10 and 11 AM and 12, 2, 3, 4, 5, and 6 PM. The price is 40 francs during the day (20 francs children under 12). Lunch service costs 300 francs (200 francs children under 12). Dinner cruises on the 8 PM service cost 550 francs (no children). Wine and service are included in the lunch and dinner prices.

Canauxrama (tel. 42–39–15–00) organizes leisurely half-day canal tours in flat-bottom barges along the picturesque but relatively unknown St-Martin and Ourcq Canals in East Paris. Departures are from 5 bis quai de la Loire, 19e (9:15 and 2:45), or from Bassin de l'Arsenal, 12e (9:45 and 2:30), opposite 50 boulevard de la Bastille. The price is 70 francs (60 francs for students and senior citizens and on weekend afternoons; 45 francs children under 12).

Opening and Closing Times

Banks are open weekdays, but there's no strict pattern to their hours of business. Generally, they're open from 9:30 to 4:30 or 5. Some banks close for lunch between 12:30 and 2.

Most Paris **museums** close one day a week—usually either Monday or Tuesday—and on national holidays. Usually, they're open from 10 to 5 or 6. Many museums close for lunch (12 to 2) and are open Sundays only in the afternoon.

Large **shops** are open from 9 or 9:30 to 6 or 7 and don't close at lunchtime. Smaller shops often open earlier (8 AM) but take a lengthy lunch break (1 to 4); small food shops are often open Sunday mornings, 9 to 1. Some corner grocery stores will stay open until about 10 PM. Most shops close all day Monday.

Tipping

Bills in bars and restaurants must, by law, include service, but it is customary to leave some small change unless you're dissatisfied. The amount of this varies—from 30 centimes for a beer to a few francs after a meal. In expensive restaurants, it's common to leave an additional 5% of the bill on the table.

Tip **taxi drivers** and **hairdressers** about 10% of the bill. Give theater and cinema **ushers** a couple of francs. In some theaters and hotels, **cloakroom attendants** may expect nothing (*pourboire interdit*—no tip); otherwise, give them 5 francs. **Washroom attendants** usually get 2–5 francs, though the sum is often posted.

If you stay more than two or three days in a hotel, it is customary to leave something for the **chambermaid**—about 10 francs per day. Expect to pay about 10 francs (5 francs in a moderately priced hotel) to the person who carries your bags or who hails you a taxi. In hotels providing room service, give 5 francs to the waiter (this does not apply if breakfast is routinely served in your room). If the chambermaid does some pressing or laundering for you, give her 5–10 francs on top of the bill.

Service station attendants get nothing for gas or oil, but 5 or 10 francs for checking tires. Train and airport **porters** get a fixed sum (6–10 francs) per bag. **Museum guides** should get 5–10 francs after a guided tour. It is standard practice to tip **bus drivers about 10 francs** after an excursion.

2 Where to Stay on a Budget

Updated by
David Downie

Winding staircases, geranium pots in the windows, a concierge who seems to have stepped from a 19th-century novel—all of these still exist in abundance in Paris hotels. Budget travelers will find that many of these charming touches exist *outside* the city's luxury hotels and world-famous hostelries. In Paris, unlike some international cities, there are wonderful hotels in all price ranges. Nevertheless, travelers with modest means should not be naive or unrealistic in their expectations. Paris is one of the most expensive cities in the world, and although a wealth of captivating little rooms exist at 750 francs a night, do not count on being captivated by a 300-franc room in a small hotel in the 13th Arrondissement.

Our criteria when selecting the hotels reviewed below were cleanliness, friendly management, value for money, and—where possible—character. A few chain hotels are listed for their price and/or convenient location. We list a fair number of hotels in outlying arrondissements (the 10th–15th, 18th–20th); although these areas boast fewer sights and less character per square block than central districts, hotels are usually considerably cheaper here. In any case you can move quickly, cheaply, and safely from one arrondissement to the next on the city's excellent transit system, making many of these off-the-beaten-path lodgings excellent bargains. Generally, there are more Right Bank hotels offering luxury—or at any rate formality—than there are on the Left Bank, where hotels tend to be smaller but often loaded with character. The Right Bank's 1st, 2nd, and 8th arrondissements are still the most sought-after for lodging, and prices here reflect this. Less expensive alternatives on the Right Bank are the fashionable Marais quarter (3rd and 4th arrondissements), where hotels have mushroomed in recent years, and the 11th and 12th, near the Opéra Bastille.

Once upon a time, obvious high and low seasons existed in Paris. Nowadays, the city is as likely to be overrun in November or February as in summer. The French in general and the Parisians in particular take their vacations in July and August, so most of the trade fairs and conventions that fill hotels the rest of the year come to a halt at this time, freeing up rooms for tourists. Prices at any hotel can vary depending on time of year—July–August and winter discounts are common. The French Tourist Office publishes a calendar showing peak periods.

Despite the huge choice of hotels here, you should always reserve well in advance, especially if you're determined to stay in a specific hotel. You can do this by telephoning ahead, then writing or faxing for confirmation. If you are asked to send a deposit, make sure you discuss refund policies before mailing your check or money order. Always ask for some form of written confirmation of your reservation, detailing the duration of your stay, the price, location and type of your room (single or double, twin beds or double), and bathroom. Shared toilets or bathrooms down the hall, though increasingly rare, are still found in many modest establishments. Never assume that what is billed as a bathroom (*salle de bain*) will necessarily contain a tub. Some rooms have toilets (what the French call *wc* or *cabinet de toilet*), some have *bidets* only—but no tub or shower. Others have a shower but no toilet, and still others have only washstands. Our reviews indicate the number of rooms with full bath facilities including tub (*baignoire*) or shower (*douche*), and number of rooms with shared baths. Make sure you know what you are getting when you book.

Almost all Paris hotels charge extra for breakfast, with prices ranging from 30 francs to over 100 francs per person in luxury establishments. Even the cheapest hotels generally assume you will be having breakfast there, and will add the breakfast charge to your bill automatically. If you don't want to have breakfast at the hotel, say so when you check in. For anything more than the standard Continental breakfast of café au lait (coffee with hot milk) and *baguette* (bread) or croissants, the price will be higher. Some hotels have especially pleasant breakfast areas, and we have noted these.

You'll notice that the French government grades hotels from four-star deluxe to one star, and that the stars appear on a shield on the hotel's facade. Theoretically, the ratings depend on amenities and price. They can be misleading, however, since many hotels prefer to be understarred for tax reasons. Generally, one- and two-star establishments offer the most affordable rooms, but some three-star hotels also have a fine price-to-quality ratio. Our gradings are based on price: Under 750F, Under 500F, and Under 300F. Prices vary considerably at individual hotels depending upon season and the type or location of the room and bathroom. We list several higher-grade hotels with some affordable rooms—smaller, without a view, with shared bath facilities, etc.—and note this wherever applicable. Rates must be posted in all rooms, and all extra charges clearly shown.

Lodging in dormitories, residence halls, or hostels is a cheap option for students. Nonstudents also can stay in hostels and—when vacancies exist—in residence halls, although the latter are technically reserved for students. Keep in mind that digs will be Spartan, and most will require that you bring your own linens or rent them on-site. You may also face minimum and maximum stays, curfews, and long lines for showers. Cash is king in these places, so don't plan on financing your stay with a credit card. Any student can take advantage of the many university lodgings, where short-term student housing is available, usually in the summer and during school holidays. To register, you must show proof of full-time student status, so an International Student Identity Card (*see* Student and Youth Travel in Chapter 1) is a wise buy. The largest dormitories are at **Cité Universitaire** (15 blvd. Jourdan, Métro: Porte Royal, tel. 44–85–35–79 or 45–89–13–37). For general information on foyers and hostels, contact the following: **Accueil des Jeunes en France** (A.J.F., 119 rue St-Martin, Métro: Hôtel de Ville, tel. 42–77–87–80); **French Youth Hostels Association** (38 blvd. Raspail, Métro: Sèvres-Babylone, tel. 45–48–69–84), and **UCRIF** (72 rue Rambuteau, Métro: Châtelet/Les Halles, tel. 40–26–57–64). For more information on hostels, *see* Student and Youth Travel in Chapter 1. We review a few especially appealing youth hostels below.

If you want a home base that's roomy enough for a family and comes with cooking facilities, a furnished rental may be the solution. Keep in mind that although this can save money, it is generally not a budget option. Rates start at about $125 a day. Among companies with rentals in Paris are **At Home Abroad** (405 E. 56th St., Suite 6H, New York, NY 10022, tel. 212/421–9165) and **Villas and Apartments Abroad** (420 Madison Ave., Suite 1105, New York, NY 10017, tel. 212/759–1025 or 800/433–3020). Companies dealing exclusively with French properties include **French Experience** (370 Lexington Ave., New York, NY 10017, tel. 212/986–1115, fax 212/986–3808) and **Chez Vous** (220 Redwood Hwy., Suite 129, Mill Valley, CA 94941, tel. 415/331–2535, fax 415/331–5296). In Paris, the best agency is **Rothray** (10 rue Nicolas Flamel, tel. 48–87–13–37).

Very reasonably priced rooms in private homes are available through **Accueil France Lodge** (5 rue du Faubourg-Montmartre, 75009 Paris, tel. 42–46–68–19, fax 42–46–65–61) and **Bed & Breakfast 1 = Connexion +** (7 rue Campagne Première, 75014 Paris, tel. 43–35–11–26, fax 40–47–69–20). Home stays with Parisian families can be arranged through **Servas** (11 John St., New York, NY 10038, tel. 212/267–0252) and **The Friendship Force** (575 South Tower, 1 CNN Center, Atlanta, GA 30303, tel. 404/522–9494).

A home exchange, in which you swap your home for a house or apartment in Paris, provides you with free lodging for your stay. Home-exchange organizations publish annual directories listing available exchanges. Arrangements for the actual exchange are made by the two parties to it, not by the organization. Principal clearinghouses include **Intervac U.S./International Home Exchange** (Box 590504, San Francisco, CA 94159, tel. 415/435–3497); the **Vacation Exchange Club** (Box 650, Key West, FL 33041, tel. 800/638–3841); and **Loan-a-Home** (2 Park La., Apt. 6E, Mount Vernon, NY 10552, tel. 914/664–7640).

Next to a free home exchange, the most economical sleep in Paris is probably camping in the Bois de Boulogne. Contact **Les Campings du Bois du Boulogne** (Alle du Bord de l'Eau, Bois de Boulogne, tel. 45–24–30–00). Rates are $15 a night for a tent for two; the campground is open year-round and accepts no advance reservations.

The following credit card abbreviations are used: AE, American Express; DC, Diners Club; MC, MasterCard; and V, Visa.

Highly recommended lodgings are indicated by a star ★.

1st Arrondissement (Louvre)
See Right Bank Lodging map

Under 750F **Britannique.** A friendly, family-owned hotel in a restored 19th-century building, the Britannique has a handsome winding staircase and nicely decorated, soundproofed rooms. Ask for a room on one of the top three floors. Rooms with shower are significantly cheaper. *20 av. Victoria, 75001, Métro: Châtelet, tel. 42–33–74–59, fax 42–33–82–65. 25 rooms with bath, 15 with shower. English spoken. AE, DC, V.*

Londres Stockholm. An appealing combination of character and comfort singles out this small hotel. The lobby has exposed oak beams, statues in niches, and rustic-looking stone walls. The freshly repainted, rough-cast white walls in the rooms are off-set by deep red carpeting. There's no restaurant or bar, but limited room service is available. Rooms are under 500 francs during low season. *13 rue St-Roch, 75001, Métro: Pyramides, tel. 42–60–15–62, fax 42–60–16–00. 29 rooms with bath, 2 with shower. English spoken. AE, MC, V.*

Tamise. Just off the rue de Rivoli and Tuileries Gardens, this small hotel was once a private town house. Modestly luxurious, it boasts many English antiques in its charming rooms. *4 rue Alger, 75001, Métro: Tuileries, tel: 42–60–51–54, fax 42–86–89–97. 15 rooms with bath, 4 with shower. English spoken. DC, V.*

Under 300F **Lille.** You won't find a less expensive base for exploring the Louvre than this hotel, located a short distance from the Cour Carrée. The facade got a face-lift a few years ago, but the somewhat shabby interior and minimal plumbing down long corridors was not upgraded. Hence the rock-bottom prices. Still, the Lille is a slice of Old Paris. There's no elevator, and not all rooms have TVs or phones. *8 rue du Pélican, 75001, Métro: Palais-Royal, tel. 42–33–33–42. 5 rooms with shower, 8 with shared bath. Some English spoken. No credit cards.*

2nd Arrondissement (Stock Exchange)
See Right Bank Lodging map

Under 750F **Choiseul-Opéra.** The historic, classical facade of the Choiseul-Opéra, located between the Opéra and place Vendôme, belies the strictly functional interior. The entrance hall, salon, and bar were remodeled in 1992, and many rooms were freshened up. Service is relaxed but efficient, and the staff are happy to try out their English on guests. There's no restaurant or bar. *1 rue Daunou, 75002, Métro: Opéra, tel. 42–61–70–41, fax 42–86–91–96. 30 rooms with bath, 15 with shower, 2 suites with bath. English spoken. AE, DC, MC, V.*

Under 450F **Tiquetonne.** Be warned: This one-star has no frills and little atmosphere, but it's clean, unbelievably cheap, and located within easy walking distance of dozens of sights. The first two stories have double-glazed windows, which you'll appreciate on noisy weekends. Shared baths are down rather gloomy corridors. *6 rue Tiquetonne, 75002, Métro: Etienne-Marcel, tel. 42–36–94–58. 30 rooms with shower, 17 with shared bath. No English spoken. No credit cards.*

3rd Arrondissement (Le Marais/Beaubourg)
See Right Bank Lodging map

Under 500F **Hôtel du Marais.** On the edge of the Marais, this small hotel in a restored old building is near the Bastille Opéra and the Picasso Museum. For extremely reasonable rates (at the low end of this price category) you get amenities generally reserved for more expensive hotels, such as minibars and color TVs in rooms. Some rooms have exposed beams; all are functional, soundproofed, and clean. *2 bis rue des Commines, 75003, Métro: Filles-du-Calvaire, tel. 48–87–78–27, fax 48–87–09–01. 12 rooms with bath, 27 with shower. Some English spoken. Facilities: minibar in rooms. AE, DC, MC, V.*

4th Arrondissement (Le Marais/Ile St-Louis)
See Right Bank Lodging map

Under 750F **Axial Beaubourg.** Opened in 1990, this three-star hotel in a 17th-century building is one of the better deals going in the Marais. There are beamed ceilings in the lobby and in the six first-floor rooms; decor is functional. The clientele is a mix of Europeans and Americans. The Beaubourg and Picasso Museums are a five-minute walk away. *11 rue du Temple, 75004, Métro: Hôtel de Ville, tel. 42–72–72–22, fax 42–72–03–53. 34 rooms with bath, 5 with shower. English spoken. AE, V.*
Bretonnerie. This small, three-star hotel is located on a tiny street in the Marais, a few minutes' walk from the Beaubourg. The snug rooms are decorated in Louis XIII style, but vary considerably in size from spacious to cramped. Some boast antiques, beamed ceilings, and marble-clad bathrooms. There's a bar and breakfast room in the vaulted cellar. The smallest rooms are less expensive. *22 rue Ste-Croix-de-la-Bretonnerie, 75004, Métro: Hôtel de Ville, tel. 48–87–77–63, fax 42–77–26–78. 30 rooms with bath, 1 with shower, 1 suite with bath. English spoken. Facilities: bar and breakfast room. MC, V. Closed late July to late Aug.*
St-Louis. The St-Louis is one of the Ile St-Louis's converted 17th-century town houses. Antique furniture and oil paintings decorate the public areas. The bedrooms are elegantly simple, with exposed beams and stone walls. Blue-gray or light brown tiles adorn bathrooms. Breakfast is served in the atmospheric cellar. Rates barely make it into our price range, but do include breakfast. *75 rue St-Louis-en-l'Ile, 75004, Métro: Pont-Marie, tel. 46–34–04–80, fax 46–34–02–13. 15 rooms with bath, 6 with shower. English spoken. No credit cards.*
★ **Vieux Marais.** As its name implies, this charming, two-star hotel lies in the heart of the Marais. Prices are at the low end of this category. The rooms and bathrooms are simply decorated in light, refreshing colors and are impeccably clean. Try to get a room overlooking the courtyard. Breakfast is served in a pretty lounge, and a second lounge with a TV is located in the cellar.

Right Bank Lodging

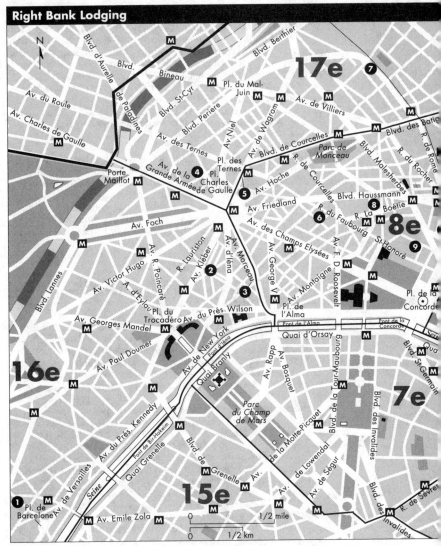

Alison, **9**
Argenson, **8**
Axial Beaubourg, **29**
Bradford, **6**
Bretonnerie, **31**
Britannique, **15**
Castex, **38**
Ceramic, **5**
Choiseul-Opéra, **17**

Garden-Hotel, **27**
Hôtel du Marais, **32**
Hôtel du Pré, **19**
Hôtel du 7ᵉ Art, **37**
Hôtel Notre-Dame, **25**
Jules-César, **41**
Keppler, **3**
Kléber, **2**
Le Fauconnier, **36**

Le Fourcy, **35**
Le Laumière, **24**
Le Maubuisson, **34**
Lille, **14**
Londres
Stockholm, **12**
Marigny, **10**
Méridional, **28**
Modern Hôtel-
Lyon, **43**

Ouest, **7**
Palma, **4**
Paris-Lyon Palace, **42**
Place des Vosges, **39**
Queen's Hotel, **1**
Régina, **13**
Regyn's
Montmartre, **23**
Résidence
Alhambra, **26**

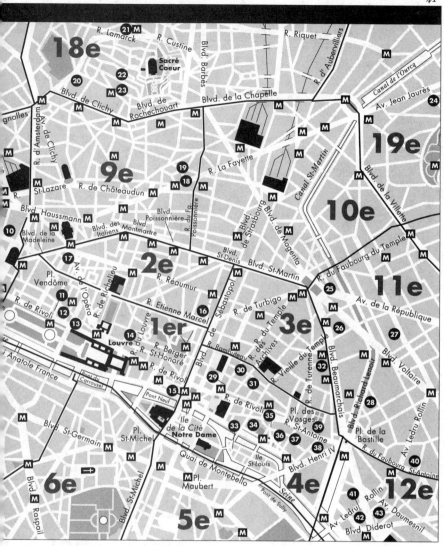

Left Bank Lodging

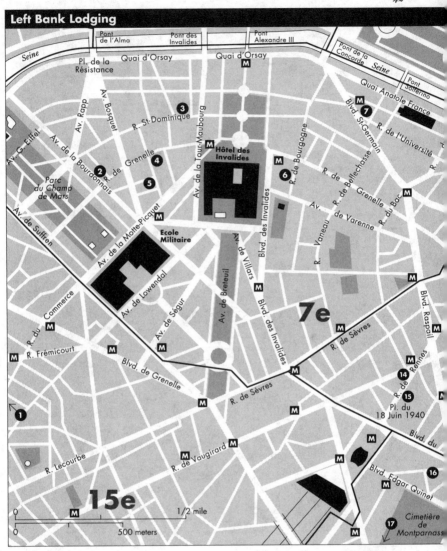

Acacias
St-Germain, **15**

Aramis-
St-Germain, **14**

Champ de Mars, **5**

Collège de France, **32**

Elysa Luxembourg, **29**

Esméralda, **33**

Fred' Hôtel, **17**

Grand Hôtel
Lévêque, **4**

Grands Ecoles, **27**

Hôtel Coypel, **24**

Hôtel des
Beaux-Arts, **25**

Hôtel du Globe, **35**

Hôtel Florida, **18**

Istria, **19**

Jardin des Plantes, **26**

Kensington, **2**

L'Abbaye
St-Germain, **13**

Lenox, **16**

Lille, **8**

Lys, **34**

Marronniers, **12**

Midi, **20**

Nainville, **1**

Oriental, **31**

Pantheon, **28**

Parc
Montsouris, **21**

Pavillon, **3**

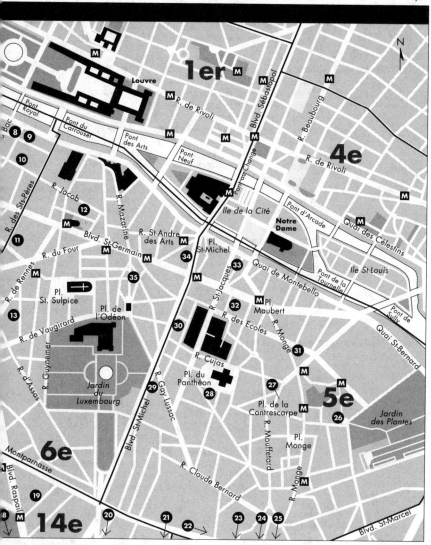

1er

Louvre

4e

R. de Rivoli

Blvd. Sébastopol

R. Beaubourg

R. de Rivoli

Pont
Royal

Pont du
Carrousel

Pont
des Arts

Pont
Neuf

Bac

R. Jacob

R. Mazarine

R. des Sts-Pères

Ile de la Cité

Notre
Dame

Pont d'Arcade

Quai des Célestins

Ile St-Louis

Blvd. St-Germain

R. St-Andre
des Arts

Pl.
St-Michel

Quai de Montebello

Pont de la
Tournelle

R. du Four

R. de Rennes

R. St-Jacques

Quai St-Bernard

Pont de
Sully

Pl.
St. Sulpice

Pl. de
l'Odéon

R. des Ecoles

Pl.
Maubert

R. Monge

R. de Vaugirard

R. Cujas

Pl. du
Panthéon

5e

Jardin
des Plantes

R. Guynemer

R. d'Assas

Jardin
du
Luxembourg

R. St-Michel

R. Gay Lussac

Pl. de la
Contrescarpe

R. Mouffetard

Pl.
Monge

R. Monge

6e

Montparnasse

Blvd. Raspail

14e

R. Claude Bernard

Blvd. St-Marcel

The staff is exceptionally courteous. *8 rue de Plâtre, 75004, Métro: Hôtel de Ville, tel. 42–78–47–22, fax 42–78–34–32. 22 rooms with bath, 8 with shower. English spoken. Facilities: TV lounge. MC, V.*

Under 500F **Place des Vosges.** A loyal American clientele swears by this
★ small, historic hotel located on a charming street just off the exquisite square of the same name. Oak-beamed ceilings and rough-hewn stone in public areas and some of the guest rooms add to the atmosphere. Ask for the top-floor room, the hotel's largest, with a view of Marais rooftops. Some rooms, the size of walk-in closets, are less expensive. There's a welcoming little breakfast room. *12 rue de Birague, 75004, Métro: Bastille, tel. 42–72–60–46, fax 42–72–02–64. 5 rooms with bath, 11 with shower. English spoken. AE, DC, V.*

Hôtel du 7e Art. The decor of this small Marais two-star hotel is 1940s–60s Hollywood movies, complete with posters and photographs (the name means "Seventh Art," what the French call filmmaking). Rooms have brown carpets and beige walls; they're small and sparsely furnished, but clean and quiet. The clientele tends to be young, and Americans are made to feel welcome. Breakfast and snacks are served in handsome ground-floor or cellar rooms with stone walls, and there's also a pleasant bar. No elevator. *20 rue St-Paul, 75004, Métro: St-Paul, tel. 42–77–04–03, fax 42–77–69–10. 6 rooms with bath, 15 with shower, 2 suites with bath. English spoken. Facilities: bar. AE, DC, MC, V.*

Under 300F **Castex.** This family-run, two-star hotel in a 19th-century build-
★ ing is a real find. It was remodeled from top to bottom in 1989, and rooms are squeaky clean. The decor is strictly functional, but the extremely friendly owners and rock-bottom prices mean the Castex is often fully booked months ahead. There's a large American clientele. The eight least expensive rooms, two per floor, share toilets on the immaculate, well-lit landings. There's no elevator, and TV is in the lobby only. *5 rue Castex, 75004, Métro: Bastille, tel. 42–72–31–52, fax 42–72–57–91. 4 rooms with bath, 23 with shower. English spoken. MC, V.*

Le Fauconnier. This youth hostel offers simple, clean beds in rooms for two, four, or six at just over 100 francs per person per night. The building, a lovely 17th-century town house, is on a small, quiet street near the Seine. Breakfast is served in a pleasant ground-floor room. There's a small patio open in summer. Most rooms have shower or basin (w.c. down the hall). An age limit for guests of 30 theoretically exists, but off-season enforcement is lax. *11 rue du Fauconnier, 75004, Métro: St-Paul, tel. 42–74–23–45. No credit cards. No reservations.*

Le Fourcy. Another MIJE youth hostel, this is 100 yards from Le Fauconnier in another 17th-century town house. It has the same look and feel as Le Fauconnier, but on a larger scale. *6 rue de Fourcy, 75004, Métro: St-Paul, tel. 42–74–23–45. No credit cards. No reservations.*

Le Maubuisson. The third MIJE youth hostel in the Marais, this one is in the former 17th-century Abbaye Royale de Maubuisson near the church of Saint-Gervais and the Hôtel-de-Ville (city hall). Rooms are for two or four, with shower or basin (shared w.c.), at comparable prices to the two hostels above. Again, the 30-year-old age limit for guests is often waived in low season. *12 rue des Barres, 75004, Métro: Hôtel-de-Ville, tel. 42–72–72–09. No credit cards. No reservations.*

American Express offers Travelers Cheques built for two.

American Express® Cheques *for Two*. The first Travelers Cheques that allow either of you to use them because both of you have signed them. And only one of you needs to be present to purchase them.

Cheques *for Two* are accepted anywhere regular American Express Travelers Cheques are, which is just about everywhere. So stop by your bank, AAA* or any American Express Travel Service Office and ask for Cheques *for Two*.

Travelers Cheques

5th Arrondissement (Latin Quarter)
See Left Bank Lodging map

Under 750F
★ **Elysa Luxembourg.** The Elysa is what the French call an *hôtel de charme*. Though the building is not large, most rooms are surprisingly spacious, and all are exquisitely maintained and refurbished yearly. Cream-colored furniture is set against pale blue or pink fabrics. You'll find a minibar in every room and a breakfast lounge serving Continental or buffet breakfasts. The Elysa is one of the rare hotels in the city with a sauna. *6 rue Gay Lussac, 75005, Métro: Luxembourg, tel. 43–25–31–74, fax 46–34–56–27. 25 rooms with bath, 5 with shower. English spoken. Facilities: sauna. AE, DC, MC, V.*

★ **Pantheon.** In a handsome 18th-century building facing the Pantheon, this excellent three-star hotel has prices at the top end of this category. Some of the charming rooms have exposed beams, balconies, and stunning views; a vaulted breakfast room and impressive lobby are additional attractions. The desk staff is very helpful. *19 pl. du Pantheon, 75005, Métro: St-Michel, tel. 43–54–32–95, fax 43–26–64–65. 32 rooms with bath. English spoken. AE, DC, V.*

Under 500F
Collège de France. The Collège de France offers peace and quiet in the heart of the Latin Quarter. Rooms are simply decorated in pale greens and light browns. The prettiest three—often booked months ahead—have oak beams and are up on the sixth floor under the eaves. Some rooms cost a little more than 500 francs, so inquire when you book. *7 rue Thénard, 75005, Métro: Maubert-Mutualité, tel. 43–26–78–36, fax 46–34–58–29. 23 rooms with bath, 6 with shower. Some English spoken. AE.*

★ **Esméralda.** Lovers of small, charming Parisian hotels will want to stay at this simple lodging, where the rooms are a little dusty but positively exude timeworn Gallic charm. Esméralda is set in a fine 17th-century building opposite Notre Dame (request a room with a view), near Square Viviani. All the rooms are small—some are midget-size. Many have copies of 17th-century furniture. Those with showers on the landing are little more than 300 francs. *4 rue St-Julien-le-Pauvre, 75005, Métro: St-Michel, tel. 43–54–19–20, fax 40–51–00–68. 16 rooms with bath, 3 with shower on the landing. Some English spoken. No credit cards.*

★ **Grands Ecoles.** Recently upgraded from no stars to two, this delightful hotel in three small old buildings is set far off the street in a beautiful garden. There are parquet floors, antiques, and a piano in the breakfast area. Most rooms have beige carpets and flowery wallpaper. You won't find a quieter, more charming hotel for the price. There's a faithful American clientele, including some backpackers. The rooms with bathroom facilities on the well-lit landings are inexpensive. *75 rue du Cardinal Lemoine, 75005, Métro: Cardinal Lemoine, tel. 43–26–79–23, fax 43–25–28–15. 29 rooms with bath, 10 with shower, 9 with shared bath. English spoken. V.*

Jardin des Plantes. Across the street from the lovely Jardin des Plantes botanical gardens on the edge of the Latin Quarter, this pleasant two-star hotel offers botanical-theme decor and low prices for its rooms with shower (those with bath are more, but still reasonable). There's a fifth-floor terrace where you can breakfast or sunbathe in summer, and a sauna and ironing room in the cellar. *5 rue Linné, 75005, Métro: Monge, tel. 47–07–06–*

20, fax 47–07–62–74. 29 rooms with bath, 4 with shower. English spoken. Facilities: sauna, bar-tearoom, terrace. AE, DC, MC, V.

Oriental. This no-frills one-star in an old building has clean rooms, and is located near the Arènes de Lutèce. Plumbing is minimal, some of it down corridors. *2 rue Arras, 75005, Métro: Jussieu, tel. 43–54–38–12, fax 40–51–86–78. 2 rooms with bath, 25 with shower, 5 with shared bath. Some English spoken. AE, MC, V.*

Sorbonne. This pretty, early 18th-century hotel, located right by the Sorbonne, was transformed in 1988 when its handsome stone facade was cleaned. Fresh flowers adorn each room, and great clusters of geraniums hang from the windows. Try for a room overlooking the little garden. Rooms with shower are at the low end of this price category. *6 rue Victor-Cousin, 75005, Métro: Luxembourg, tel. 43–54–58–08, fax 40–51–05–18. 11 rooms with bath, 26 with shower. English spoken. MC, V.*

Under 300F **Port Royal Hôtel.** This cheerful, tidy, family-run establishment stands on the tree-lined boulevard de Port-Royal, on the Latin Quarter's nether frontier. Double rooms with shower or bath (still priced under 300 francs) boast comfortable beds and a rose-hued decor far sprucer than those usually found in accommodations in this price range. Streetside rooms are soundproofed. Breakfast (20 francs extra and obligatory) is served in a pleasant *salle à manager*, or, on fine days, in a leafy courtyard. Guests housed above the fourth floor are charged extra for breakfast served in the room, since the hotel has no elevator. *8 blvd. de Port-Royal, 75005, Métro: Gobelins, tel. 43–31–70–06. 16 rooms with bath or shower, 29 with shared bath. No English spoken. No credit cards.*

6th Arrondissement (Luxembourg)
See Left Bank Lodging map

Under 750F **Saints-Pères.** The Saints-Pères is an old favorite, offering peace
★ and quiet in the heart of St-Germain. Several rooms in this 17th-century town house are decorated in authentic period style; most rooms look out over the hotel garden, where breakfast and tea are served. Affordable rooms are near the top of this price range; others are higher, so inquire when you book. There's no restaurant, but the cane-and-bamboo bar is an ever-popular rendezvous. *65 rue des Saints-Pères, 75006, Métro: Sèvres, tel. 45–44–50–00, fax 45–44–90–83. 30 rooms with bath, 4 with shower, 3 suites with bath. English spoken. Facilities: bar. MC, V.*

Aramis-St-Germain. Despite its location on busy rue de Rennes, the Aramis-St-Germain, opened only in 1985, has proved a hit. All windows are double-glazed (keeping out street noise), and rooms are individually decorated with wallpapers and fabrics. Several have Jacuzzis. There's no restaurant. Harvey's Piano Bar on the first floor is popular. Some rooms are expensive, so ask when you call. *124 rue de Rennes, 75006, Métro: Rennes, tel. 45–48–03–75, fax 45–44–99–29. 36 rooms with bath, 6 with shower. English spoken. Facilities: bar, parking. AE, DC, MC, V.*

★ **Marronniers.** There are few better places in Paris than the Marronniers for great value and atmosphere. Located on appealing rue Jacob, the hotel is reached through a small courtyard. All rooms are light and full of character. Those on the attic floor have sloping ceilings, uneven floors, and terrific views over the church of St-Germain-des-Prés. The vaulted cellars have been converted into two atmospheric lounges. *21 rue Jacob, 75006, Métro: St-Germain-des-Prés, tel. 43–25–30–60, fax 40–46–83–56. 17 rooms with bath, 20 with shower. English spoken. Facilities: bar. No credit cards.*

Under 500F   **Acacias St-Germain.** This three-star hotel in a 19th-century building near Montparnasse was completely remodeled in 1992. It offers spotlessly clean rooms decorated in summery fabrics and colors, and a small, flower-filled patio. Check into the remarkable low-season and weekend discounts; high-season prices are over 500 francs. *151 bis rue de Rennes, 75006, Métro: Montparnasse, tel. 45–48–97–38, fax 45–44–63–57. 24 rooms with bath, 17 with shower. English spoken. Facilities: 24-hour room service, parking. AE, DC, V.*

Lys. This one-star hotel is tucked into a centuries-old building on a quiet street that's a stone's throw from place St-Michel. The recently remodeled rooms come in all shapes and sizes but are clean, charming, and affordable. *23 rue Serpente, 75006, Métro: St-Michel, tel. 43–26–97–57. 4 rooms with bath, 18 with shower. Some English spoken. No credit cards.*

Under 300F   **Hôtel du Globe.** This offers loads of Left Bank atmosphere packed into minimal space. Best suited to those who travel light (don't even attempt to negotiate the narrow, winding stairs with a suitcase much bigger than a carryon), the minuscule rooms are artfully arranged to make the most of every square inch. A shower, sink, and toilet, for example, are tucked behind a folding door (no detail of your ablutions will escape your roommate). Rooms with bath (more than 300 francs) offer slightly more space. Closets are small or nonexistent. However, the colorful bathrooms are spotless, and the decor is pleasingly whimsical, with pretty details such as crocheted bed covers. Fresh flowers greet guests at the entrance. *15 rue des Quatre-Vents, 75006, Métro: Odéon, tel. 46–33–62–69. 6 rooms with bath, 14 with shower. No English spoken. No credit cards. Closed Aug. 6–28.*

7th Arrondissement (Invalides)
See Left Bank Lodging map

Under 750F   **Université.** This appealingly converted 17th-century town
★   house is located between boulevard St-Germain and the Seine. Rooms have their original fireplaces and are decorated with English and French antiques. Though there's no restaurant, you can rent the vaulted cellar for parties. Drinks and snacks are served all day in the bar or, in good weather, in the courtyard. Only rooms with shower make it into this price range. *22 rue de l'Université, 75007, Métro: Bac, tel. 42–61–09–39, fax 42 60–40–84. 20 rooms with bath, 7 with shower. English spoken. Facilities: bar. No credit cards.*

Lille. Located practically next door to the Musée d'Orsay, the Lille is a small two-star hotel in a fully modernized old building. Rooms are simply but pleasantly decorated, and their rates are at the low end of this price category. *40 rue de Lille, 75007, Métro: Musée d'Orsay, tel. 42–61–29–09, fax 42–61–53–97. 7 rooms with bath, 13 with shower. English spoken. Facilities: bar. AE, DC, V.*

Quai Voltaire. Long a favorite of Americans, this two-star, charming hotel offers history (Baudelaire and Wagner were guests) and views from its 28 Seine-side rooms. Because of room-by-room renovation, some new rooms are large and comfortable (under 750 francs), while the older, well-worn rooms with minimal bath facilities cost less. *19 Quai Voltaire, 75005, Métro: Bac, tel. 42-61-50-91, fax 42-61-62-66. 24 rooms with bath, 7 with shower, 2 with shared bath. English spoken. Facilities: bar. AE, DC, V.*

Varenne. The Varenne stands in a flower-filled courtyard set back from the street; windows of rooms facing the road are double-glazed to reduce noise. Decor is contemporary—and at times basic—with oak furniture and colorful curtains and wallpaper. Rooms with shower are at the low end of this category. *44 rue de Bourgogne, 75007, Métro: Varenne, tel. 45-51-45-55, fax 45-51-86-63. 14 rooms with bath, 10 with shower. English spoken. AE, V.*

Under 500F **Champ de Mars.** This simple, clean two-star hotel has one-star prices. Don't expect luxury or atmosphere, just a very good deal, in a nice neighborhood near the Eiffel Tower and Invalides. *7 rue Champ de Mars, 75007, Métro: Ecole Militaire, tel. 45-51-52-30. 19 rooms with bath, 6 with shower. Some English spoken. MC, V. Closed two weeks in mid-Aug.*

Kensington. Perhaps the main reason for wanting to stay in this small two-star hotel is the superb view of the Eiffel Tower from the two top floors. Rooms are tiny and uninspiring, with white Formica, but they are freshly decorated and always impeccably clean; all have double-glazed windows. There's no restaurant, but limited room service is available. Rooms with shower have rock-bottom rates. *79 av. de la Bourdonnais, 75007, Métro: Ecole-Militaire, tel. 47-05-74-00, fax 47-05-25-81. 12 rooms with bath, 14 with shower. English spoken. AE, DC, MC, V.*

★ **Pavillon.** The entrance to the family-run Pavillon lies behind a garden at the end of an alley off rue St-Dominique, guaranteeing peace and quiet. Although some rooms in this former 19th-century convent are tiny, all have been redecorated and feature Laura Ashley wallpaper and old prints. Breakfast is served in the little courtyard in summer. There's no elevator, but the hotel is only two stories high. Rooms with bath are out of this price range. *54 rue St-Dominique, 75007, Métro: Invalides, tel. 45-51-42-87, fax 45-51-32-79. 3 rooms with bath, 15 with shower. English spoken. AE, MC, V.*

Solférino. Located across the street from the Musée d'Orsay, the Solférino is a charming little hotel with a variety of rooms, the cheapest being those with shower only and shared bath. The rooms' decor is light and summery, and the breakfast room–lounge is lit by a skylight. *91 rue de Lille, 75007, Métro: Musée d'Orsay, tel. 47-05-85-54, fax 45-55-51-16. 22 rooms with bath, 5 with shower, 5 with shower and shared w.c. English spoken. MC, V. Closed Christmas–New Year's.*

Under 300F **Grand Hôtel Lévêque.** A superb location near the Ecole-Militaire and a charming welcome are the Lévêque's biggest assets. Many of the airy, high-ceilinged rooms were recently renovated; while they vary in size, all are immaculate, as are the tiled bathrooms. The bright front rooms overlook a car-free market street filled with enticing food shops. Rooms that open onto the back courtyard are a few francs cheaper. If you are burdened with heavy luggage, book a room on a lower floor, since there is no elevator. *29 rue Cler, 75007, Métro: Ecole-*

Militaire, tel. 47–05–49–15. 35 rooms with shower, 15 with shared bath. English spoken. Facilities: lounge. MC, V.

8th Arrondissement (Champs-Elysées)
See Right Bank Lodging map

Under 750F   **Alison.** Conveniently located near the place de la Madeleine on a pleasant side street, the Alison is a small, friendly hotel in a 19th-century building. The rooms are decorated in simple, modern style. *21 rue de Surène, 75008, Métro: Madeleine, tel. 42–65–54–00, fax 42–65–08–17. 24 rooms with bath, 11 with shower. English spoken. Facilities: bar. AE, DC, V.*

Bradford. The turn-of-the-century, family-run Bradford is an upscale hotel, and only its rooms with shower qualify as affordable. An old wooden elevator carries you from the flower-filled lobby to the spacious, comfortable rooms, some equipped with Louis XVI-style furniture, brass beds, and fireplaces. *10 rue St-Philippe-du-Roule, 75008, Métro: St-Philippe-du-Roule, tel. 45–63–20–20, fax 45–63–20–07. 36 rooms with bath, 12 with shower, 2 suites with bath. English spoken. Facilities: bar. AE, DC, MC, V.*

Under 500F   **Argenson.** This friendly, family-run hotel provides what may
★ well be the best value in the swanky 8th Arrondissement. Some of the city's greatest sights are just a 10-minute walk away. Old furniture, molded ceilings, and skillful flower arrangements add to the charm. An ongoing room-by-room renovation means new bathrooms in many. The best rooms have full bath; reserve well in advance for one of these. *15 rue d'Argenson, 75008, Métro: Miromesnil, tel. 42–65–16–87. 5 rooms with bath, 19 with shower, 3 with shared bath. Some English spoken. DC, MC, V.*

Ceramic. These are the lowest rates you'll pay this close to the Arc de Triomphe—just a few hundred yards away. The hotel has a handsome Belle Epoque tiled facade and a crystal chandelier in the reception area. The rooms haven't been remodeled in some time but are still comfortable. Those facing the street (among them 412, 422, 442) boast bay windows and intricate plaster moldings. Those facing the courtyard are quieter but less appealing. *34 av. de Wagram, 75008, Métro: Etoile, tel. 42–27–20–30, fax 46–22–95–83. 27 rooms with bath, 26 with shower. English spoken. MC, V.*

Marigny. Not much has changed here since Marcel Proust lodged in this small, pleasant 19th-century hotel just minutes from the Madeleine and among the area's cheapest. Rooms with bath are out of this price category. *11 rue de l'Arcade, 75008, Métro: Madeleine, tel. 42–66–42–71. 11 rooms with bath, 15 with shower, 6 with shared bath. English spoken. MC, V.*

9th Arrondissement (Opéra)
See Right Bank Lodging map

Under 500F   **Hôtel du Pré.** Located near the pretty square Montholon, slightly off the beaten track, this three-star hotel was thoroughly remodeled in the 1980s. Its reasonable prices, charming and sunny public areas, comfortable rooms done in summery colors, and large bathrooms make it a very good deal. *10 rue Pierre-Sémard, 75009, Métro: Poissonière, tel. 42–81–37–11,* fax 40–23–98–28. 22 rooms with bath, 19 with shower. English spoken. Facilities: bar. AE, V.

Riboutté-Lafayette. This small, cozy two-star hotel in a 19th-century building near the busy rue La Fayette is family-run and filled with charming bric-a-brac and old furniture. The clean, sunny rooms are decorated in pastel colors, and those on the top floor have sloping ceilings. 5 rue Riboutté, 75009, Métro: Cadet, tel. 47–70–62–36, fax 48–00–91–50. 15 rooms with bath, 9 with shower. English spoken. V.

11th Arrondissement (Bastille)
See Right Bank Lodging map

Under 750F **Méridional.** This three-star hotel in a 19th-century building is a five-minute walk from either the Bastille or the Marais. It's located on a handsome but busy tree-lined boulevard. Though the lobby is a bit garish, the comfortable, quiet rooms are simply decorated in earth tones. The hotel was entirely remodeled in 1991. Prices are lower in winter. 36 blvd. Richard Lenoir, 75011, Métro: Bréguet-Sabin, tel. 48–05–75–00, fax 43–57–42–85. 26 rooms with bath, 10 with shower. English spoken. AE, DC, V.

Under 500F **Garden-Hotel.** Set on a pretty garden square in a quiet residential neighborhood just 10 minutes from Père-Lachaise cemetery, this family-run, two-star hotel has little character but is spotlessly clean. Rooms in front have lovely views; all units have double-glazed windows and color TVs and are soberly decorated with brown carpets and beige walls. Note that bathtubs are half-size in rooms with baths. The breakfast room decor leaves much to be desired. 1 rue du Général-Blaise, 75011, Métro: Saint-Ambroise or Voltaire, tel. 47–00–57–93, fax 47–00–45–29. 3 rooms with bath, 39 with shower. No English spoken. No credit cards.

★ **Résidence Alhambra.** This hotel is on the edge of the historical Marais quarter and is conveniently close to five Métro lines. The Alhambra's gleaming white exterior and flower-filled window boxes provide a bright spot in an otherwise drab neighborhood. The smallish guest rooms are painted in fresh pastel shades and have marble-topped breakfast tables. The lobby is filled with plants and leather armchairs. Most rooms have color TV. 13 rue de Malte, 75011, Métro: République, tel. 47–00–35–52, fax 43–57–98–75. 10 rooms with bath, 48 with shower. English spoken. MC, V.

Résidence Trousseau. Built in the late 1980s, this hotel-residence is on a quiet street that's a 15-minute walk east of the Bastille. It offers well-equipped but smallish rooms, all with kitchenettes. There isn't much atmosphere, and the neighborhood isn't particularly interesting, but the price, facilities, and comfort are right. Rates are lower for longer stays. Note that some rooms have convertible sofabeds instead of standard double beds. 13 rue Trousseau, 75011, Métro: Faidherbe-Chaligny, tel. 48–05–55–55, fax 48–05–83–97. 66 rooms with bath. English spoken. Facilities: kitchenettes, parking, minigolf, billiard table, self-service laundry. AE, DC, MC, V.

Under 300F **Hôtel Notre-Dame.** A delicate Art Nouveau marquee adorns the Notre-Dame's freshly painted facade. Inside, a pleasant (English-speaking) manager extends a courteous welcome. The cheerful rooms, done in pastel tones, are fairly spacious for the price, and offer such welcome amenities as comfortable new mattresses, soundproofed windows, telephones, and TVs. Excellent métro and bus connections to every part of town are close at hand on the place de la République. You'll pay a little more than 300 francs if you want a private bath or shower and w.c. *51 rue de Malte, 750011, Métro: République, tel. 47-00-78-76, fax 43-55-32-31. 10 rooms with bath, 14 with shower, 27 with shared bath. English spoken. MC, V.*

12th Arrondissement (Gare de Lyon)
See Right Bank Lodging map

Under 750F **Modern Hôtel-Lyon.** This three-star, family-run hotel, conveniently located between the Bastille and the Gare de Lyon, changed ownership in 1992. As a result, rooms have been remodeled and redecorated in light colors, and many bathrooms are being upgraded. The new owners are as friendly and helpful as their predecessors. *3 rue Parrot, 75012, Métro: Gare de Lyon, tel. 43-43-41-52, fax 43-43-81-16. 36 rooms with bath, 12 with shower. English spoken. Facilities: bar. AE, MC, V.*

Paris-Lyon Palace. Located near the Gare de Lyon, this attractive three-star hotel has modern, strictly functional rooms, but the large, plant-filled lobby is decorated in an appealing Art Deco style. There's no restaurant, but the bar is open from lunch till 1 AM. Service is notably warm. *11 rue de Lyon, 75012, Métro: Gare de Lyon, tel. 43-07-29-49, fax 46-28-91-55. 64 rooms with bath, 64 with shower. English spoken. Facilities: bar. AE, DC, MC, V.*

Under 500F **Jules-César.** The address may be unfashionable, but the Bastille, Jardin des Plantes, and Ile St-Louis are just a short walk away, and the Gare de Lyon is just around the corner. The hotel, built in 1914, has been restored. The lobby is rather glitzy, but the guest rooms are more subdued. Rooms facing the street are larger than those in the back and have a somewhat better view. *52 av. Ledru-Rollin, 75012, Métro: Gare de Lyon, tel. 43-43-15-88, fax 43-43-53-60. 4 rooms with bath, 44 with shower. English spoken. MC, V.*

13th Arrondissement (Les Gobelins)
(See Left Bank Lodging map)

Under 500F **Résidence les Gobelins.** Located five minutes from the Latin Quarter, this simple, small two-star hotel on a quiet street offers pleasant rooms in warm, coordinated colors. The breakfast room faces a small flower-filled garden. There's cable TV in every room. *9 rue des Gobelins, 75013, Métro: Gobelins, tel. 47-07-26-90, fax 43-31-44-05. 18 rooms with bath, 14 with shower. English spoken. AE, DC, MC, V.*

Under 300F **Hôtel Coypel.** The Coypel's management is currently upgrading this modest but bright and clean hotel set on a quiet street off the avenue des Gobelins in the 13th Arrondissement. Wooden floors are a bit creaky, but rooms have ample closet space, and newer units feature double-glazed windows. Rooms with numbers ending in "1" are the most spacious and comfortable. If you're willing to do without a private bath, you can rent a double room for under 150 francs (there is an extra charge for use of the shower—15 francs buys eight minutes of hot water). The hotel has a charming, helpful staff. *2 rue Coypel, 75013, Métro: Place d'Italie, tel. 43-31-18-08. 12 rooms with shower, 28 with shared bath. English spoken. MC, V.*

Hôtel des Beaux-Arts. The peaceful, family-style ambience and low prices compensate for the out-of-the-way location in a residential area near Paris's Chinatown. Added pluses include a courtyard with gazebo for summer breakfasts and a large, quiet park across the street. Good housekeeping is evident in the (compact) rooms and halls. The most attractive accommodations are on the top floor under the eaves, though they would probably be hot in summer. Three métro lines and several convenient bus routes run from the nearby place d'Italie. Proprietor Mme. Foutrel advises guests to book well in advance, since she has considerable repeat business. *2 rue Toussaint-Féron, 75013, Métro: Tolbiac, tel. 44–24–22–60. 11 rooms with shower, 14 with shared bath. No English spoken. AE, MC, V.*

14th Arrondissement (Montparnasse)
See Left Bank Lodging map

Under 750F   **Istria.** This small, charming two-star hotel was once a Montparnasse artists' hangout. Totally rebuilt in 1988 around a flower-filled courtyard on a quiet street, it is now a family-run establishment with simple, clean, and comfortable rooms decorated in soft, summery colors. *29 rue Campagne-Première, 75014, Métro: Raspail, tel. 43–20–91–82, fax 43–22–48–45. 4 rooms with bath, 22 with shower. English spoken. AE, MC, V.*

Lenox Montparnasse. You'll want to stay in this new hotel mainly to take advantage of its location in the heart of Montparnasse; it's just around the corner from the famous Dôme and Coupole brasseries, and close to the Luxembourg Gardens. Try for one of the south-facing rooms; they are noticeably lighter and fresher than the others. The best rooms have original fireplaces, old mirrors, and exposed beams; others are decorated in functional modern styles. All have gleaming white-tile bathrooms. There's no restaurant, but snacks are served in the bar, and room service is available. *15 rue Delambre, 75014, Métro: Edgar-Quinet, tel. 43–35–34–50, fax 43–20–46–64. 36 rooms with bath, 10 with shower, 6 suites with bath. English spoken. Facilities: bar. AE, DC, MC, V.*

Under 500F   **Midi.** This hotel is close to both Montparnasse and the Latin Quarter, and there are Métro and RER stations nearby. Don't be put off by the nondescript facade and reception area; most of the rooms are adequately furnished, and those facing the street are both large and quiet. Request room 32, if possible, and avoid the cheapest rooms, which are quite dingy and unattractive. *4 av. Réné-Coty, 75014, Métro: Denfert-Rochereau, tel. 43–27–23–25, fax 43–21–24–58. 20 rooms with bath, 21 with shower, 9 with shared bath. Some English spoken. No credit cards.*

Parc Montsouris. This modest two-star hotel in an early 1900s building is on a charming and quiet residential street next to the lovely Parc Montsouris; it's a five-minute walk to the RER station. Remodeled throughout in 1991, its smallish rooms are decorated with pastel colors and modern furniture. Some rooms with shower are very inexpensive. *4 rue du Parc-Montsouris, 75014, Métro: RER Cité-Universitaire, tel. 45–89–09–72, fax 45–80–92–72. 18 rooms with bath, 17 with shower, 7 suites with bath. English spoken. AE, MC, V.*

Under 300F   **Fred'Hôtel.** Friendly, personalized service and thoughtful amenities in most rooms (radio, TV, hair dryers) bring travelers to this out-of-the-way hotel, set on an unprepossessing street three métro stops south of Montparnasse. The recently renovated rooms (some are more than 300 francs) are clean and cheerful enough, though the color schemes occasionally jar. More important, guests' peace and comfort are aided by double-glazed windows, carpeted floors, and beds with good-quality mattresses. There's an elevator here as well. The management gladly arranges sightseeing tours and restaurant reservations. *11 av. Villemain, 75014, Métro: Plaisance, tel. 45–43–24–18, fax 45–43–27–26. 10 rooms with bath, 12 with shower, 2 with shared bath. English spoken. Facilities: lounge. AE, DC, MC, V.*

Hôtel Floridor. Short on charm and cheer, the Floridor is nonetheless a good value, offering affordable prices and a convenient location, with direct connections to Orly (Orlybus) and Roissy (via RER) virtually at the doorstep. An elevator just wide enough for one person leads to functional, adequately sized guest rooms. Units overlooking the square are soundproofed; all are equipped with telephone and TV. Rooms with bath are a little more expensive, and tubs are half-size, so you're better off going with a shower. Breakfast is extra and obligatory. *28 pl. Denfert-Rochereau, 75014, Métro and RER: Denfert-Rochereau, tel. 43–21–35–53, fax 43–27–65–81. 5 rooms with bath, 40 with shower, 3 with shared bath. No English spoken. No credit cards.*

15th Arrondissement (Front de Seine)

Under 300F **Nainville Hôtel.** The Nainville belongs to Paris's vanishing breed of small, family-run hotels-cum-cafés. Most of the rooms here are singles, suited for commercial travelers; but there are a few double rooms with private showers, satellite TV, and a view of the verdant Square Violet next door. An atmosphere of provincial calm reigns over the spic-and-span little rooms; fresh paint and sparkling windows give evidence of careful housekeeping, but the eclectic decor and hideous carpet may grate on some nerves. *53 rue de l'Eglise, 75015, Métro: Félix-Faure, tel. 45–57–35–80. 5 rooms with shower, 32 with shared bath. English spoken. No credit cards. Closed mid-July–Aug.*

16th Arrondissement (Trocadéro/Bois de Boulogne)
See Right Bank Lodging map

Under 750F **Kléber.** Located just a short walk from Etoile and Trocadéro, the little Kléber benefits greatly from the calm and greenery of nearby place des Etats-Unis. Decor is strictly modern throughout, but the thick blue carpets, set against beige walls, create a warm atmosphere. The hotel is impeccably clean. Though there's no restaurant, there's a comfortable first-floor lounge and bar. Rooms on the 2nd and 5th floors have balconies. Only those with showers are affordable. *7 rue de Belloy, 75016, Métro: Etoile, tel. 47–23–80–22, fax 49–52–07–20. 11 rooms and 1 suite with bath, 10 rooms with shower. English spoken. Facilities: bar, parking. AE, DC, MC, V.*

Under 500F **Keppler.** Ideally located on the edge of the 8th and 16th arrondissements near the Champs-Elysées, this small two-star hotel in a 19th-century building boasts many three-star features (room service, small bar) at extremely reasonable prices. The spacious and airy rooms are simply decorated with modern furnishings. *12 rue Keppler, 75016, Métro: Kléber, tel. 47–20–65–*

05, fax 47–23–02–29. 31 rooms with bath, 18 with shower. English spoken. Facilities: bar. AE, MC, V.

Queen's Hotel. One of only a handful of hotels located in the desirable residential district around rue la Fontaine, Queen's is within walking distance of the Seine and the Bois de Boulogne. The hotel is small and functional, but standards of comfort and service are high. Flowers on the facade add an appealing touch. Most rooms with shower are well under 500 francs. *4 rue Bastien-Lepage, 75016, Métro: Michel-Ange-Auteuil, tel. 42–88–89–85, fax 40–50–67–52. 7 rooms with bath, 15 with shower. English spoken. MC, V.*

17th Arrondissement (Monceau/Clichy)
See Right Bank Lodging map

Under 500F **Ouest.** Although this unpretentious hotel overlooks the railroad near Pont-Cardinet station, you can be sure of a quiet night's sleep, since all the rooms are soundproofed. Some are lighter and more spacious than others, so be sure to make your preference known. The area may not have much to interest tourists, but Montmartre, Parc Monceau, and the Grands Magasins are all within easy reach. Rates for rooms with shower are at the low end of this price range. *165 rue de Rome, 75017, Métro: Rome, tel. 42–27–50–29, fax 42–27–27–40. 17 rooms with bath, 31 with shower. English spoken. Facilities: parking, bar. MC, V.*

★ **Palma.** This prim and proper two-star hotel located between the Arc de Triomphe and Porte Maillot is run by the friendly and efficient Couderc family. Small and charming, it is one of the best modest hotel deals in the city. Ask for a top-floor room with a view. All rooms have cable TV with CNN. Breakfast is included in the price. *46 rue Brunel, 75017, Métro: Argentine, tel. 45–74–74–51, fax 45–74–40–90. 15 rooms with bath, 22 with shower. English spoken. MC, V.*

18th Arrondissement (Montmartre)
See Right Bank Lodging map

Under 500F **Regyn's Montmartre.** Despite small rooms (all recently renovated), this small, owner-run hotel on Montmartre's place des Abbesses is rapidly gaining an enviable reputation for simple, comfortable accommodations. Try for one of the rooms on the upper floors, with great views over the city. Guests are predominantly young. *18 pl. des Abbesses, 75018, Métro: Abbesses, tel. 42–54–45–21, fax 42–54–45–21. 14 rooms with bath, 8 with shower. English spoken. MC, V.*

Timhotel Montmartre. The reason for listing what is only one of eight Timhotels in Paris is simply the location of the Montmartre member of the chain—right in the leafy little square where Picasso lived at the turn of the century. Rooms are basic and functional, though the Montmartre theme is continued by the Toulouse-Lautrec posters. *11 rue Ravignan, 75018, Métro: Abbesses, tel. 42–55–74–79, fax 42–55–71–01. 6 rooms with bath, 57 with shower. English spoken. AE, DC, MC, V.*

Utrillo. Newly renovated, the Utrillo is on a quiet side street at the foot of Montmartre. The decor is appealing, with prints in every room and a marble-topped breakfast table. Because the color white is emphasized throughout, the hotel seems light, clean, and more spacious than it actually is. Prices are well below 500 francs. *7 rue Aristide-Bruant, 75018, Métro: Blanche,* *tel. 42–58–13–44, fax 42–23–93–88. 5 rooms with bath, 25 with shower. English spoken. Facilities: sauna. AE, DC, MC, V.*

Under 300F **Résidence Hôtel Pacific.** These rooms and studios equipped with refrigerators, microwaves, TVs, and telephones provide an economical alternative to traditional hotel accommodations if you plan to spend a week or more in Paris. However, the location in northern Montmartre is not ideal for hurried sightseers: Sacré-Coeur is a good 10-minute walk away, and the place de la Concorde is nine métro stops distant. But if you have time to spare, you'll enjoy the colorful market on the nearby rue du Poteau, and the many cafés filled with equally colorful locals. The Pacific is furnished in functional style; maid service and clean linen are provided once a week (more often at extra cost). If your room is on the fifth floor, you may well regret the absence of an elevator. *77 rue du Ruisseau, 75018, Métro: Jules-Joffrin, tel. 42–62–53–00, fax 46–06–09–82. 41 rooms with shower, 3 with shared bath. English spoken. MC, V.*

19th Arrondissement (La Villette)
See Right Bank Lodging map

Under 300F **Le Laumière.** Though it's located some ways from downtown, the low rates of this family-run, two-star hotel, close to the tumbling Buttes-Chaumont park, are hard to resist. Most rooms are functional only, but some of the larger ones overlook the garden. The staff is exceptionally helpful. Shared baths (both showers and w.c.) are on well-lit landings. Rooms with bath are a little more than 300 francs, but others are well under. *4 rue Petit, 75019, Métro: Laumière, tel. 42–06–10–77, fax 42–06–72–50. 18 rooms with bath, 28 with shower, 8 with shared bath. English spoken. AE, DC, MC, V.*

Splurges

★ **L'Abbaye St-Germain.** This delightful hotel is a former 18th-century convent near St-Sulpice, in the heart of the Left Bank. The first-floor rooms open onto flower-filled gardens. Some rooms on the top floor have oak beams and alcoves. The entrance hall is sturdily authentic, with stone vaults. All bathrooms are decorated with colored marble. The bar is for guests only. *10 rue Cassette, 75006, Métro: St-Sulpice, tel. 45–44–38–11, fax 45–48–07–86. 42 rooms and 4 suites, all with bath. English spoken. Facilities: bar. MC, V.*

Régina. Set in the handsome place des Pyramides, this Art Nouveau gem stuffed with fine antiques is pleasantly old-fashioned. Request a room overlooking the Louvre and the Tuileries Gardens. *2 pl. des Pyramides, 75001, Métro: Tuileries, tel. 42–60–31–10, fax 40–15–95–16. 120 rooms and 10 suites, all with bath. English spoken. Facilities: restaurant (closed August), bar. AE, DC, MC, V.*

3 Exploring Paris

Paris is a city of vast, noble perspectives and winding, hidden streets. This combination of the pompous and the intimate is a particularly striking and alluring feature of Paris. The French capital is also, for the tourist, a practical city: It is relatively small as capitals go, with many of its major sites and museums within walking distance of one another.

In fact, the best method of getting to know Paris is on foot, although public transportation—particularly the métro subway system—is excellent. Buy a *Plan de Paris* booklet: a city map-guide with a street-name index that also shows métro stations. Note that all métro stations have a detailed neighborhood map just inside the entrance.

Paris owes both its development and much of its visual appeal to the river Seine, which weaves through its heart. Each bank of the Seine has its own personality; the Rive Droite (Right Bank), with its spacious boulevards and haughty buildings, generally has a more sober and genteel feeling to it than the more carefree and bohemian Rive Gauche (Left Bank) to the south.

Paris's historical and geographical heart is Notre Dame Cathedral on the Ile de la Cité, the larger of the Seine's two islands (the other is the Ile St-Louis). The city's principal tourist axis is less than 4 miles long, running parallel to the north bank of the Seine from the Arc de Triomphe to the Bastille.

If you are an avid museum goer, you can save time and money with the **Museum Pass.** This one-, three-, or five-day pass allows you to view the permanent collections of 65 museums and monuments including the Louvre, in Paris and the surrounding area an unlimited number of times. The pass is sold at any of the participating museums and monuments (many of which are described below), the main métro and RER stations, the tourist office (127 av. des Champs-Elysées, 75008), and **Musée & Compagnie** (49 rue Etienne Marcel, 75001) and comes with an information-packed leaflet and a métro plan. A one-day pass is 60 francs, a three-day pass is 120 francs, and a five-day pass is 170 francs. You can also buy the pass in the United States before you go, but the cost will be slightly higher. Contact **Marketing Challenges International, Inc.** (10 E. 21st St., Suite 600, New York, N.Y. 10010, tel. 212/529–8484, fax 212/460–8287). A one-day pass is $17, three-day is $29, and five-day is $39.

Monuments and museums are sometimes closed for lunch, usually between 12 and 2, and one day a week, usually Monday or Tuesday. Check before you set off.

We've divided our coverage of Paris into six tours, but there are several "musts" that any first-time visitor to Paris is loath to miss: the Eiffel Tower, the Champs-Elysées, the Louvre, and Notre Dame. It would be a shame, however, not to explore the various *quartiers*, or districts, each with its own personality and charm.

The Historic Heart

Numbers in the margin correspond to points of interest on the Historic Heart map.

Of the two islands in the Seine—the Ile St-Louis (*see* The Marais and Ile St-Louis, *below*) and Ile de la Cité—it is the Ile de la Cité that forms the historic heart of Paris. It was here, for obvious reasons of defense, and in the hope of controlling the trade that passed along the Seine, that the earliest inhabitants of Paris, the Gaulish tribe of the Parisii, settled in about 250 BC. They called their little home Lutetia, meaning "settlement surrounded by water." Whereas the Ile St-Louis is today largely residential, the Ile de la Cité remains deeply historic, the result not just of more than 2,000 years of habitation, but of the fact that this is the site of the most important and one of the most beautiful churches in France—the great brooding cathedral of Notre Dame. Few of the island's other medieval buildings have survived to the present, most having fallen victim to town planner Baron Haussmann's ambitious rebuilding of the city in the mid-19th century. But among the rare survivors are the jewel-like Sainte-Chapelle, a vision of shimmering stained glass, and the Conciergerie, the grim former city prison.

Another major attraction on this tour—the Louvre—came into existence in the mid-13th century, when Philippe-Auguste built it as a fortress to protect the city's western flank. It was not until pleasure-loving François I began a partial rebuilding of this original rude fortress in the early 16th century that today's Louvre began gradually to take shape. A succession of French rulers was responsible for this immense, symmetrical structure, now the largest museum in the world, as well as the easiest to get lost in.

If Notre Dame and the Louvre represent Church and State, respectively, the third major attraction we cover—Les Halles

Paris Exploring *(Boxes Refer to Detail Maps)*

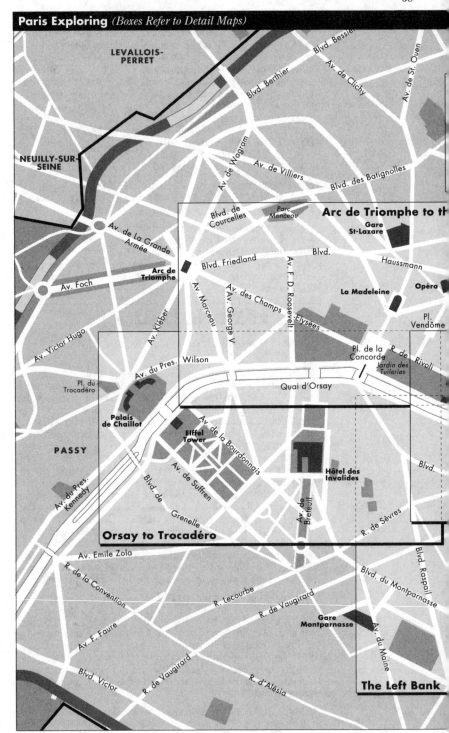

LEVALLOIS-PERRET

NEUILLY-SUR-SEINE

Blvd. Bessier

Blvd. Berthier

Av. de Clichy

Av. de St. Ouen

Blvd. de Courcelles

Parc Monceau

Av. de Wagram

Av. de Villiers

Blvd. des Batignolles

Arc de Triomphe to th

Gare St-Lazare

Av. de la Grande Armée

Blvd. Friedland

Blvd.

Haussmann

Opéra

Av. Foch

Arc de Triomphe

Av. Marceau

Av. des Champs

Av. F. D. Roosevelt

La Madeleine

Pl. Vendôme

Av. Kléber

Av. George V

Elysées

Pl. de la Concorde

R. de Rivoli

Av. Victor Hugo

Av. du Pres. Wilson

Wilson

Quai d'Orsay

Jardin des Tuileries

Pl. du Trocadéro

Palais de Chaillot

Eiffel Tower

Av. de la Bourdonnais

PASSY

Av. de Suffren

Hôtel des Invalides

Blvd.

Av. du Pres. Kennedy

Blvd. de

Grenelle

Av. de Breteuil

R. de Sèvres

Orsay to Trocadéro

Av. Emile Zola

R. de la Convention

R. Lecourbe

R. de Vaugirard

Blvd. du Montparnasse

Blvd. Raspail

Av. F. Faure

Blvd. Victor

R. de Vaugirard

R. d'Alésia

Gare Montparnasse

Av. du Maine

The Left Bank

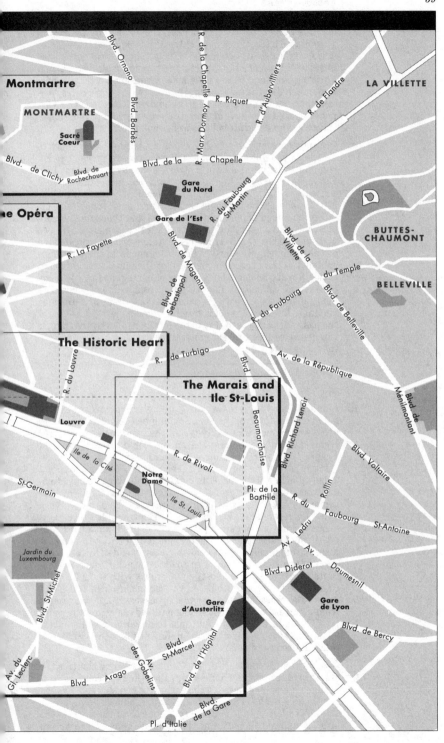

Montmartre

MONTMARTRE

Sacré Coeur

Blvd. Ornano

Blvd. Barbès

Blvd. de Clichy

Blvd. de Rochechouart

e Opéra

R. La Fayette

R. de la Chapelle

R. Riquet

R. d'Aubervilliers

R. de Flandre

LA VILLETTE

R. Marx Dormoy

Blvd. de la · Chapelle

Gare du Nord

Gare de l'Est

R. du Faubourg St-Martin

Blvd. de Magenta

Blvd. de Sébastopol

Blvd. de la Villette

du Temple

Blvd. de Belleville

R. du Faubourg

BUTTES-CHAUMONT

BELLEVILLE

The Historic Heart

R. du Louvre

R. de Turbigo

Blvd.

Av. de la République

The Marais and Ile St-Louis

Louvre

Ile de la Cité

Notre Dame

St-Germain

R. de Rivoli

Ile St. Louis

Beaumarchaise

Blvd. Richard Lenoir

Pl. de la Bastille

R. du Faubourg St-Antoine

Rollin

Blvd. Voltaire

Blvd. de Ménilmontant

Jardin du Luxembourg

Blvd. St-Michel

Av. du Gl. Leclerc

Blvd.

Arago

Av. des Gobelins

Blvd. St-Marcel

Blvd. de l'Hôpital

Gare d'Austerlitz

Av. Ledru

Av.

Blvd. Diderot

Daumesnil

Gare de Lyon

Blvd. de Bercy

Blvd. de la Gare

Pl. d'Italie

(pronounced *lay al*)—stands for the common man. For centuries, this was Paris's central market, replenished by an army of wagons and later, trucks, which caused astounding traffic jams in the city's already congested streets. The market was closed in 1969 and replaced by a striking shopping mall, the Forum. The surrounding streets have since undergone a transformation, much like the neighboring Marais, with shops, cafés, restaurants, and chic apartment buildings. However, the vast public spaces here have attracted a large vagrant population to the area, and general shabbiness has emerged.

Old and new blend and clash in Paris, contrasts that are hard to escape as you follow this tour. The brash modernity of the Forum, for example, stands in contrast to the august church of St-Eustache nearby. The Louvre itself has not been spared controversy: While Louis XIV's harmoniously imposing Cour Carrée, one of the supreme architectural achievements of his reign, has been painstakingly restored and thousands of cobblestones have been laid in place of tarmac, a mixture of awe and outrage has greeted the glass pyramid on the opposite side of the complex. Similarly, the incongruous black-and-white columns in the classical courtyard of Richelieu's neighboring Palais Royal present a further case of daring modernity or architectural vandalism, depending on your point of view. The Parisians take seriously their role as custodians of a glorious heritage, but they are not content to remain mere guardians of the past. If the city is to stay in the forefront of urban change, it is imperative that present generations bequeath something to the future. Well, so some say.

Toward the Louvre

The tour begins at the western tip of the Ile de la Cité, at the ❶ sedate **Square du Vert Galant.** Nothing is controversial here, not even the statue of the Vert Galant himself, literally the vigorous—by which was really meant the amorous—adventurer Henri IV, sitting foursquare on his horse. Henri, King of France from 1589 until his assassination in 1610, was something of a dashing figure, by turns ruthless and charming, a stern upholder of the absolute rights of monarchy, and a notorious womanizer. He is probably best remembered for his cynical remark that *Paris vaut bien une messe* ("Paris is worth a mass"), a reference to his readiness to renounce his Protestantism as a condition of gaining the throne of predominantly Catholic France, and indeed of being allowed to enter the city. A measure of his canny statesmanship was provided by his enactment of the Edict of Nantes in 1598, by which French Protestants were accorded (almost) equal rights with their Catholic counterparts. It was Louis XIV's renunciation of the Edict nearly 100 years later that led to the massive Huguenot exodus from France, greatly to the economic disadvantage of the country. The square itself is a fine spot to linger on a sunny afternoon. It is also the departure point for the glass-topped *vedette* tour boats on the Seine.

Crossing the Ile de la Cité, just behind the Vert Galant, is the ❷ oldest bridge in Paris, confusingly called the **Pont Neuf,** or New Bridge. It was completed in the early 17th century and was the first bridge in the city to be built without houses lining either side. Turn left onto it. Visible to the north of the river is the large-windowed **Samaritaine** department store. Once across the river, turn left again and walk down to rue Amiral-de-Coligny. Opposite you is the massive eastern facade of the Louvre. It is Baroque dignity and coherence with no frills, a suitably imposing entrance to the rigorous classicism of the Cour Carrée beyond.

However, before heading for the Louvre, stay on the right-hand sidewalk and duck into the church of **St-Germain l'Auxerrois.** This was the French royal family's Paris church, used by them right up to 1789, in the days before the Revolution, when the Louvre was a palace rather than a museum. The fluid stonework of the facade reveals the influence of 15th-century Flamboyant Gothic, the final, exuberant fling of the Gothic before the classical takeover of the Renaissance. Notice the unusually wide windows in the nave, light flooding through them, and the equally unusual double aisles. The triumph of classicism is evident, however, in the fluted columns around the choir, the area surrounding the altar. These were added in the 18th century and are characteristic of the desire of 18th-century clerics to dress up medieval buildings in the architectural raiment of their day.

The Louvre

The best times to avoid crowds at the Louvre are during lunchtime between 12:30 and 2:30 or on Monday and Wednesday evenings, when it stays open till 9:45. Admission charge is reduced by almost half on Sundays.

In 1984, President François Mitterrand launched his Grand Louvre Project, a plan for restoration of the museum that includes the extension and modernization of the museum interior, renovation of the Palais du Louvre, and the restoration of the Carrousel gardens between the museum and the Tuileries Gardens. By 1993, the bicentennial of the opening of the Louvre, most of the facades had been cleaned, the museum's collection extended into the Richelieu wing, and construction of an underground garage and shopping arcade begun. The project is not scheduled for completion until 1996, so don't be surprised to see construction crews and steam shovels marring the otherwise superb locale when you visit.

The Louvre colonnade across the road from St-Germain l'Auxerrois screens one of Europe's most dazzling courtyards, the **Cour Carrée,** a monumental, harmonious, and superbly rhythmical ensemble. It has something of the assured feel of an Oxford or Cambridge quadrangle, though on a much grander scale. In the **crypt** under it, excavated in 1984, sections of the defensive towers of the original, 13th-century fortress can be seen.

If you enter the museum via the quai du Louvre entrance, saunter through the courtyard and pass under the **Pavillon de l'Horloge**—the Clock Tower—and you come face to face with the Louvre's most controversial development, I. M. Pei's notorious **glass pyramid,** surrounded by three smaller pyramids. It's more than just a grandiloquent gesture, a desire on the part of Mitterrand, who commissioned it, to make his mark on the city. First, the pyramid marks the new, and much needed, entrance to the Louvre; it also houses a large museum shop, café, and restaurant. Second, it acts as the terminal point for the most celebrated city view in Europe, a majestic vista stretching

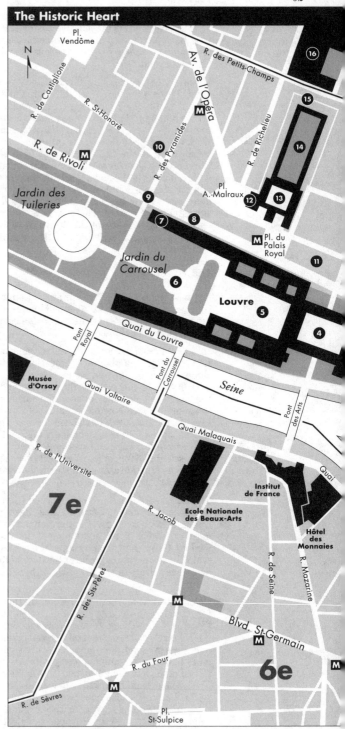

The Historic Heart

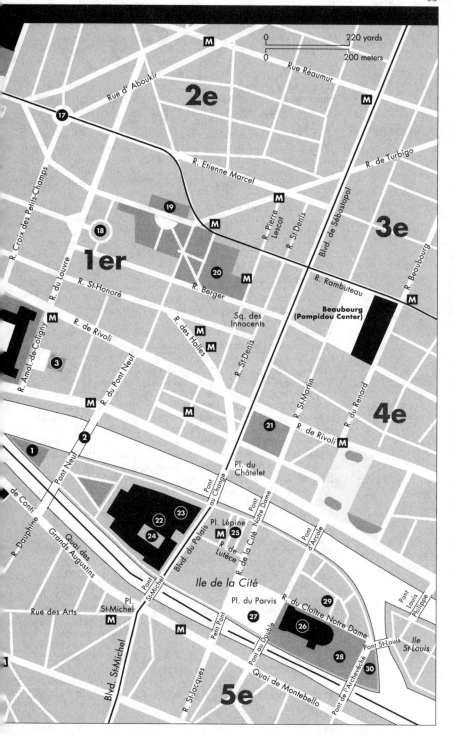

through the Arc du Carrousel, the Tuileries Gardens, across place de la Concorde, up the Champs-Elysées to the towering Arc de Triomphe, and ending at the giant modern arch at La Tête Défense, 2½ miles more to the east. Needless to say, the architectural collision between classical stone blocks and pseudo-Egyptian glass panels has caused a furor. Adding insult to injury, at least as far as many Parisians are concerned, is the shocking fact that Pei isn't even a Frenchman! Before making up your mind, however, it may help to remember that the surrounding buildings in this part of the Louvre are mainly earnest 19th-century pastiche, whose pompous solemnity neither jars nor excites. Furthermore, though it may seem a coherent, unified structure, today's Louvre is the end product of many generations of work. The earliest parts of the building date from the reign of François I at the beginning of the 16th century. Down the years, Henri IV (1589–1610), Louis XIII (1610–1643), Louis XIV (1643–1715), Napoléon (1804–1814), and Napoléon III (1852–1870) have all contributed to the construction. Before rampaging revolutionaries burned part of it down during the bloody Paris Commune of 1871, the building was even larger. The open section facing the Tuileries Gardens was originally the Palais des Tuileries, the main Paris residence of the royal family.

The uses to which the building has been put have been almost equally varied. Though Charles V (1364–1380) made the Louvre his residence, later French kings preferred to live elsewhere, mainly in the Loire Valley. Even after François I decided to make the Louvre his permanent home, and accordingly embarked on an ambitious rebuilding program (most of which came to nothing), the Louvre never became more than a secondary palace. When, in 1682, Louis XIV decided to move the French court out of the city to Versailles, despite having previously initiated a major program of rebuilding at the Louvre, it seemed that the Louvre would never be more than a home for minor courtiers. Indeed, during the remainder of Louis's reign, the palace underwent a rapid decline. Its empty apartments were taken over by a rabble of artists; little shacklike shops were set up against the walls; and chimneys projected higgledy-piggledy from the severe lines of the facades. Louis XV (1715–1774), thanks in large measure to the financial shrewdness of his chief minister, Marigny, then inaugurated long-overdue renovations, though he, too, preferred to live at Versailles. The Louvre's association with the French crown was not to last much longer. It was from the Tuileries Palace that Louis XVI and Marie Antoinette fled in 1791, two years after the start of the Revolution, only to be arrested and returned to Paris for their executions. The palace was taken over by the Revolutionary leaders—the Convention first, then the Directory. At the very end of the century, Napoléon, initially as first consul, subsequently as emperor, initiated a further program of renovation and rebuilding and established the Louvre first and foremost as a museum rather than as a palace. This did not, however, prevent the three remaining French kings—Louis XVIII (1814–1824), who has the dubious distinction of having been the only French monarch to have died in the Louvre; Charles X (1824–1830); and Louis-Philippe (1830–1848)—from making the Louvre their home. The latter pair suffered the indignity of expulsion at the hands of the dreaded Paris mob in the uprisings of 1830 and 1848, respectively.

Today, of course, you'll want to see the Louvre not just to walk through a central part of French history, or even to marvel at the French gift for creating buildings that convey the pomp and prestige they consider their nation's due; rather, you'll be drawn here to see the extraordinary collections assembled under its roofs. Paintings, drawings, antiquities, sculpture, furniture, coins, jewelry—the quality and the sheer variety are intimidating. The number-one attraction for most is Leonardo da Vinci's enigmatic *Mona Lisa*, "La Joconde" to the French. But there are numerous other works of equal quality. The collections are divided into seven sections: Oriental antiquities; Egyptian antiquities; Greek and Roman antiquities; sculpture; paintings, prints, and drawings; furniture; and objets d'art. What follows is no more than a selection of favorites, chosen to act as key points for your exploration. If you have time for only one visit, they will give some idea of the riches of the museum. With the rearrangement of the museum far from complete— the rue de Rivoli wing, which used to house the French Finance Ministry, is to become part of the museum by 1994—it's not possible to say with certainty just what works will be on display where. Study the plans at the entrance to get your bearings, and pick up a map to take with you.

Paintings: French paintings dominate the picture collection. Here are the highlights, in chronological order:

The Inspiration of the Poet, by Poussin (1594–1665), is a sturdy example of the Rome-based painter's fascination with the classical world and of the precision of his draftsmanship. The coloring, by contrast, is surprisingly vivid, almost Venetian.

Cleopatra Landing, by Claude (1600–1682), presents an altogether more poetic vision of the ancient world, delicately atmospheric, with the emphasis on light and space rather than on the nominal subject matter.

The Embarkation for the Island of Cythera, by Watteau (1684–1721), concentrates on creating an equally poetic mood, but there is an extra layer of emotion: The gallant gentlemen and their courtly women seem drugged by the pleasures about to be enjoyed, but disturbingly aware of their transitory nature, too.

The Oath of the Horatii, by David (1748–1825), takes a much sterner view of classical Rome; this is neoclassicism—severe, uncompromising, and austere. The moral content of the painting takes precedence over purely painterly qualities; it also held an important political message for contemporaries, championing the cause of Republicanism.

La Grande Odalisque, by Ingres (1780–1867), is the supreme achievement by this habitually staid "academic" artist; sensuous yet remote and controlled. Here, exoticism and the French classical tradition gel to produce a strikingly elegant image.

The Raft of the Medusa, by Géricault (1791–1824), presages a much more gloomily Romantic view of the human state, nightmarish despite its heroism and grand scale.

The Massacre at Chios, by Delacroix (1798–1863), is a dashing example of the painter's brilliant coloring and free handling. The rigid orthodoxies of French academic painting are decisively rejected in favor of a dramatically Romantic approach.

Among works by non-French painters, pride of place must go to the *Mona Lisa*, if only by virtue of its fame. The picture is smaller than you might expect and kept behind protective glass; it is invariably surrounded by a crowd of worshipers. The Italian Renaissance is also strongly represented by Fra Angelico, Mantegna, Raphael, Titian, and Veronese. Holbein, Van Eyck, Rembrandt, Hals, Brueghel, and Rubens underline the achievements of northern European painting. The Spanish painters El Greco, Murillo, Velázquez, and Goya are also well represented.

Sculpture: Three-dimensional attractions start with marvels of ancient Greek sculpture such as the soaring *Venus of Samothrace,* from the 3rd century BC, and the *Venus de Milo,* from the 2nd century BC. The strikingly realistic *Seated Scribe* dates from around 2000 BC. Probably the best-loved exhibit is Michelangelo's pair of *Slaves,* intended for the unfinished tomb of Pope Julius II.

Furniture and Objets d'Art: The number-one attraction is the **French crown jewels,** a glittering display of extravagant jewelry, including the 186-karat Regent diamond. Among the collections of French furniture, don't miss the grandiose 17th- and 18th-century productions of Boulle and Riesener, marvels of intricate craftsmanship and typical of the elegant luxury of the best French furniture. The series of immense Gobelins tapestries may well be more to the taste of those with a fondness for opulent decoration. *Palais du Louvre, tel. 40–20–50–50. Admission: 35 frs adults, 20 frs 18–25 years, over 60, and on Sun.; children under 18 free. Open Thurs.–Sun. 9–6, Mon. and Wed. 9 AM–9:45 PM. Some sections open some days only.*

North of the Louvre

Stretching westward from the main entrance to the Louvre and the glass pyramid is an expanse of stately, formal gardens. These are the **Tuileries Gardens** (*see* From the Arc de Triomphe ❻ to the Opéra, *below*). Leading to them is the **Arc du Carrousel,** a small relation of the distant Arc de Triomphe and, like its big brother, put up by Napoléon. To the north, in the Pavillon de ❼ Marsan, the northernmost wing of the Louvre, is the **Musée des Arts Décoratifs,** which houses over 50,000 objects charting the course of French furniture and applied arts through the centuries. The Musée de la Publicité, with its collection of 50,000 posters, stages temporary exhibits within the museum. *107 rue de Rivoli. Admission: 23 frs. Open Wed.–Sat. 12:30–6, Sun. 12–6.*

Running the length of the Louvre's northern side is Napoléon's ❽ elegant, arcaded **rue de Rivoli,** a street whose generally dull tourist shops add little to their surroundings. Cross it and ❾ you're in **place des Pyramides** and face-to-face with its gilded statue of Joan of Arc on horseback. The square is a focal point for city tour buses.

Walk up rue des Pyramides and take the first left, rue St-❿ Honoré, to the Baroque church of **St-Roch.** The church was begun in 1653 but completed only in the 1730s, the decade of the coolly classical facade. Classical playwright Corneille (1606–1684) is buried here; a commemorative plaque honoring him is located at the left of the entrance. It's worth having a look inside the church to see the bombastically Baroque altarpiece in the circular Lady Chapel at the far end.

Double back along rue St-Honoré to place du Palais-Royal. On the far side of the square, opposite the Louvre, is the **Louvre des Antiquaires,** a chic shopping mall housing upscale antiques shops. It's a minimuseum in itself. Its stylish, glass-walled corridors deserve a browse even if you have no intention of buying.

Retrace your steps to place André-Malraux, with its exuberant fountains. The Opéra building is visible down the avenue of the same name, while, on one corner of the square, at rue de Richelieu, is the **Comédie Française.** This theater is the time-honored setting for performances of classical French drama, with tragedies by Racine and Corneille and comedies by Molière regularly on the bill. The building itself dates from 1790, but the Comédie Française company was created by that most theatrical of French monarchs, Louis XIV, back in 1680. Those who understand French and who have a taste for the mannered, declamatory style of French acting—it's a far cry from method acting—will appreciate an evening here. (*See* The Arts and Nightlife, Chapter 6, for details on how to get tickets.)

To the right of the theater is the unobtrusive entrance to the gardens of the **Palais-Royal.** The buildings of this former palace—royal only in that all-powerful Cardinal Richelieu (1585–1642) magnanimously bequeathed them to Louis XIII—date from the 1630s. In his early days as king, Louis XIV preferred the relative intimacy of the Palais-Royal to the intimidating splendor of the Louvre. He soon decided, though, that his own intimidating splendor warranted a more majestic setting; hence, of course, that final word in un-intimacy, Versailles.

Today, the Palais-Royal is home to the French Ministry of Culture and is not open to the public. But don't miss the **Jardin du Palais-Royal,** gardens bordered by arcades harboring discreet boutiques and divided by rows of perfectly trimmed little trees. They are a surprisingly little-known oasis in the gray heart of the city. It's hard to imagine anywhere more delightful for dozing in the afternoon sun. As you walk into the gardens, there's not much chance that you'll miss the black-and-white striped, truncated columns in the courtyard or the revolving silver spheres that slither around in the two fountains at either end, the controversial work of architect Daniel Buren. Long gone are the days when this dignified spot was the haunt of prostitutes and gamblers, a veritable sink of vice, in fact. It's hard to imagine anywhere much more respectable these days. Walk up to the end, away from the main palace, and peek into the opulent, Belle Epoque, glass-lined interior of **Le Grand Véfour.** This is more than just one of the swankiest restaurants in the city; it's probably the most sumptuously appointed, too.

Around the corner from here, on rue de Richelieu, stands France's national library, the **Bibliothèque Nationale.** It contains over 7 million printed volumes. A copy of every book and periodical printed in France must, by law, be sent here. Visitors can admire Robert de Cotte's 18th-century courtyard and peep into the 19th-century reading room. The library galleries stage exhibits from time to time from the collections. *58 rue de Richelieu. Open daily 10–8.*

From the library, walk southeast along rue des Petits-Champs to the circular **place des Victoires.** It was laid out in 1685 by Mansart, a leading proponent of 17th-century French classicism, in honor of the military victories of Louis XIV, that indefatigable warrior whose near-continuous battles may have brought much prestige to his country but came perilously close to bringing it to bankruptcy, too. Louis is shown prancing on a plunging steed in the center of the square; it's a copy, put up in 1822 to replace the original destroyed in the Revolution. You'll find some of the city's most upscale fashion shops here and on the surrounding streets.

Head south down rue Croix des Petits-Champs. You'll pass the undistinguished bulk of the Banque de France on your right. The second street on the left leads to the circular, 18th-century **Bourse du Commerce,** or Commercial Exchange. Alongside it is a 100-foot-high fluted column, all that remains of a mansion built here in 1572 for Catherine de Médicis. The column is said to have been used as a platform for stargazing by Catherine's astrologer, Ruggieri.

You don't need to scale Ruggieri's column to be able to spot the bulky outline of the church of **St-Eustache,** away to the left. Since the demolition of the 19th-century iron and glass market halls at the beginning of the '70s, an act that has since come to be seen as little short of vandalism, St-Eustache has reemerged as a dominant element on the central Paris skyline. It is a huge church, the "cathedral" of Les Halles, built, as it were, as the market people's Right Bank reply to Notre Dame on the Ile de la Cité. St-Eustache dates from a couple of hundred years later than Notre Dame. With the exception of the feeble west front, added between 1754 and 1788, construction lasted from 1532 to 1637, spanning the twilight of Gothic and the rise of the Renaissance. As a consequence, the church is a curious architectural hybrid. Its exterior flying buttresses, for example, are solidly Gothic. Its column orders, rounded arches, and comparatively simple and thick window tracery are unmistakably classical. Few buildings bear such eloquent witness to stylistic transition. St-Eustache also features occasional organ concerts. *2 rue du Jour, tel. 46–27–89–21, for concert information. Open daily.*

Nothing now remains of either the market halls or the rumbustious atmosphere that led 19th-century novelist Emile Zola to dub Les Halles *le ventre de Paris* ("the belly of Paris"). Today, the vast site is part shopping mall and part garden. The latter, which starts by the provocative, king-size sculpture *Hand* in front of St-Eustache, is geared for children. They'll also love the bush shaped like a rhinoceros.

The once-grimy facades of the buildings facing Les Halles have been expensively spruced up to reflect the mood of the shiny new **Forum des Halles,** the multilevel mall. Just how long the plastic, concrete, glass, and mock-marble of this gaudy mall will stay shiny is anyone's guess. Much of the complex is already showing signs of wear and tear, a state of affairs not much helped by the hordes of down-and-outs who invade it toward dusk. Nonetheless, the multitude of shops gathered at the Forum makes it somewhere no serious shopper will want to miss. The sweeping white staircase and glass reflections of the central courtyard have a certain photogenic appeal.

Leave by square des Innocents to the southeast; its 16th-century Renaissance fountain has recently been restored. As you make your way toward boulevard de Sébastopol, you can see the futuristic funnels of the Beaubourg jutting above the sur-

rounding buildings (*see* The Marais and Ile St-Louis, *below*).
Head right, toward the Seine. Just before you reach place du
Châtelet on the river, you'll see the **Tour St-Jacques** to your left.
This richly worked, 170-foot stump, now used for meteorologi-
cal purposes and not open to the public, is all that remains of a
16th-century church destroyed in 1797.

The Ile de la Cité

From place du Châtelet, cross back over the Seine on the Pont
au Change to the Ile de la Cité. To your right looms the imposing **Palais de Justice,** the Law Courts, built by Baron Haussmann in his characteristically weighty classical style about
1860. You can wander around the building, watching the bustle
of the lawyers, or attend a court hearing. But the real interest
here is the medieval part of the complex, spared by Haussmann
in his otherwise wholesale destruction of the lesser medieval
buildings of the Ile de la Cité. There are two buildings you'll
want to see: the Conciergerie and the Sainte-Chapelle.

The **Conciergerie,** the northernmost part of the complex, was
originally part of the royal palace on the island. Most people
know it, however, as a prison, the grim place of confinement for
Danton, Robespierre, and, most famously, Marie Antoinette
during the French Revolution. From here, all three, and count-
less others who fell afoul of the Revolutionary leaders, were
taken off to place de la Concorde and the guillotine. The name
of the building is derived from the governor, or *concierge*, of the
palace, whose considerable income was swollen by the privilege he enjoyed of renting out shops and workshops. Inside,
you'll see the guardroom, complete with hefty Gothic vaulting
and intricately carved columns, and the Salle des Gens
d'Armes, an even more striking example of Gothic monumen-
tality. From there, a short corridor leads to the kitchen, with
its four vast fireplaces. Those with a yen to throw a really memorable party can rent the room. The cells, including that in
which Marie Antoinette was held, and the chapel, where objects connected with the ill-fated queen are displayed, complete the tour. *Admission: 25 frs adults, 16 frs students and
senior citizens. Joint ticket with Sainte-Chapelle: 40 frs. Open
daily 9:30–6:30, 10–4:30 in winter.*

The other perennial crowd puller in the Palais de Justice is the
Sainte-Chapelle, the Holy Chapel. It was built by the genial and
pious Louis IX (1226–1270), whose good works ensured his
subsequent canonization. He constructed it to house what he
took to be the Crown of Thorns from Christ's crucifixion and
fragments of the True Cross, all of which he had bought from
the impoverished Emperor Baldwin of Constantinople at phenomenal expense. Architecturally, for all its delicate and ornate exterior decoration—notice the open latticework of the
pencil-like *flèche*, or spire, on the roof—the design of the building is simplicity itself. In essence, it's no more than a thin, rec-
tangular box, much taller than it is wide. But think of it
primarily as an oversize reliquary, an ornate medieval casket
designed to house holy relics.

The building is actually two chapels in one. The plainer, first-
floor chapel, made gloomy by insensitive mid-19th-century res-
torations (which could do with restoration themselves), was for
servants and lowly members of the court. The upper chapel, in-

finitely more spectacular, was for the king and more important members of the court. This is what you come to see. You reach it up a dark spiral staircase. Here, again, some clumsy 19th-century work has added a deadening touch, but the glory of the chapel—the stained glass—is spectacularly intact. The chapel is airy and diaphanous, the walls glowing and sparkling as light plays on the windows. Notice how the walls, in fact, consist of at least twice as much glass as masonry: The entire aim of the architects was to provide the maximum amount of window space. The Sainte-Chapelle is one of the supreme achievements of the Middle Ages and will be a highlight of your visit to Paris. Come early in the day to avoid the dutiful crowds that trudge around it. Better still, try to attend one of the regular, candle-lit concerts given here. *Tel. 43–54–30–09, for concert information. Admission: 25 frs adults, 14 frs students and senior citizens. Joint ticket with Conciergerie: 40 frs. Open daily 9:30–6:30; winter, daily 10–5.*

Take rue de Lutèce opposite the Palais de Justice down to place ❷❺ Louis-Lépine and the bustling **Marché aux Fleurs,** the flower market. There's an astoundingly wide range of flowers on sale and, on Sundays, there are birds, too—everything from sparrows to swans. *Open daily 9–7.*

Notre Dame

Around the corner, looming above the large, traffic-free place du Parvis (*kilometre zéro* to the French, the spot from which all distances to and from the city are officially measured), is the most enduring symbol of Paris, its historic and geographic ❷❻ heart, the **Cathédrale Notre Dame.** The building was started in 1163, with an army of stonemasons, carpenters, and sculptors working on a site that had previously seen a Roman temple, an early Christian basilica, and a Romanesque church. The chancel and altar were consecrated in 1182, but the magnificent sculptures surrounding the main doors were not put into position until 1240. The north tower was finished 10 years later. Despite various changes in the 17th century, principally the removal of the rose windows, the cathedral remained substantially unaltered until the French Revolution. Then, the statues of the kings of Israel were hacked down by the mob, chiefly because they were thought to represent the despised royal line of France, and everything inside and out that was deemed "anti-Republican" was stripped away. An interesting postscript to this destruction occurred in 1977, when some of the heads of these statues were discovered salted away in a bank vault on boulevard Haussmann. They'd apparently been hidden there by an ardent royalist who owned the small mansion that now forms part of the bank. The restored heads are now on display in the Musée de Cluny (*see* The Left Bank, *below*). *Admission free.*

By the early 19th century, the excesses of the Revolution were over, and the cathedral went back to fulfilling its religious functions again. Napoléon crowned himself emperor here in May 1804. (David's heroic painting of this lavish ceremony can be seen in the Louvre.) Full-scale restoration started in the middle of the century, the most conspicuous result of which was the construction of the spire, the flèche, over the roof. It was then, too, that Haussmann demolished the warren of little buildings in front of the cathedral, creating the place du Parvis. The

Portal of the Last
Judgment, **1**
Portal to the Virgin, **2**
Portal of St. Anne, **3**
Le Brun, **4**
St. Stephen's Portal, **5**
South Rose Window, **6**
Our Lady of Paris, **7**
Le Sueur, **8**
North Rose Window, **9**
Cloister Portal, **10**

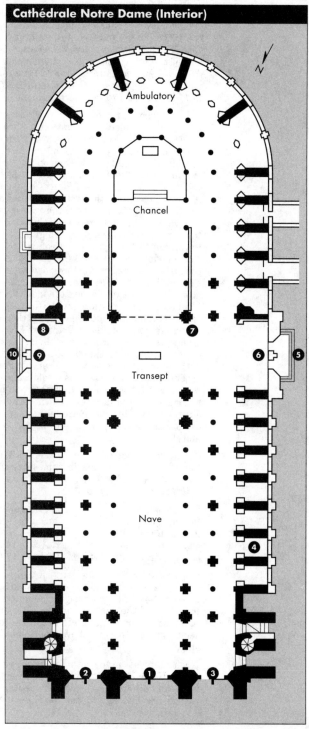

Cathédrale Notre Dame (Interior)

Ambulatory

Chancel

Transept

Nave

㉗ Crypte Archéologique, the archaeological museum under the square, contains remains unearthed during excavations here in the 1960s. Slides and models detail the history of the Ile de la Cité. The foundations of the 3rd-century Gallo-Roman rampart and of the 6th-century Merovingian church can also be seen. *Place du Parvis. Admission: 25 frs adults (40 frs including tower of Notre Dame), 14 frs age 18–24 and over 60, 6 frs age 7–17. Open daily 10–6:30, 10–5 in winter.*

Place du Parvis provides the perfect place from which to gaze at the facade, divided neatly into three levels. At the first-floor level are the three main entrances, or portals: the Portal of the Virgin on the left, the Portal of the Last Judgment in the center, and the Portal of Ste-Anne on the right. All three are surmounted by magnificent carvings—most of them 19th-century copies of the originals—of figures, foliage, and biblical scenes. Above this level are the restored statues of the kings of Israel, the Galerie des Rois. Above the gallery is the great rose window, and, above that, the Grand Galerie, at the base of the twin towers. Between them, you can glimpse the flèche. The south tower houses the great bell of Notre Dame, as tolled by Quasimodo, Victor Hugo's fictional hunchback. The interior of the cathedral, with its vast proportions, soaring nave, and gentle, multicolored light filtering through the stained-glass windows, inspires awe, despite the inevitable throngs of tourists. Visit early in the morning, when the cathedral is at its lightest and least crowded. You come first to the massive, 12th-century columns supporting the twin towers. Look down the nave to the transepts—the arms of the church—where, at the south (right) entrance to the chancel, you'll glimpse the haunting, 12th-century statue of Notre Dame de Paris, Our Lady of Paris. The chancel itself owes parts of its decoration to a vow taken by Louis XIII in 1638. Still without an heir after 23 years of marriage, he promised to dedicate the entire country to the Virgin Mary if his queen produced a son. When the longed-for event came to pass, Louis set about redecorating the chancel and choir.

On the south side of the chancel is the **Treasury,** with a collection of garments, reliquaries, and silver and gold plate. *Admission: 15 frs adults, 10 frs students and senior citizens, 5 frs children. Open daily 10–5:45.*

The 387-step climb to the top of the **towers** is worth the effort for the close-up view of the famous gargoyles—most of them added in the 19th century—and the expansive view over the city. *Entrance via north tower. Admission: 30 frs adults, 16 frs students and senior citizens. Open daily 10–4:30.*

On the subject of views, no visit to Notre Dame is complete **㉘** without a walk behind the cathedral to **Square Jean XXIII,** located between the river and the building. It offers a breathtaking sight of the east end of the cathedral, ringed by flying buttresses, surmounted by the spire. From here, the building seems almost to float above the Seine like some vast, stone ship.

If your interest in the cathedral is not yet sated, duck into the **㉙ Musée Notre Dame.** It displays paintings, engravings, medallions, and other objects and documents, all of which trace the cathedral's history. *10 rue du Cloître-Notre-Dame. Admis-*

sion: 10 frs, 6 frs students and senior citizens, 4 frs children under 14. Open Wed. and weekends only, 2:30–6.

There's a final pilgrimage you may like to make on the Ile de la Cité to the **Mémorial de la Déportation,** located at square de l'Ile-de-France, at the eastern tip of the island. Here, in what was once the city morgue, you'll find the modern crypt, dedicated to those French men and women who died in Nazi concentration camps. You may find a visit to the quiet garden above it a good place to rest and to muse on the mysterious dichotomy that enables the human race to construct buildings of infinite beauty and to treat its fellow men with infinite cruelty. *Admission free. Open daily 9–6, 9–dusk in winter.*

The Marais and Ile St-Louis

Numbers in the margin correspond to points of interest on the Marais and Ile St-Louis map.

This tour includes two of the oldest and most historic neighborhoods in Paris: the Marais—once a marshy area north of the Seine, today about the most sought-after residential and business district of the city—and the Ile St-Louis, the smaller of the two islands in the Seine. It also includes a side trip to the Bastille, site of the infamous prison stormed on July 14, 1789, an event that came to symbolize the beginning of the French Revolution. Largely in commemoration of the bicentennial of the Revolution in 1989, the Bastille area has been renovated.

Renovation is one of the key notes of this tour, especially around the Marais; the word *marais*, incidentally, means marsh or swamp. Well into the '70s, this was one of the city's poorest areas, filled with dilapidated tenement buildings and squalid courtyards. Today, most of the Marais's spectacular *hôtels particuliers*—loosely, "mansions," one-time residences of aristocratic families—have been restored and transformed into museums. The grubby streets of the Jewish quarter, around the rue des Rosiers, is about the only area to remain undeveloped. The area's regeneration was sparked by the building of the Beaubourg, arguably Europe's most vibrant—and architecturally whimsical—cultural center. The gracious architecture of the 17th and early 18th centuries, however, sets the tone for the rest of the Marais. Try to visit during the Festival du Marais, held every June and July, when concerts, theater, and ballet are performed.

The history of the Marais began when Charles V, king of France in the 14th century, moved the French court from the Ile de la Cité. However, it wasn't until Henri IV laid out the place Royale, today the place des Vosges, in the early 17th century, that the Marais became *the* place to live. Aristocratic dwellings began to dot the neighborhood, and their salons filled with the *beau monde*. But following the French Revolution, the Marais rapidly became one of the most deprived, dissolute areas in Paris. It was spared the attentions of Baron Haussmann, the man who rebuilt so much of Paris in the mid-19th century, so that, though crumbling, its ancient golden-hued buildings and squares remained intact.

Hôtel de Ville to Beaubourg

❶ Begin your tour at the **Hôtel de Ville**, the city hall, overlooking the Seine. The building is something of a symbol for the regeneration of the Marais, since much of the finance and direction for the restoration of the area has been provided by the Parisian municipal authorities. As the area has been successfully redeveloped, so the prestige of the mayor of Paris has grown with it. In fact, until 1977, Paris was the only city in France without a mayor; with the creation of the post and the election to it of Jacques Chirac, leader of the right-of-center Gaullist party, the position has become pivotal in both Parisian and French politics. It comes as no surprise, therefore, that Chirac has overseen a thoroughgoing restoration of the Hôtel de Ville, both inside and out. You can't go inside, but stand in the traffic-free square in front of it and ponder the vicissitudes that have plagued the Parisian municipal authorities down the years and the dramas that have been played out here. It was here, in 1357, that Etienne Marcel, cloth merchant and prominent city father, attempted to exploit the chaos of the Hundred Years War—the titanic struggle between France and England for control of France—by increasing the power of what he hoped would be an independent Paris. And it was just one year later that his supporters had him assassinated here, believing that his ambitions had outstripped their common interests. There's a statue of Marcel in the little garden on the south side of the building overlooking the Seine. The square was also used for numerous public executions. Most victims were hanged, drawn, and quartered; the lucky ones were burned at the stake. It was also here, during the Revolution, that Robespierre, fanatical leader of the Terror, came to suffer the fate of his many victims when a furious mob sent him to the guillotine in 1794. Following the short-lived restoration of the Bourbon monarchy in 1830, the building became the seat of the French government, a role that came to a sudden end with the uprisings in 1848. In the Commune of 1871, the Hôtel de Ville was burned to the ground. Today's exuberant building, based closely on the Renaissance original, went up between 1874 and 1884. In 1944, following the liberation of Paris from Nazi rule, General de Gaulle took over the leadership of France here.

From the Hôtel de Ville, head north across rue de Rivoli and up rue du Temple. On your right, you'll pass one of the city's most popular department stores, the **Bazar de l'Hôtel de Ville**, or BHV, as it's known. The first street on your left, rue de la Verrerie, will take you down to rue St-Martin and the church of **St-Merri**, an ornate mid-16th-century structure. Its dark interior can be fun to explore, though it contains nothing of outstanding interest. You may find the stores, restaurants, and galleries of rue St-Martin more diverting.

❹ The **Beaubourg/Pompidou Center** or, to give it its full name, the Centre National d'Art et de Culture Georges-Pompidou, is next. Georges Pompidou (1911–1974) was the president of France who inaugurated the project. If nothing else, the Beaubourg is an exuberant melting pot of culture, which casts its net far and wide: Anything goes here. The center hosts an innovative and challenging series of exhibits, in addition to housing the largest collection of modern art in the world. It boasts an avowedly open-door policy toward the public—witness the long hours—and a determination to bring in the crowds by whatever means possible. On the other hand, there's little getting away from the fact that the building itself has been the target of much unfavorable rhetoric. Unveiled in 1977, the Beaubourg is by far the most popular museum in the world, attracting upward of 8 million visitors a year; but it has begun to show its age in no uncertain terms. The much-vaunted, gaudily painted service pipes that snake up the exterior—painted the same colors that were used to identify them on the architects' plans—need continual repainting. The plastic tubing that encloses the exterior escalators is cracked and grimy. The skeletal supports in the interior are peeling and dirty. In essence, the massive solemnity of a building like the Louvre makes the brashness of the Beaubourg seem cheap, many now maintain. Does the Beaubourg display gross architectural bad manners, contemptuously ignoring the elegant proportions of the surrounding streets? Or is it a bold and potent architectural statement, feeling no need to apologize for its uncompromising nature?

❺ You'll approach the center across **plateau Beaubourg,** a substantial square that slopes gently down toward the main entrance. In summer, it's thronged with musicians, mime artists, dancers, fire-eaters, acrobats, and other performers. Probably the single most popular thing to do at the Beaubourg is to ride the escalator up to the roof, with the Parisian skyline unfolding as you are carried through its clear plastic piping. There is a sizable restaurant and café on the roof. The major highlight inside is the modern art collection on the fourth floor. The emphasis is largely on French artists; American painters and sculptors are conspicuous by their absence. Movie buffs will want to take in the cinémathèque, a movie theater showing near-continuous programs of classic films from the world over. There are also magnificent reference facilities, among them a language laboratory, an extensive collection of tapes, videos, and slides, an industrial design center, and an acoustics and musical research center. The bookshop on the first floor stocks a wide range of art books, many in English, plus postcards and posters. *Beaubourg, plateau Beaubourg, tel. 42–77–12–33. Admission free. Admission to art museum: 28 frs, 32 frs for special exhibitions in the Grande Galerie. Open Wed.–Mon. noon–10 PM, weekends 10 AM–10 PM; closed Tues. Guided tours in English weekdays 3:30, weekends 11 during summer and Christmas seasons only.*

You can leave plateau Beaubourg by its southwestern corner—to your right as you face the building—and head down little rue Ste-Croix de la Bretonnerie to visit the Marais's Jewish quarter; it represents an intriguing element of Parisian ethnic history but, especially since some relatively recent bomb attacks, is a rather cloistered quarter of the Marais.

You'll see the more obvious of the area's historical highlights if you take rue Rambuteau, which runs along the north side of the center (to your left as you face the building). The **Quartier de l'Horloge,** the Clock Quarter, opens off the plateau here. An entire city block has been rebuilt, and, though its shops and cafés make a brave attempt to bring it to life, it retains a resolutely artificial quality. The mechanical clock around the corner on rue Clairvaux will amuse kids, however. Saint George defends Time against a dragon, an eagle-beaked bird, or a monstrous crab (symbolizing earth, air, and water, respectively) every

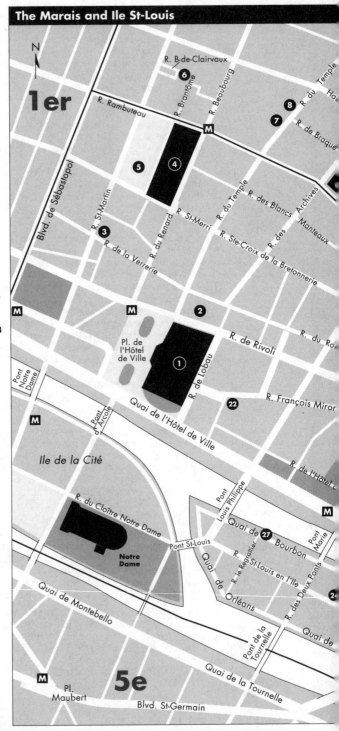

The Marais and Ile St-Louis

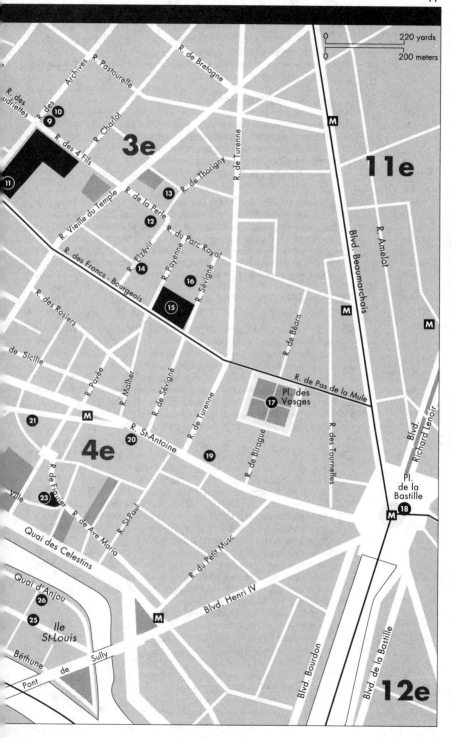

hour, on the hour. At noon, 6 PM, and 10 PM, he takes on all three at once. On the other side of the Quartier de l'Horloge, at 11 rue Brantôme, is **AS-ECO,** the only all-night supermarket in the city; note that it's closed on Sundays. However, it's more fun shopping in the little market at the beginning of rue Rambuteau.

Around the Marais

You are now poised to plunge into the elegant heart of the Marais. You won't be able to get into many of the historic homes here—the private hôtels particuliers—but this won't stop you from admiring their stately facades. And don't be afraid to push through the heavy formal doors—or *porte-cochères*—to glimpse the discreet courtyards that lurk behind them.

7 From the Clock Quarter, continue down rue Rambuteau and take the first left, up rue du Temple, to the **Hôtel d'Avaux** at no. 71, built in 1640. The immense entrance is decorated with the sculpted heads of what, in 17th-century France, passed for sav-
8 ages. A few doors up, at no. 79, is the **Hôtel de Montmor,** dating from the same period. It was once the scene of an influential literary salon—a part-social and part-literary group—that met here on an impromptu basis and included the philosopher Descartes (1596–1650) and the playwright Molière (1622–1673). Note the intricate ironwork on the second-floor balcony.

9 Head east on rue des Haudriettes to the little-known **Musée de la Chasse et de la Nature,** housed in one of the Marais's most stately mansions, the Hôtel de Guénégaud. The collections include a series of immense 17th- and 18th-century pictures of dead animals, artfully arranged, as well as a wide variety of guns and stuffed animals (you might want to pass this by if you are a vegetarian or an opponent of blood sports). *60 rue des Archives, tel. 42–72–86–43. Admission: 25 frs adults, 5 frs. children under 16. Open Wed.–Mon. 10–12:30 and 1:30–5:30.*

Next door, at 58 rue des Archives, two fairy-tale towers stand
10 on either side of the Gothic entrance (1380) to the **Hôtel de Clisson.** In the mid-15th century this was the Paris base of the Duke of Bedford, regent of France after Henry V's demise, during the English occupation of Paris, a phase of the Hundred Years War that lasted from 1420 to 1435. At the end of the 17th century, it was bought by the glamorous princess of Soubise, a grande dame of Parisian literary society. She later moved into the neighboring Hôtel de Soubise, now the **Archives Nationales.**
11 Its collections today form part of the **Musée de l'Histoire de France,** whose entrance is at the southern end of the Archives Nationales. There are thousands of intricate historical documents, many complete with impressive red seals. The highlights are the Edict of Nantes (1598), the wills of Louis XIV and Napoléon, and the Declaration of Human Rights. Louis XVI's diary is also in the collection, containing his sadly ignorant entry for July 14, 1789, the day the Bastille was stormed and, for all intents and purposes, the day the French Revolution can be said to have begun: *Rien* ("nothing"), he wrote. You can also visit the apartments of the prince and princess de Soubise; don't miss them if you have any interest in the lifestyles of 18th-century French aristocrats. *60 rue des Francs-Bourgeois, tel. 40–27–62–18. Admission: 12 frs adults, children under 18 free. Open Wed.–Mon. 1:45–5:45.*

Continue east on rue des Francs-Bourgeois, turning left onto rue Vielle du Temple and passing the Hôtel de Rohan (on your left, on the corner), built for the archbishop of Strasbourg in 1705. Turn right onto rue de la Perle and walk down to the ⑫ **Musée de la Serrure,** the Lock Museum. It's sometimes also called the **Musée Bricard,** a name you'll recognize on many French locks and keys. The sumptuous building in which the collections are housed is perhaps more interesting than the assembled locks and keys within; it was built in 1685 by Bruand, the architect of Les Invalides *(see* From Orsay to Trocadéro, *below).* But those with a taste for fine craftsmanship will appreciate the intricacy and ingenuity of many of the older locks. One represents an early security system—it would shoot anyone who tried to open it with the wrong key. Another was made in the 17th century by a master locksmith who was himself held under lock and key while he labored over it—the task took him four years. *1 rue de la Perle, tel. 42–77–79–62. Admission: 10 frs. Open Mon.–Fri. 2–5; closed Sat., Sun., Aug., and last week of Dec.*

⑬ From here it is but a step to the Hôtel Salé, today the **Musée Picasso,** opened in the fall of 1985 and so far showing no signs of losing its immense popularity. Be prepared for long lines at any time of year. The building itself, put up between 1656 and 1660 for financier Aubert de Fontenay, quickly became known as the Hôtel Salé—*salé* meaning salted—as a result of the enormous profits made by de Fontenay as the sole appointed collector of the salt tax. The building was restored by the French government at phenomenal expense as a permanent home for the pictures, sculptures, drawings, prints, ceramics, and assorted works of art given to the government by Picasso's heirs after the painter's death in 1973 in lieu of death duties. What's notable about the collection—other than the fact that it's the largest assemblage of works by Picasso in the world—is that these were works that Picasso himself owned; works, in other words, that he especially valued. There are pictures from every period of his life, adding up to a grand total of 230 paintings, 1,500 drawings, and nearly 1,700 prints, as well as works by Cézanne, Miró, Renoir, Braque, Degas, Matisse, and others. If you have any serious interest in Picasso, this is not a place you'd want to miss. The positively palatial surroundings of the Hôtel Salé add greatly to the pleasures of a visit. *5 rue de Thorigny, tel. 42–71–25–21. Admission: 26 frs. Open Thurs.–Mon. 9:30–6.*

Head back down rue de Thorigny and cross to rue Elzévir, op-⑭ posite. Halfway down on the left is the **Musée Cognacq-Jay,** opened here in 1990 after being transferred from its original home on boulevard des Capucines near the Opéra. The museum is devoted to the arts of the 18th century and contains outstanding furniture, porcelain, and paintings (notably by Watteau, Boucher, and Tiepolo). *8 rue Elzévir, tel. 40–27–07–21. Admission: 12 frs, 6 frs students and children. Open Tues.–Sun. 10–5:30.*

Continue down rue Elzévir to **rue des Francs-Bourgeois.** Its name—Street of the Free Citizens—comes from the homes for the poor, or almshouses, built here in the 14th century, whose inhabitants were so impoverished that they were allowed to be "free" of taxes. In marked contrast to the street's earlier pover-⑮ ty, the substantial **Hôtel Carnavalet** became the scene, in the late 17th century, of the most brilliant salon in Paris, presided over by Madame de Sévigné. She is best known for the hundreds of letters she wrote to her daughter during her life; they've become one of the most enduring chronicles of French high society in the 17th century, and the Carnavalet was her home for the last 20 years of her life. In 1880, the hotel was transformed into the **Musée Carnavalet**, or Musée Historique de la Ville de Paris. As part of the mammoth celebrations for the bicentennial of the French Revolution, in July 1989, the museum annexed the neighboring **Hôtel Peletier St-Fargeau.** Together the two museums chronicle the entire history of the city of Paris, with material dating from the city's origins until 1789 housed in the Hôtel Carnavalet, and objects from that time to the present in the Hôtel Peletier St-Fargeau. Parts of the older collections are quite interesting, albeit repetitive. There are large numbers of maps and plans, quantities of furniture, and a substantial assemblage of busts and portraits of Parisian worthies down the ages. The sections on the Revolution, on the other hand, are extraordinary and include some riveting models of guillotines and a number of objects associated with the royal family's final days, including the chess set that the prisoners used to pass the time, and the king's razor. *23 rue de Sévigné, tel. 42–72–21–13. Admission: 40 frs adults, 30 frs students and senior citizens. Open Tues.–Sun. 10–5:30; closed Mon.*

Now walk a minute or two farther along rue des Francs-Bourgeois to **place des Vosges.** Place des Vosges, or place Royale as it was originally known, is the oldest square in Paris. Laid out by Henri IV at the beginning of the 17th century, it is the model on which all later city squares, that most French of urban developments, are based. It stands on the site of a former royal palace, the Palais des Tournelles, which was abandoned by the French queen, Italian-born Catherine de Médicis, when her husband, Henri II, was killed in a tournament here in 1559. The square achieves a harmony and a balance that make it deeply satisfying. The buildings have been softened by time, their pale pink stones crumbling slightly in the harsh Parisian air, their darker stone facings pitted with age. The combination of symmetrical town houses and the trim green square, bisected in the center by gravel paths and edged with plane trees, makes place des Vosges one of the more pleasant places to spend a hot summer's afternoon in the city. On these days, it will usually be filled with children playing in shafts of sunlight, with the roar of the traffic a distant hum.

Place des Vosges was always a highly desirable address, reaching a peak of glamour in the early years of Louis XIV's reign, when the nobility were falling over themselves for the privilege of living here. Notice the two larger buildings in the center of the north and south sides. The one on the south side was the king's pavilion; the one on the north was the queen's pavilion. The statue in the center is of Louis XIII. It's not the original; that was melted down in the Revolution, the same period when the square's name was changed in honor of the French district of the Vosges, the first area of the country to pay the new revolutionary taxes. You can tour the **Maison de Victor Hugo** at no. 6 (admission 12 frs, 6.50 frs students; open Tues.–Sun. 10–5:40), where the French author lived between 1832 and 1848. The collections here may appeal only to those with a specialized knowledge of the workaholic French writer.

Around the Bastille

From place des Vosges, follow rue de Pas de la Mule and turn
(18) right down boulevard Beaumarchais until you reach **place de la
Bastille,** site of the infamous prison destroyed at the beginning
of the French Revolution. Until 1988, there was little more to
see at place de la Bastille than a huge traffic circle and the
Colonne de Juillet, the July Column. As part of the country-
wide celebrations for July 1989, the bicentennial of the French
Revolution, an **opera house** (Opéra de la Bastille) was put up on
the south side of the square. Designed by Argentinian-born
Carlos Ott, it seats more than 3,000 and boasts five moving
stages. This ambitious project has inspired substantial redevelopment on the surrounding streets, especially along rue de
Lappe—once a haunt of Edith Piaf—and rue de la Roquette.
What was formerly a humdrum neighborhood is rapidly becoming one of the most sparkling and attractive in the city. Stream-
lined art galleries, funky jazz clubs, Spanish-style *tapas* bars—
very chic in Paris these days—and classy restaurants set the
tone. For a taste of the new Bastille-style nightlife, try **Balajo**
(9 rue de Lappe); it's the liveliest place here, with music (either
disco or live) nightly. Don't expect things to get too lively before 11 PM, however.

The Bastille, or, more properly, the Bastille St-Antoine, was a
massive building, protected by eight immense towers and a
wide moat (its ground plan is marked by paving stones set into
the modern square). It was built by Charles V in the late 14th
century. He intended it not as a prison but as a fortress to
guard the eastern entrance to the city. By the reign of Louis
XIII (1610–1643), however, the Bastille was used almost exclu-
sively to house political prisoners. Voltaire, the Marquis de
Sade, and the mysterious Man in the Iron Mask were all incar-
cerated here, along with many other unfortunates. It was this
obviously political role—specifically, the fact that the prisoners were nearly always held by order of the king—that led to
the formation of the "furious mob" (in all probability no more
than a largely unarmed rabble) to break into the prison on July
14, 1789, kill the governor, steal what firearms they could find,
and set free the seven remaining prisoners.

Later in 1789, the prison was knocked down. A number of the
original stones were carved into facsimiles of the Bastille and
sent to each of the provinces as a memento of royal oppression.
The key to the prison was given by Lafayette to George Washington, and it has remained at Mt. Vernon ever since. Nonetheless, the power of legend being what it is, what soon became
known as the "storming of the Bastille" was elevated to the status of a pivotal event in the course of the French Revolution,
one that demonstrated decisively the newfound power of a long-
suffering population. Thus it was that July 14 became the
French national day, an event celebrated with great nationalis-
tic fervor throughout the country. It's very much more than
just a day off or an excuse for a cookout. Needless to say, the
place to be, especially in the evening, is place de la Bastille.

The July Column commemorates a more substantial political
event: the July uprising of 1830, which saw the overthrow of the
repressive Charles X, the Bourbon king about whom it was said
only too truthfully that "the Bourbons learnt nothing, and for-
got nothing." It's sometimes hard to imagine the turmoil that

was a feature of French political life from the Revolution of 1789 right through the 19th century (and, arguably, well into the 20th). After the fall of Napoléon in 1815, the restoration of a boneheaded monarchy, personified first by Louis XVIII, then by Charles X, virtually guaranteed that further trouble was in store. Matters came to a head in July 1830 with the Ordinances of St-Cloud, the most contentious of which was to restrict the franchise—the right to vote—to a handful of landowners. Charles was duly toppled in three days of fighting at the end of the month—the Three Glorious Days—and a new, constitutionally elected monarch, Louis-Philippe, took the throne. His reign was hardly more distinguished, despite attempts to curry favor among the populace. Nor was it noticeably more liberal. Louis-Philippe did, nonetheless, have the July Column built as a memorial, stipulating that 500 of those killed in the fighting of 1830 were to be buried under it. When, in 1848, Louis-Philippe himself was ousted, the names of a handful of the Parisians killed in the fighting of 1848 were then added to those already on the column. (Louis-Philippe and his wife, disguised as Mr. and Mrs. William Smith, fled to Britain and threw themselves on the mercy of the young Queen Victoria.)

Toward the Ile St-Louis

There's more of the Marais to be visited between place de la Bastille and the Ile St-Louis, the last leg of this tour. Take wide **⑲** rue St-Antoine to the **Hôtel de Sully,** site of the **Caisse Nationale des Monuments Historiques,** the principal office for the administration of French historic monuments. Guided visits to sites and buildings all across the city begin here, though all of them are for French-speakers only. Still, it's worth stopping here to look at the stately, 17th-century courtyard with its richly carved windows and lavish ornamentation. The bookshop just inside the gate has a wide range of publications on Paris, many of them in English (open daily 10–12:45 and 1:45–6). You can also wander around the gardens.

Those with a fondness for the Baroque should duck into the ear-**⑳** ly 17th-century church of **St-Paul-St-Louis,** a few blocks west on rue St-Antoine. Its abundant decoration, which would be easier to appreciate if the church were cleaned, is typical of the Baroque taste for opulent detail.

㉑ The **Hôtel de Beauvais,** located on rue François Miron, is a Renaissance-era hôtel particulier dating from 1655. It was built for one Pierre de Beauvais and financed largely by a series of discreet payments from the king, Louis XIV. These surprisingly generous payments—the Sun King was normally parsimonious toward courtiers—were de Beauvais's reward for having turned a blind eye to the activities of his wife, Catherine-Henriette Bellier, in educating the young monarch in matters sexual. Louis, who came to the throne in 1643 at the age of 4, was 14 at the time Catherine-Henriette gave him the benefit of her wide experience; she was 40.

Continue down rue François Miron. Just before the Hôtel de **㉒** Ville is the site of one of the first churches in Paris, **St-Gervais-St-Protais,** named after two Roman soldiers martyred by the Emperor Nero in the 1st century AD. The original church—no trace remains of it now—was built in the 7th century. The present church, a riot of Flamboyant-style decoration, went up be-

tween 1494 and 1598, making it one of the last Gothic construc-
tions in the country. Some find this sort of late-Gothic architecture a poor, almost degraded, relation of the pure styles of the
12th and 13th centuries. Does it carry off a certain exuberance,
or is it simply a mass of unnecessary decoration? You'll want to
decide for yourself. Pause before you go in, to look at the facade, put up between 1616 and 1621. Where the interior is late
Gothic, the exterior is one of the earliest examples of classical,
or Renaissance, style in France. It's also the earliest example
of French architects' use of the classical orders of decoration on
the capitals (topmost sections) of the columns. Those on the
first floor are plain and sturdy Doric; the more elaborate Ionic
is used on the second floor; while the most ornate of all—Corinthian—is used on the third floor. The church hosts occasional
organ and choral concerts. *Tel. 47–26–78–38 for concert information. Open Tues.–Sun. 6:30 AM–8 PM; closed Mon.*

Don't cross the Seine to Ile St-Louis yet: Take rue de l'Hôtel de
Ville to where it meets rue de Figuier. The painstakingly re-
㉓ stored **Hôtel de Sens** (1474) on the corner is one of a handful of
Parisian homes to have survived since the Middle Ages. With
its pointed corner towers, Gothic porch, and richly carved decorative details, it is a strange mixture, half defensive strong-
hold, half fairy-tale château. It was built at the end of the 15th
century for the archbishop of Sens. Later, its best-known occupants were Henri IV and his queen, Marguerite, philanderers
both. While Henri dallied with his mistresses—he is said to
have had 56—at a series of royal palaces, Marguerite entertained her almost equally large number of lovers here. Today
the building houses a fine arts library, the **Bibliothèque Forney**
(admission free; open Tues.–Fri. 1:30–8:30, Sat. 10–8:30).

The Ile St-Louis

㉔ Cross pont Marie to the **Ile St-Louis,** the smaller of the two islands in the heart of Paris, linked to the Ile de la Cité by pont
St-Louis. The contrast between the islands is striking, considering how close they are. Whereas the Ile de la Cité, the oldest
continuously inhabited part of the city, is steeped in history
and dotted with dignified, old buildings, the Ile St-Louis is a
discreet residential district, something of an extension of the
Marais. Once thought to be an unimportant backwater and an
area curiously out-of-sync with the rest of the city, Ile St-Louis
is now a highly desirable address; a little old-fashioned, perhaps, certainly rather stuffy, but with its own touch of class.
There are no standouts here and no great sights, but for idle
strolling, window-shopping, or simply sitting on one of the little quays and drinking in the views while you watch the river
swirl by, the Ile St-Louis exudes a quintessentially Parisian
air. Come early in the day if you want to sample the full flavor of
this elegant haven.

The most striking feature of the island is its architectural uni-
ty, which stems from the efforts of a group of early 17th-cen-
tury property speculators. At that time, there were two islands
here, the Ile Notre Dame and Ile aux Vaches—the cows' island,
a reference to its use as grazing land. The speculators, led by an
energetic engineer named Christophe Marie (after whom the
pont Marie was named), bought the two islands, joined them
together, and divided the newly formed Ile St-Louis into build-

ing plots. Louis Le Vau (1612–1670), the leading Baroque architect in France, was commissioned to put up a series of imposing town houses, and by 1664 the project was largely complete.

There are three things you'll want to do here. One is to walk along **rue St-Louis en l'Ile,** which runs the length of the island. People still talk about its quaint, village-street feel, although this village street is now lined with a high-powered array of designer boutiques and a constant throng of tourists patroling its length. Many of them stop at **Berthillon** (31 rue St-Louis en l'Ile) for legendary, highly flavored ice cream. Though its products can be sampled at other cafés in Paris, this little shop is still the place to come—as the long lines will attest.

The second place to visit is the **Hôtel de Lauzun.** It was built in about 1650 for Charles Gruyn, who accumulated an immense fortune as a supplier of goods to the French army, but who landed in jail before the house was even completed. In the 19th century, the revolutionary critic and visionary poet Charles Baudelaire (1821–1867) had an apartment here, where he kept a personal cache of stuffed snakes and crocodiles. In 1848, the poet Théophile Gautier (1811–1872) moved in, making it the meeting place of the Club des Haschischines, the Hashish-Eaters' Club; novelist Alexander Dumas and painter Eugène Delacroix were both members. The club came to represent more than just a den of drug-takers and gossip, for these men believed passionately in the purity of art and the crucial role of the artist as sole interpreter of the chaos of life. Art for art's sake—the more exotic and refined the better—was their creed. Anything that helped the artist reach heightened states of perception was applauded by them. Now the building is used for receptions by the mayor of Paris. *17 quai d'Anjou, tel. 43–54–27–14. Admission: 22 frs. Open Easter–Oct., weekends only 10–5:30.*

The third and most popular attraction is a walk along the quays. The most lively, **quai de Bourbon,** is at the western end, facing the Ile de la Cité. There are views of Notre Dame from here and of the Hôtel de Ville and church of St-Gervais-St-Protais on the Right Bank. It can be an almost eerie spot in the winter, when it becomes deserted. In the summer, rows of baking bodies attest to its enduring popularity as the city's favorite sunbathing spot.

From the Arc de Triomphe to the Opéra

Numbers in the margin correspond to points of interest on the Arc de Triomphe to the Opéra map.

This tour takes in grand, opulent Paris: the Paris of imposing vistas, long, arrow-straight streets, and plush hotels and jewelers. It begins at the Arc de Triomphe, standing foursquare at the top of the most famous street in the city, the Champs-Elysées. You'll want to explore both its commercial upper half and its verdant lower section. The hinterland of the Champs-Elysées, made up of the imposing streets leading off it, is equally stylish. You're within striking distance of the Seine here (and a ride on a Bateau Mouche) to the south, and the cheerful, crowded Faubourg St-Honoré to the north. This is not so much an area for museums as for window-shopping and monument-gazing. Dazzling vistas open up from place de la Concorde, place de la Madeleine, and L'Etoile. Fashion shops, jewelers, art galleries, and deluxe hotels proliferate. This is also where the French president resides in his "palace" (not a very Repub-lican term, but then French presidents enjoy regal lifestyles) just off the Champs-Elysées.

Local charm is not, however, a feature of this exclusive sector of western Paris, occupying principally the 8th Arrondissement. It's beautiful and rich—and a little impersonal. Frenchmen moan that it's losing its character, and, as you notice the num-ber of fast-food joints along the Champs-Elysées, you'll know what they mean. In short: Visit during the day, and head else-where in search of Parisian ambience and an affordable meal in the evening.

The Arc de Triomphe and Champs-Elysées

Place Charles de Gaulle is known by Parisians as **L'Etoile,** the star—a reference to the streets that fan out from it. It is one of Europe's most chaotic traffic circles, and short of a death-defy-ing dash, your only way of getting to the Arc de Triomphe in the middle is to take an underground passage from the Champs-Elysées or avenue de la Grande Armée.

❶ The colossal, 164-foot **Arc de Triomphe** was planned by Napo-léon—who believed himself to be the direct heir to the Roman emperors—to celebrate his military successes. Unfortunately, Napoléon's strategic and architectural visions were not entire-ly on the same plane, and the Arc de Triomphe proved some-thing of a white elephant. When it was required for the triumphal entry of his new empress, Marie-Louise, into Paris in 1810, it was still only a few feet high. To save face, a dummy arch of painted canvas was put up.

Empires come and go, and Napoléon's had been gone for over 20 years before the Arc de Triomphe was finally finished in 1836. It boasts some magnificent sculpture by François Rude, such as the *Departure of the Volunteers,* better known as *La Mar-seillaise,* situated to the right of the arch when viewed from the Champs-Elysées. After showing alarming signs of decay, the structure received a thorough overhaul in 1989 and is now back to its original neo-Napoléonic splendor. The view from the top illustrates the star effect of Etoile's 12 radiating avenues and enables you to admire the vista down the Champs-Elysées to-ward place de la Concorde and the distant Louvre. In the other direction, you can see down avenue de la Grande Armée toward La Tête Défense and its severe modern arch, surrounded by im-posing glass and concrete towers. There is a small museum half-way up the arch devoted to its history. France's Unknown Soldier is buried beneath the archway; the flame is rekindled every evening at 6:30. *Pl. Charles-de-Gaulle. Admission: 31 frs adults, 17 frs students and senior citizens, 6 frs children. Open daily 10–5:30, 10–5 in winter. Closed public holidays.*

The cosmopolitan pulse of Paris beats strongest on the grace-fully sloping, 1¼-mile-long **Champs-Elysées.** It was originally laid out in the 1660s by the landscape gardener Le Nôtre as a garden sweeping away from the Tuileries, but you will see few signs of these pastoral origins as you stroll past the cafés, res-

The Arc de Triomphe to the Opéra

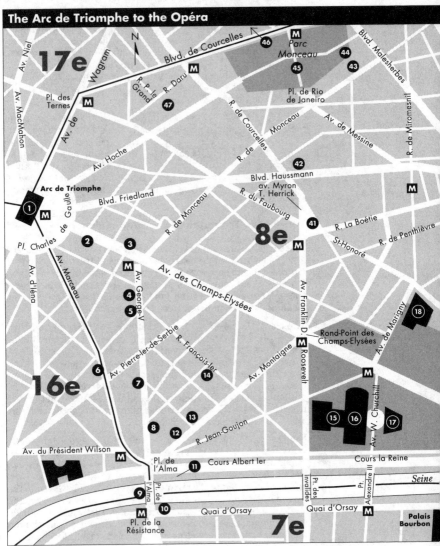

American Cathedral of the Holy Trinity, **7**

Arc de Triomphe, **1**

Atelier de Gustave Moreau, **37**

Bateaux Mouches, **11**

Crazy Horse Saloon, **8**

Crillon, **26**

Eglise de la Madeleine, **20**

Fauchon, **22**

Galeries Lafayette, **33**

Gare St-Lazare, **38**

George V, **5**

Grand Palais, **16**

Hédiard, **23**

Jardin des Tuileries, **29**

Les Egouts, **10**

Lido, **3**

Maison de la Vigne et du Vin de France, **14**

Marks & Spencer, **35**

Maxim's, **24**

Musée Cernuschi, **44**

Musée de l'Orangerie, **28**

Musée du Jeu de Paume, **27**

Musée Jacquemart-André, **42**

Musée Jean-Jacques Henner, **46**

Musée Nissim de Camondo, **43**

Olympia, **31**

Opéra, **32**

Palais de la Découverte, **15**

440 yards
400 meters

R. d. Rome
R. du Rocher
R. des Londres
R. d'Amsterdam
Av. de Clichy
R. de la Rochefoucauld
R. d'Aumale

Gare
St-Lazare

38

40

36

37

R. de Châteaudun
R. Chaussée d'Antin
R. Taitbout

9e

Pl.
St-Augustin

Blvd. Haussmann

R. Pasquier

39

34

35

33

R. Auber

32

Pl.
de l'Opéra

Blvd. Malesherbes

R. Tronchet

23

22

Eglise de la
Madeleine

31

Blvd. des
Capucines

Blvd. des Italiens

R. d'Aguesseau

19

R. Boissy d'Anglas

21

20

Blvd. de la
Madeleine

R. des
Capucines

R. de la Paix

R. du Quatre Septembre

2e

R. St-Honoré

Pl. de la
Madeleine

26

24

R. Royale

Pl. de la
Concorde

25

27

30

Pl.
Vendôme

R. de Castiglione

R. St-Honoré

Av. de l'Opéra

R. des Petits Champs

R. de Richelieu

1er

28

Jardin des
Tuileries

29

R. de Rivoli

Pl. de la Concorde

Quai des Tuileries

Jardin du
Carrousel

Louvre

taurants, airline offices, car showrooms, movie theaters, and chic arcades that occupy its upper half.

② Start off by stopping in at the main **Paris Tourist Office** at no. 127. It's at the Arc de Triomphe end of the Champs-Elysées, on the right-hand side as you arrive from Etoile. It is an invaluable source of information on accommodations, places to visit, and entertainment—both in Paris and in the surrounding Ile-de-France region. *Open daily 9–8, 9–9 on weekdays in summer, 9–6 on Sun. out of season.*

The Champs-Elysées occupies a central role in French national celebrations. It witnesses the finish of the Tour de France bicycle race on the last Sunday of July. It is also the site of vast ceremonies on July 14, France's national, or Bastille, day, and November 11, Armistice Day. Its trees are often decked with the French *tricolore* and foreign flags to mark visits from heads of state.

Three hundred yards down on the left, at 116b, is the famous **③** **Lido** nightclub: Foot-stomping melodies in French and English and champagne-soaked, topless razzmatazz pack in the crowds **④** every night. In contrast are the red-awninged **Prince de Galles ⑤** (Prince of Wales) and the blue-awninged **George V,** two of the city's top hotels on avenue George-V, a right-hand turn off Champs-Elysées. Continue down avenue George-V, and turn **⑥** right down Pierre Ier-de-Serbie to the church of **St-Pierre de Chaillot** on avenue Marceau. The monumental frieze above the entrance, depicting scenes from the life of St. Peter, is the work of Henri Bouchard and dates from 1937.

Returning to avenue George-V, continue toward the slender **⑦** spire of the **American Cathedral of the Holy Trinity,** built by G. S. Street between 1885 and 1888. *Open weekdays 9–12:30 and 2–5, Sat. 9–noon. Services: weekdays 9 AM, Sun. 9 AM and 11 AM; Sun. school and nursery. Guided tours Sun. and Wed. 12:30.*

⑧ Continue down to the bottom of the avenue, passing the **Crazy Horse Saloon** at no. 12, one of Paris's most enduring and spectacular night spots, to place de l'Alma and the Seine.

⑨ The **pont de l'Alma** (Alma bridge) is best known for the chunky stone "Zouave" statue carved into one of the pillars. Zouaves were Algerian infantrymen recruited into the French army who were famous for their bravura and colorful uniforms. (The term came to be used for volunteers in the Union Army during the American Civil War.) There is nothing quite so glamorous, or colorful, about the Alma Zouave, however, whose hour of glory comes in times of watery distress: Parisians use him to judge the level of the Seine during heavy rains. As recently as the spring of 1988, the Zouave was submerged up to his chest, and the roads running along the riverbanks were under several feet of water.

⑩ Just across the Alma bridge, on the left, is the entrance to **Les Egouts,** the Paris sewers (admission: 25 frs adults, 20 frs students and senior citizens; open Sat.–Wed. 11–5). Brave the unpleasant—though tolerable—smell and follow the underground passages and footbridges along the sewers' banks. Signs note the streets above you, and detailed panels and displays illuminate the history of waste disposal in Paris, which boasts the second largest sewer system in the world (after

Chicago's). If you prefer a less malodorous tour of the city, stay on the Right Bank and head down the sloping side road to the left of the bridge, for the embarkation point of the **Bateaux Mouches**. These popular motorboats set off every half hour, heading east to the Ile St-Louis and then back west, past the Eiffel Tower, as far as the Allée des Cygnes and its miniature version of the Statue of Liberty. *Bateau Mouche* translates, misleadingly, as "fly boat"; but the name Mouche actually refers to a district of Lyon where the boats were originally manufactured.

Stylish avenue Montaigne leads from the Seine back toward the Champs-Elysées. The newly cleaned facade of the **Théâtre des Champs-Elysées** is a forerunner of the Art Deco style. The theater dates from 1913 and was the first major building in France to be constructed in reinforced concrete. *15 av. Montaigne.*

A few buildings along is the **Plaza Athénée** hotel (the "Plaza"), a favorite hangout for the *beau monde* who frequent the neighboring haute couture houses. Around the corner on the rue François-Ier is the **Maison de la Vigne et du Vin de France.** This is the classy central headquarters of the French wine industry and a useful source of information about wine regions. Bottles and maps are on display. *21 rue François-Ier, tel. 47–20–20–76. Admission free. Open weekdays 9–12:30 and 1:30–6.*

Double back on rue François-Ier as far as Place François-Ier, then turn left onto rue Jean-Goujon, which leads to avenue Franklin D. Roosevelt, another spacious boulevard between Champs-Elysées and the river. Halfway down it is the entrance to the **Palais de la Découverte** (Palace of Discovery), whose scientific and technological exhibits include working models and a planetarium. *Av. Franklin-D-Roosevelt. Admission: 21 frs adults, 11 frs children under 18 (15 frs/10 frs extra for planetarium). Open Tues.–Sat. 9:30–6, Sun. 10–7.*

This "Palace of Discovery" occupies the rear half of the **Grand Palais.** With its curved glass roof, the Grand Palais is unmistakable when approached from either the Seine or the Champs-Elysées and forms an attractive duo with the **Petit Palais** on the other side of avenue Winston Churchill. Both these stone buildings, adorned with mosaics and sculpted friezes, seem robust and venerable. In fact, they were erected with indecent haste prior to the Paris World Fair of 1900. As with the Eiffel Tower, there was never any intention that they would be anything other than temporary additions to the city. But once they were up, no one seemed inclined to take them down. Together with the exuberant, lamp-lit Alexandre III bridge nearby, they recapture the opulence and frivolity of the Belle Epoque—the *fin de siècle* overripeness with which Paris is still so strongly associated. Today, the atmospheric iron and glass interior of the Grand Palais plays regular host to major exhibitions. Admire the view from the palaces across the Alexandre III bridge toward the Hôtel des Invalides. *Av. Winston Churchill. Admission varies according to exhibition. Usually open daily 10:30–6:30, and often until 10 PM Wed.*

The **Petit Palais** has a beautifully presented permanent collection of French painting and furniture, with splendid canvases by Courbet and Bouguereau. Temporary exhibits are often held here, too. The sprawling entrance gallery contains several enormous turn-of-the-century paintings on its walls and ceilings. *Av. Winston Churchill. Admission: 12 frs adults, 6 frs children. Open Tues.–Sun. 10–5:30.*

From the Rond-Point des Champs-Elysées, head down avenue de Marigny to rue du Faubourg St-Honoré, a prestigious address in the world of luxury fashion and art galleries. You'll soon spot plenty of both, but may be perplexed at the presence of crash barriers and stern policemen. Their mission: to protect **⑱** the French president in the **Palais de l'Elysée.** This "palace," where the head of state lives, works, and receives official visitors, was originally constructed as a private mansion in 1718. Although you catch a glimpse of the palace forecourt and facade through the Faubourg St-Honoré gateway, it is difficult to get much idea of the building's size or of the extensive gardens that stretch back to the Champs-Elysées. (Incidentally, when Parisians talk about "l'Elysée," they mean the President's palace; the Champs-Elysées is known simply as "les Champs," the fields.) The Elysée has known presidential occupants only since 1873; before then, Madame de Pompadour (Louis XV's influential mistress), Napoléon, Josephine, the Duke of Wellington, and Queen Victoria all stayed here. President Félix Faure died here in 1899 in the arms of his mistress. The French government—the Conseil des Ministres—attends to more public affairs when it meets here each Wednesday morning. *Not open to the public.*

Toward place de la Concorde

⑲ **St. Michael's English Church,** close to the British Embassy on rue du Faubourg St-Honoré, is a modern building whose ugliness is redeemed by the warmth of the welcome afforded to all visitors, English-speaking ones in particular. *5 rue d'Aguesseau, tel. 47–42–70–88. Services Thurs. 12:45 and Sun. 10:30 (with Sunday school) and 6:30; supervised nursery for younger children in the morning.*

Continue down rue du Faubourg St-Honoré to rue Royale. This classy street, lined with jewelry stores, links place de la **⑳** Concorde to the **Eglise de la Madeleine** (closed Sun. 1:30–3:30), a sturdy neoclassical edifice that was nearly selected as Paris's first train station (the site of what is now the Gare St-Lazare, just up the road, was eventually chosen). With its rows of uncompromising columns, the Madeleine looks more like a Greek temple than a Christian church. Inside, the only natural light comes from three shallow domes. The walls are richly and harmoniously decorated, and gold glints through the murk. The church was designed in 1814 but not consecrated until 1842. The portico's majestic Corinthian colonnade supports a gigantic pediment with a sculptured frieze of the Last Judgment. From the top of the steps, you can admire the view down rue Royale across place de la Concorde to the Palais Bourbon. From the bottom of the steps, another view leads up boulevard Malesherbes to the dome of the church of St-Augustin.

Alongside the Madeleine, between the church and L'Ecluse, is **㉑** a **ticket kiosk** (open Tues.–Sat. 12:30–8) selling tickets for same-day theater performances at greatly reduced prices. Be- **㉒** **㉓** hind the church are **Fauchon** and **Hédiard,** two stylish delicatessens that are the ultimate in posh nosh. At the end of the rue Royale, just before place de la Concorde, is the legendary

㉔ **Maxim's** restaurant. Unless you choose to eat here—an expensive and not always rewarding experience—you won't be able to see the interior decor, a riot of crimson velvets and florid Art Nouveau furniture.

There is a striking contrast between the sunless, locked-in feel ㉕ of the high-walled rue Royale and the broad, airy **place de la Concorde.** This huge square is best approached from the Champs-Elysées: The flower beds, chestnut trees, and sandy sidewalks of the avenue's lower section are reminders of its original leafy elegance. Place de la Concorde was built in the 1770s, but there was nothing in the way of peace or concord about its early years. Between 1793 and 1795, it was the scene of over a thousand deaths by guillotine; victims included Louis XVI, Marie Antoinette, Danton, and Robespierre. The obelisk, a present from the viceroy of Egypt, was erected in 1833. The handsome, symmetrical, 18th-century buildings facing the ㉖ square include the deluxe hotel **Crillon,** though there's nothing so vulgar as a sign to identify it—just an inscribed marble plaque above the doorway.

Facing one side of place de la Concorde are the **Tuileries Gardens.** Two smallish buildings stand sentinel here. To the left, ㉗ nearer rue de Rivoli, is the **Musée du Jeu de Paume,** fondly known to many as the former home of the Impressionists (now in the Musée d'Orsay). After extensive renovation, the Jeu de Paume reopened in 1991 as a home to brash temporary exhibits of contemporary art. *Admission: 30 frs adults, 20 frs students and senior citizens. Open Tues. noon–9:30, Wed.–Fri. 12–7, weekends 10–7.* The other, identical building, nearer the Seine, ㉘ is the recently restored **Musée de l'Orangerie,** containing some early 20th-century paintings by Monet (including his vast, eight-paneled *Water Lilies*), Renoir, and other Impressionists. *Place de la Concorde. Admission: 26 frs adults, 14 frs students and senior citizens. Open Wed.–Mon. 9:45–5:15; closed Tues.*

㉙ As gardens go, the **Jardin des Tuileries** is typically French: formal and neatly patterned, with statues, rows of trees, gravel paths, and occasional patches of grass trying to look like lawns. These may benefit from the overhaul ordered by Culture Minister Jack Lang for the early '90s. It is a charming place to stroll and survey the surrounding cityscape. To the north is the disciplined, arcaded rue de Rivoli; to the south, the Seine and the gold-hued Musée d'Orsay with its enormous clocks; to the west, the Champs-Elysées and Arc de Triomphe; to the east, the Arc du Carrousel and the Louvre, with its glass pyramid.

Place Vendôme and the Opéra

㉚ **Place Vendôme,** north of the Jardin des Tuileries, is one of the world's most opulent squares. Mansart's rhythmic, perfectly proportioned example of 17th-century urban architecture has shone in all its golden-stoned splendor since being cleaned a few years ago. Many other things shine here, too—in jewelers' display windows and on the dresses of guests of the top-ranking **Ritz** hotel. Napoléon had the square's central column made from the melted bronze of 1,200 cannons captured at the battle of Austerlitz in 1805. That's him standing vigilantly at the top. Painter Gustave Courbet headed the Revolutionary hooligans who, in 1871, toppled the column and shattered it into thousands of metallic pieces.

Cross the square and take rue des Capucines on your left to
③ boulevard des Capucines. The **Olympia** music hall is still going
strong, though it has lost some of the luster it acquired as the
stage for such great postwar singers as Edith Piaf and Jacques
Brel.

② The **Opéra,** begun in 1862 by Charles Garnier at the behest of
Napoléon III, was not completed until 1875, five years after the
emperor's political demise. It is often said to typify the Second
Empire style of architecture, which is to say that it is a pompous hodgepodge of styles, imbued with as much subtlety as a
Wagnerian cymbal crash. After paying the entry fee, you can
stroll around at leisure. The monumental foyer and staircase
are boisterously impressive, a stage in their own right, where,
on first nights, celebrities preen and prance. If the lavishly up-
holstered auditorium (ceiling painted by Marc Chagall in 1964)
seems small, it is only because the stage is the largest in the
world—over 11,000 square yards, with room for up to 450 performers. The **Musée de l'Opéra** (Opéra museum), containing a
few paintings and theatrical mementos, is unremarkable. *Admission: 28 frs, 15 frs children. Open daily 10–4:30, but closed
occasionally for rehearsals; call 47–42–57–50 to check.*

Around the Opéra

Behind the Opéra are the *grands magasins*, Paris's most re-
③ nowned department stores. The nearer of the two, the **Galeries
Lafayette,** is the most outstanding, if only because of its vast,
shimmering, turn-of-the-century glass dome. The domes at the
③ corners of **Printemps,** farther along boulevard Haussmann, to
the left, can be best appreciated from the outside; there is a
③ splendid view from the store's rooftop cafeteria. **Marks & Spencer,** across the road, provides a brave outpost for British goods,
such as ginger biscuits, bacon rashers, and Cheddar cheese.

③ The **Trinité** church, several blocks north of the Opéra, is not an
unworthy 19th-century effort at neo-Renaissance style. Its
central tower is of dubious aesthetic merit but is a recognizable
feature in the Paris skyline (especially since its cleaning in
1986). The church was built in the 1860s and is fronted by a
pleasant garden.

③ The nearby **Atelier de Gustave Moreau** was the town house and
studio of painter Gustave Moreau (1826–1898), doyen of the
Symbolist movement that strove to convey ideas through images. Many of the ideas Moreau was trying to express remain
obscure to the general public, however, even though the artist
provided explanatory texts. But most onlookers will be content
admiring his extravagant colors and flights of fantasy, which
reveal the influence of Persian and Indian miniatures. Fantastic details cover every inch of his canvases, and his canvases
cover every inch of wall space, making a trip to the museum one
of the strangest artistic experiences in Paris. Go on a sunny
day, if possible; the low lighting can strain the eyes even more
than Moreau's paintings can. *14 rue de la Rochefoucauld. Admission: 17 frs adults, 10 frs children and senior citizens. Open
Thurs.–Sun. 10–12:45 and 2–5:15, Mon. and Wed. 11–5:15.*

③ Rue St-Lazare leads from Trinité to the **Gare St-Lazare,** whose
imposing 19th-century facade has been restored. In the days of
steam and smoke, the station was an inspiration to several Impressionist painters, notably Monet. Note an eccentric sculp-

ture to the right of the facade—a higgledy-piggledy accumulation of clocks.

㊴ The leafy, intimate **Square Louis XVI,** off boulevard Haussmann between St-Lazare and St-Augustin, is perhaps the nearest Paris gets to a verdant, London-style square—if you discount the bombastic mausoleum in the middle. The unkempt chapel marks the initial burial site of Louis XVI and Marie Antoinette after their turns at the guillotine on place de la Concorde. Two stone tablets are inscribed with the last missives of the doomed royals—touching pleas for their Revolutionary enemies to be forgiven. When compared to the pomp and glory of Napoléon's memorial at the Invalides, this tribute to royalty (France was ruled by kings until 1792 and again from 1815 to 1848) seems trite and cursory. *Open daily 10–noon and 2–6, 10–4 in winter.*

Before leaving the square, take a look at the gleaming 1930s-style facade of the bank at the lower corner of rue Pasquier. It has some amusing stone carvings halfway up, representing various exotic animals.

㊵ A mighty dome is the most striking feature of the innovative iron-and-stone church of **St-Augustin,** dexterously constructed in the 1860s within the confines of an awkward, V-shaped site. The use of metal girders obviated the need for exterior buttressing. The dome is bulky but well-proportioned and contains some grimy but competent frescoes by the popular 19th-century French artist William Bouguereau.

㊶ Rue La Boétie leads to another church, **St-Philippe du Roule,** built by Chalgrin between 1769 and 1784. Its austere classical portico dominates a busy square. The best thing inside this dimly lit church is the 19th-century fresco above the altar by Théodore Chassériau, featuring the Descent from the Cross.

㊷ Make your way back to boulevard Haussmann via avenue Myron T. Herrick. The **Musée Jacquemart-André** features Italian Renaissance and 18th-century art in a dazzlingly furnished, late-19th-century mansion. *158 blvd. Haussmann, tel. 42–89–04–91. Admission: 18 frs. Open Wed.–Sun. 1–6.*

Rue de Courcelles and a right on rue de Monceau will lead to place de Rio de Janeiro. Before venturing into the Parc Monceau at the far end of avenue Ruysdaël, continue along rue de Monceau to the **Musée Nissim de Camondo.** Inside, you will find the stylish interior of an aristocratic Parisian mansion in the style of Louis XVI, dating from the last days of the regal Ancien Régime. *63 rue de Monceau. Admission: 18 frs adults, 12 frs students and senior citizens. Open Wed.–Sun. 10–noon and 2–5.*

㊹ Rue de Monceau and boulevard Malesherbes lead to the **Musée Cernuschi,** whose collection of Chinese art ranges from neolithic pottery (3rd century BC) to funeral statuary, painted 8th-century silks, and contemporary paintings. *7 av. Velasquez. Admission: 12 frs. Open Tues.–Sun. 10–5:40.*

㊺ The **Parc Monceau,** which can be entered from avenue Velasquez, was laid out as a private park in 1778 and retains some of the fanciful elements then in vogue, including mock ruins and a phony pyramid. In 1797, Garnerin, the world's first-recorded parachutist, staged a landing in the park. The rotunda, known as the Chartres Pavilion, was originally a tollhouse and has well-worked iron gates.

Leave the Parc Monceau by these gates and follow rue Phals-
㊻ bourg and avenue de Villiers to the **Musée Jean-Jacques Henner.** Henner (1829–1905), a nearly forgotten Alsatian artist, here receives a sumptuous tribute. His obsessive fondness for milky-skinned, auburn-haired female nudes is displayed in hundreds of drawings and paintings on the three floors of this gracious museum. *43 av. de Villiers. Admission: 14 frs. Open Tues.–Sun. 10–noon and 2–5.*

Boulevard de Courcelles, which runs along the north side of the Parc Monceau, leads west to rue Pierre-le-Grand (Peter the Great Street). At the far end of that street, at 12 rue Daru, loom the unlikely gilt onion domes of the Russian Orthodox ca-
㊼ thedral of **St-Alexandre Nevsky,** erected in neo-Byzantine style in 1860. Inside, the wall of icons that divides the church in two creates an atmosphere seldom found in Roman Catholic or Protestant churches.

From Orsay to Trocadéro

Numbers in the margin correspond to points of interest on the Orsay to Trocadéro map.

The Left Bank has two faces: the cozy, ramshackle Latin Quarter (*see* The Left Bank, *below*) and the spacious, stately 7th Arrondissement. This tour covers the latter, then heads back across the Seine for a look at the museums and attractions clustered around the place du Trocadéro. The latest addition to the area is already the most popular: the Musée d'Orsay. Crowds flock to this stylishly converted train station to see the Impressionists, but also discover important examples of other schools of 19th- and early 20th-century art.

The atmosphere of the 7th Arrondissement is set by the National Assembly, down the river from Orsay, opposite place de la Concorde. French deputies meet here to hammer out laws and insult each other. They resume more civilized attitudes when they return to the luxurious ministries that dot the nearby streets. The most famous is the Hôtel Matignon, official residence of the French prime minister.

The majestic scale of many of the area's buildings is totally in character with the daddy of them all, the Invalides. Like the Champ de Mars nearby, the esplanade in front of the Invalides was once used as a parade ground for Napoléon's troops. In a coffin beneath the Invalides dome, M. Bonaparte dreams on.

Musée d'Orsay

❶ The **Musée d'Orsay** opened in December 1986. It is devoted to the arts (mainly French) produced between 1848 and 1914, and its collections are intended to form a bridge between the classical collections of the Louvre and the modern collections of the Beaubourg. The building began in 1900 as a train station for routes between Paris and the southwest of France. By 1939, the Gare d'Orsay had become too small for mainline travel, and intercity trains were transferred to the Gare d'Austerlitz. Gare d'Orsay became a suburban terminus until, in the 1960s, it closed for good. After various temporary uses (a theater and auction house among them), the building was set for demolition. However, the destruction of the 19th-century Les Halles (market halls) across the Seine provoked a furor among conservationists, and in the late 1970s, President Giscard d'Estaing, with an eye firmly on establishing his place in the annals of French culture, ordered Orsay to be transformed into a museum. The architects Pierre Colboc, Renaud Bardou, and Jean-Paul Philippon were commissioned to remodel the building, while Gae Aulenti, known for her renovation of the Palazzo Grassi in Venice, was hired to redesign the interior.

Exhibits take up three floors, but the visitor's immediate impression is of a single, vast, stationlike hall. The use of an aggressively modern interior design in a building almost a century old has provoked much controversy, which you'll want to resolve for yourself.

The chief artistic attraction is the Impressionists, whose works are displayed on the top floor, next to the museum café. Renoir, Sisley, Pissarro, and Monet are all well represented. Highlights for many visitors are Monet's *Poppy Field* and Renoir's *Le Moulin de la Galette*. The latter differs from many Impressionist paintings in that Renoir worked from numerous studies and completed it in his studio rather than painting it in the open air. Nonetheless, its focus on the activities of a group of ordinary Parisians amusing themselves in the sun on a Montmartre afternoon is typical of the spontaneity, the sense of the fleeting moment captured, that are the very essence of Impressionism. Where Monet, the only one of the group to adhere faithfully to the tenets of Impressionism throughout his career, strove to catch the effects of light, Renoir was more interested in the human figure.

The postimpressionists—Cézanne, van Gogh, Gauguin, and Toulouse-Lautrec—are all also represented on this floor. Some may find the intense, almost classical serenity of Cézanne the dominant presence here; witness his magnificent Mont Sainte-Victoire series, in which he paints and repaints the same subject, in the process dissolving form until the step to abstract painting seems almost an inevitability. Others will be drawn by the vivid simplicity and passion of van Gogh, or by the bold, almost pagan rhythms of Gauguin.

On the first floor, you'll find the work of Manet and the delicate nuances of Degas. Pride of place, at least in art historical terms, goes to Manet's *Déjeuner sur l'Herbe*, the painting that scandalized Paris in 1863 at the Salon des Refusés, an exhibit organized by those artists refused permission to show their work at the Academy's official annual exhibit. The painting shows a nude woman and two clothed men picnicking in a park. In the background, another naked girl bathes in a stream. Manet took the subject, poses and all, from a little-known Renaissance print in the Louvre. In that, of course, the clothed men wore contemporary 16th-century garb. In Manet's painting, the men also wear contemporary clothing, that of mid-19th-century France, complete with gray trousers and frock coats. What would otherwise have been thought a respectable "academic" painting thus became deeply shocking: two clothed men with two naked women! The loose, bold brushwork, a far cry from the polished styles of the Renaissance, added insult to artistic injury. Another reworking by Manet of a classical motif

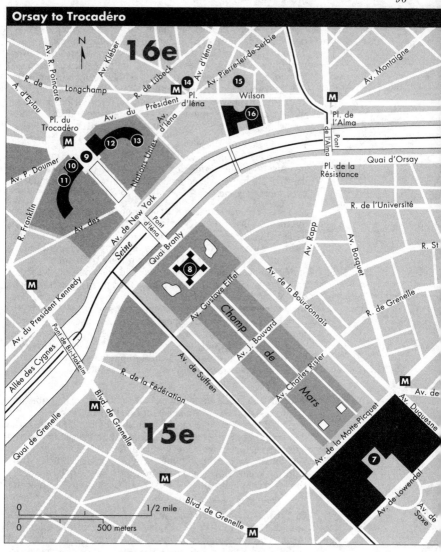

0   1/2 mile
0   500 meters

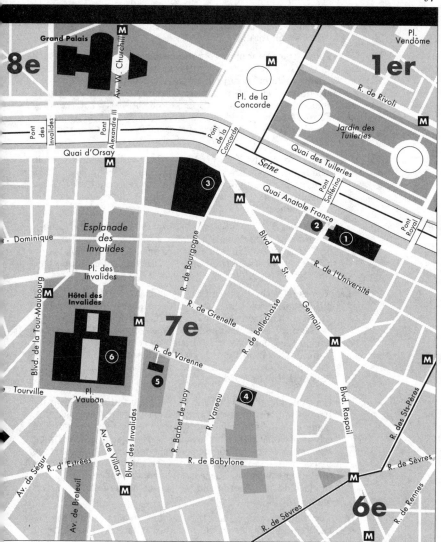

Grand Palais

8e

Av. W. Churchill

Pl. Vendôme

1er

M

Pl. de la Concorde

R. de Rivoli

M

Jardin des Tuileries

Pont des Invalides

Pont Alexandre III

Quai d'Orsay

Pont de la Concorde

Quai des Tuileries

M

Seine

Pont Solférino

Quai Anatole France

Pont Royal

M

③

M

②

①

- Dominique

Esplanade des Invalides

Pl. des Invalides

R. de Bourgogne

Blvd. St. Germain

R. de l'Université

M

M

Hôtel des Invalides

Blvd. de la Tour-Maubourg

M

R. de Grenelle

R. de Bellechasse

M

7e

M

M

R. de Varenne

⑥

⑤

Tourville

Pl. Vauban

R. Barbet de Jouy

R. Vaneau

④

Blvd. Raspail

R. des Sts-Pères

M

Av. de Ségur

R. d'Estrées

Av. de Villars

Blvd. des Invalides

R. de Babylone

R. de Sèvres

6e

R. de Rennes

Av. de Breteuil

M

R. de Sèvres

M

is his reclining nude, *Olympia*. Gazing boldly out from the canvas, she was more than respectable 19th-century Parisian proprieties could stand.

Those who prefer more correct academic paintings should look at Puvis de Chavannes's larger-than-life, classical canvases. The pale, limpid beauty of his figures is enjoying considerable attention after years of neglect. Those who are excited by more modern developments will make for the early 20th-century Fauves (meaning wild beasts, the name given them by an outraged critic in 1905)—particularly Matisse, Derain, and Vlaminck.

Sculpture at the Orsay means, first and foremost, Rodin (though there's more to enjoy at the Musée Rodin, *see below*). Two further highlights are the faithfully restored BelleEpoque restaurant and the model of the entire Opéra quarter, displayed beneath a glass floor.

The Musée d'Orsay, otherwise known as M.O., is already one of Paris's star attractions. Crowds are smaller at lunchtime and on Thursday evenings. *1 rue de Bellechasse. Admission: 31 frs adults, 16 frs students and senior citizens and on Sun. Open Tues.–Sat. 10–6, Thurs. 10–9:30, and Sun. 9–6.*

❷ Across from the Musée d'Orsay stands the **Musée de la Légion d'Honneur.** French and foreign decorations are displayed in this stylish mansion by the Seine (officially known as the Hôtel de Salm). The original building, constructed in 1786, burned during the Commune in 1871 and was rebuilt in 1878. *2 rue de Bellechasse. Admission: 10 frs. Open Tues.–Sun. 2–5.*

Toward the Invalides

Continue along the left bank of the Seine to the 18th-century ❸ **Palais Bourbon** (directly across from place de la Concorde), home of the Assemblée Nationale (French Parliament). The colonnaded facade, commissioned by Napoléon, is a sparkling sight after a recent cleaning program (jeopardized at one stage by political squabbles as to whether cleaning should begin from the left or the right). There is a fine view from the steps across to place de la Concorde and the church of the Madeleine. *Not open to the public.*

The quiet, distinguished 18th-century streets behind the Palais Bourbon are filled with embassies and ministries. The most famous, reached via rue de Bourgogne and rue de Varenne, is ❹ the **Hôtel Matignon,** residence of the French Prime Minister, and Left Bank counterpart to the President's Elysée Palace. "Matignon" was built in 1721 but has housed heads of government only since 1958. From 1888 to 1914, it was the embassy of the Austro-Hungarian Empire. *57 rue de Varenne. Neither house nor garden is open to the public.*

Another glorious town house along rue de Varenne is the Hôtel ❺ Biron, better known as the **Musée Rodin.** The splendid house, with its spacious vestibule, broad staircase, and light, airy rooms, retains much of its 18th-century atmosphere and makes a handsome setting for the sculpture of Auguste Rodin (1840–1917). You'll doubtless recognize the seated *Thinker (Le Penseur)*, with his elbow resting on his knee, and the passionate *Kiss*. There is also an outstanding white marble bust of

Austrian composer Gustav Mahler, as well as numerous examples of Rodin's obsession with hands and erotic subjects.

The second-floor rooms, which contain some fine paintings by Rodin's friend Eugène Carrière (1849–1906), afford views of the large garden behind the house. Don't go without visiting the garden: It is exceptional both for its rose bushes (over 2,000 of them, representing 100 varieties) and for its sculpture, including a powerful statue of the novelist Balzac and the despairing group of medieval city fathers known as the *Burghers of Calais. 77 rue de Varenne. Admission: 21 frs, 10 frs Sun. Open Easter–Oct., Tues.–Sun. 10–6; Nov.–Easter, Tues.– Sun. 10–5.*

❻ From the Rodin Museum, you can see the **Hôtel des Invalides,** along rue de Varenne. It was founded by Louis XIV in 1674 to house wounded (or "invalid") veterans. Although no more than a handful of old soldiers live at the Invalides today, the military link remains in the form of the **Musée de l'Armée**—one of the world's foremost military museums—with a vast collection of arms, armor, uniforms, banners, and military pictures down through the ages.

The **Musée des Plans-Reliefs,** housed on the fifth floor of the right-hand wing, contains a fascinating collection of scale models of French towns made to illustrate the fortifications planned by Vauban in the 17th century. (Vauban was a superb military engineer who worked under Louis XIV.) The largest and most impressive is Strasbourg, which takes up an entire room. Not all of Vauban's models are here, however. As part of a cultural decentralization program, France's socialist government of the early 1980s decided to pack the models (which had languished for years in dusty neglect) off to Lille in northern France. Only half the models had been shifted when a conservative government returned to office in 1986 and called for their return. Ex-Prime Minister Pierre Mauroy, the socialist mayor of Lille, refused, however, and the impasse seems set to continue.

The museums are not the only reason for visiting the Invalides. The building itself is an outstanding monumental ensemble in late-17th-century Baroque, designed by Bruand and Mansart. The main, cobbled courtyard is a fitting scene for the parades and ceremonies still occasionally held here. The most impressive dome in Paris towers over the **Eglise du Dôme** (church of the Dome). Before stopping here, however, visit the 17th-century **Eglise St-Louis des Invalides,** the Invalides's original church, and the site of the first performance of Berlioz's *Requiem* in 1837.

The Dôme church was built onto the end of Eglise St-Louis but was blocked off from it in 1793—no great pity perhaps, as the two buildings are vastly different in style and scale. It was designed by Mansart and built between 1677 and 1735. The remains of Napoléon are here, in a series of no fewer than six coffins, one inside the next, within a bombastic tomb of red porphyry, ringed by low reliefs and a dozen statues symbolizing Napoléon's campaigns. Among others commemorated in the church are French World War I hero Marshal Foch; Napoléon's brother Joseph, erstwhile king of Spain; and fortification-builder Vauban, whose heart was brought to the Invalides at Napoléon's behest. *Hôtel des Invalides. Admission: 32 frs adults, 20 frs children. Open daily 10–6; 10–5 in winter. A son-et-lumière (sound-and-light) show in English is held in the main courtyard on evenings throughout the summer.*

Cross the pleasant lawns outside the Dôme church to place Vauban. Follow avenue de Tourville to the right, and turn left onto avenue de la Motte-Picquet.

The Eiffel Tower and the Trocadéro

❼ A few minutes' walk will bring you face-to-face with the Eiffel Tower. Spare a thought for the **Ecole Militaire** on your left; it is 18th-century architecture at its most harmonious. It is still in use as a military academy and therefore not open to the public.

❽ The pleasant expanse of the **Champ de Mars** makes an ideal approach to the **Eiffel Tower,** whose colossal bulk (it's far bigger and sturdier than pictures suggest) becomes evident the nearer you get. It was built by Gustave Eiffel for the World Exhibition of 1889, the centennial of the French Revolution, and was still in good shape to celebrate its own 100th birthday. Recent restoration hasn't made the elevators any faster (lines are inevitable), but the new nocturnal illumination is fantastic—every girder highlighted in glorious detail.

Such was Eiffel's engineering wizardry that even in the strongest winds his tower never sways more than 4½ inches. Today, it is Paris's best-known landmark and exudes a feeling of permanence. As you stand beneath its huge legs, you may have trouble believing that it nearly became 7,000 tons of scrap-iron when its concession expired in 1909. Only its potential use as a radio antenna saved the day; it now bristles with a forest of radio and television transmitters. If you're full of energy, stride up the stairs as far as the third deck. If you want to go to the top, you'll have to take the elevator. The view at 1,000 feet may not beat that from the Tour Maine-Montparnasse (*see* The Left Bank, *below*), but the setting makes it considerably more romantic. *Pont d'Iéna. Cost by elevator: 2nd floor, 17 frs; 3rd floor, 34 frs; 4th floor, 51 frs. Cost by foot: 8 frs (2nd and 3rd floors only). Open July–Aug., daily 9 AM–midnight; Sept.–June, daily 9:30 AM–11 PM.*

❾ Just across the Pont d'Iena from the Eiffel Tower, on the heights of Trocadéro, is the muscular, sandy-colored **Palais de Chaillot**—a cultural center built in the 1930s to replace a Moorish-style building constructed for the World Exhibition of 1878. The gardens between the Palais de Chaillot and the Seine contain an aquarium and some dramatic fountains. The terrace between the two wings of the palace offers a wonderful view of the Eiffel Tower.

❿ The Palais de Chaillot contains four large museums, two in each wing. In the left wing (as you approach from the Seine) are the Musée de l'Homme and the Musée de la Marine. The **Musée de l'Homme,** on the second and third floors, is an earnest anthropological museum with primitive and prehistoric artifacts from throughout the world. *Admission: 25 frs adults, 15 frs chil-*

⓫ *dren. Open Wed.–Mon. 9:45–5.* The **Musée de la Marine,** on the first floor, is a maritime museum with a salty collection of ship models and seafaring paraphernalia, illustrating French naval history right up to the age of the nuclear submarine. *Admis-*

sion: 28 frs adults, 14 frs senior citizens, students, and children. Open Wed.–Mon. 10–6.

⑫ The other wing is dominated by the **Musée des Monuments Français,** without question the best introduction to French medieval architecture. This extraordinary museum was founded in 1879 by architect-restorer Viollet-le-Duc (the man who more than anyone was responsible for the extensive renovation of Notre Dame). It pays tribute to French buildings, mainly of the Romanesque and Gothic periods (roughly 1000–1500), in the form of painstaking copies of statues, columns, archways, and frescoes. It is easy to imagine yourself strolling among ruins as you pass through the first-floor gallery. Substantial sections of a number of French churches and cathedrals are represented here, notably Chartres and Vézelay. Mural and ceiling paintings—copies of works in churches around the country—dominate the other three floors. The value of these paintings has become increasingly evident as many of the originals continue to deteriorate. On the ceiling of a circular room is a reproduction of the painted dome of Cahors cathedral, giving the visitor a more vivid sense of the skills of the original medieval painter than the cathedral itself. *Admission: 16 frs, 8 frs on Sun. Open Wed.–Mon. 9:45–5:15.*

⑬ The **Musée du Cinéma,** located in the basement of this wing, traces the history of motion pictures since the 1880s. *Admission: 22 frs. Open Wed.–Mon. Guided tours only, at 10, 11, 2, 3, and 4.*

The area around the Palais de Chaillot offers a feast for museum lovers. The **Musée Guimet** (down avenue du Président Wilson, at place d'Iéna) has three floors of Indo-Chinese and Far Eastern art, initially amassed by 19th-century collector Emile Guimet. Among the museum's bewildering variety of exhibits are stone buddhas, Chinese bronzes, ceramics, and painted screens. *6 pl. d'Iéna. Admission: 26 frs adults, 14 frs students and senior citizens. Open Wed.–Mon. 9:45–5:15.*

⑮ Some 200 yards down avenue Pierre-Ier-de-Serbie is the **Palais Galliera,** home of the small, and some would say overpriced, Museum of Fashion and Costume. This stylish, late-19th-century town house hosts revolving exhibits of costume, design, and accessories, usually based on a single theme. *10 av. Pierre-Ier-de-Serbie. Admission: 25 frs adults, 15 frs students and senior citizens. Open Tues.–Sun. 10–5:40.*

⑯ The **Musée d'Art Moderne de la Ville de Paris** has both temporary exhibits and a permanent collection of modern art, continuing where the Musée d'Orsay leaves off. Among the earliest works are Fauvist paintings by Vlaminck and Derain, followed by Picasso's early experiments in Cubism. No other Paris museum exudes such a feeling of space and light. Its vast, unobtrusive, white-walled galleries provide an ideal background for the bold statements of 20th-century art. Loudest and largest are the canvases of Robert Delaunay. Other highlights include works by Braque, Rouault, Gleizes, Da Silva, Gromaire, and Modigliani. There is also a large room devoted to Art Deco furniture and screens, where Jean Dunand's gilt and lacquered panels consume oceans of wall space. Skip the expensive museum café but visit the excellent bookshop specializing in 19th- and 20th-century art and architecture, with many books in English. *11 av. du Président Wilson. Admission: 15 frs, half-*

price on Sun. for permanent exhibitions only. Open Tues.–
Sun. 10–5:30, Wed. 10–8:30.

The Left Bank

*Numbers in the margin correspond to points of interest on the
Left Bank map.*

References to the Left Bank have never lost their power to
evoke the most piquant of all images of Paris. Although the bohemian strain the area once nurtured has lost much of its vigor,
people who choose it today as a place to live or work are, in effect, turning their backs on the formality and staidness of the
Right Bank.

The Latin Quarter is the geographic and cerebral hub of the
Left Bank, populated mainly by Sorbonne students and academics who fill the air of the cafés with their ideas—and their
tobacco smoke. (The university began as a theological school in
the Middle Ages and later became the headquarters of the University of Paris; in 1968, the student revolution here had an ex-
plosive effect on French politics, resulting in major reforms in
the education system.) The name Latin Quarter comes from
the university tradition of studying and speaking in Latin, a
tradition that disappeared during the Revolution.

Most of the St-Germain cafés, where the likes of Sartre, Picasso, Hemingway, and de Beauvoir spent their days and nights,
are patronized largely by tourists now, and anyone expecting
to capture the feeling of this quarter when it was the epicenter
of intellectual and artistic life in Paris will be disappointed. Yet
the Left Bank is far from dead. It is a lively and colorful district, rich in history and character, with a wealth of bookshops,
art stores, museums, and restaurants.

St-Michel to St-Germain

❶ **Place St-Michel** is a good starting point for exploring the rich
slice of Parisian life, from its most ancient to its most modern,
that the Left Bank offers. Leave your itineraries at home, and
wander along the neighboring streets lined with restaurants,
cafés, galleries, old bookshops, and all sorts of clothing stores,
from tiny boutiques to haute couture showrooms.

If you follow quai des Grands Augustins and then quai de Conti
west from St-Michel, you will be in full view of the Ile de la Cité
and the Louvre, and you may catch a glimpse of the imposing
dome of the Temple de l'Oratoire (built in 1621 and once one of
the most important churches in France) across the Seine. The
Hôtel des Monnaies (the mint), the Institut de France (home of
the Académie Française), and the Ecole National des Beaux-
Arts (Paris's fine-arts academy) together comprise a magnificent assembly of buildings on the river embankment that lies
west of Paris's oldest bridge, the Pont Neuf.

For a route crowded more with humanity and less with car and
bus traffic, pick up the pedestrian rue St-André des Arts at the
❷ southwest corner of place St-Michel. **Studio St-André des Arts,**
at no. 30, is one of Paris's most popular experimental cinemas.
Just before you reach the Carrefour de Buci crossroads at the
❸ end of the street, turn onto the **Cour du Commerce St-André.**
Jean-Paul Marat printed his revolutionary newspaper, *L'Ami*

du Peuple, at no. 8; and it was here that Dr. Guillotin conceived the idea for a new, "humane" method of execution that was used during the Revolution—it was rumored that he practiced it on sheep first—and that remained the means of executing convicted criminals in France until President Mitterrand abolished it in 1981.

Down a small passageway on the left stands one of the few remaining towers of the 12th-century fortress wall built by Philippe-Auguste. The passage leads you to the **Cour de Rohan,** a series of three cloistered courtyards that were part of the hotel of the archbishops of Rouen, established in the 15th century; the name has been corrupted over the years to Rohan.

Rejoin the Cour du Commerce St-André and continue to the **Carrefour de Buci,** once a notorious Left Bank landmark. By the 18th century, it contained a gallows, an execution stake, and an iron collar for punishing troublemakers. In September 1792, the Revolutionary army used this daunting site to enroll its first volunteers, and many Royalists and priests lost their heads here during the bloody course of the Revolution. There's nothing sinister, however, about the Carrefour today. Brightly colored flowers spill onto the sidewalk at the **Grange à Buci** flower shop, on the corner of rue Grégoire-de-Tours. **Rue de Buci** has one of the best markets in Paris. *Open Tues.–Sun. till 1 PM.*

Several interesting, smaller streets of some historical significance radiate from the Carrefour. **Rue de l'Ancienne-Comédie,** which cuts through to the busy place de l'Odéon, is so named because it was the first home of the now legendary French theater company, the Comédie Française. The street was named in 1770, the very year the Comédie left for the Tuileries palace. The company moved again later to the Odéon, before heading to its present home by the Palais-Royal (*see* The Historic Heart, *above*).

Across the street from the company's first home (no. 14) is the oldest café in Paris, **Le Procope.** Opened in 1686 by an Italian named Francesco Procopio (only three years before the Odéon itself opened), it has been a watering hole for many of Paris's most famous literary sons and daughters over the centuries; Diderot, Voltaire, Balzac, George Sand, Victor Hugo, and Oscar Wilde were some of its more famous and infamous regulars. Ben Franklin is said to have stopped in whenever business brought him to Paris. The fomenters of the French Revolution met at the Procope, too, so it is possible that old Ben may have crossed paths with the likes of Marat, Danton, Desmoulins, and Robespierre. Napoléon's hat, forgotten here, was encased in a glass dome. In 1988, Paris's second-largest restaurant group, Frères Blanc, bought the Procope (now really more of a restaurant), claiming to want to give it a "new lease on life and a new literary and cultural vocation."

Stretching north from the Carrefour de Buci toward the Seine is the **rue Dauphine,** the street that singer Juliet Greco put on the map when she opened the Tabou jazz club here in the '50s. It attracted a group of young intellectuals who were to become known as the Zazous, a St-Germain movement promoting the jazz culture, complete with all-night parties and free love. The cult author Boris Vian liked to play his trumpet through the night, an activity that did little to endear him to the club's

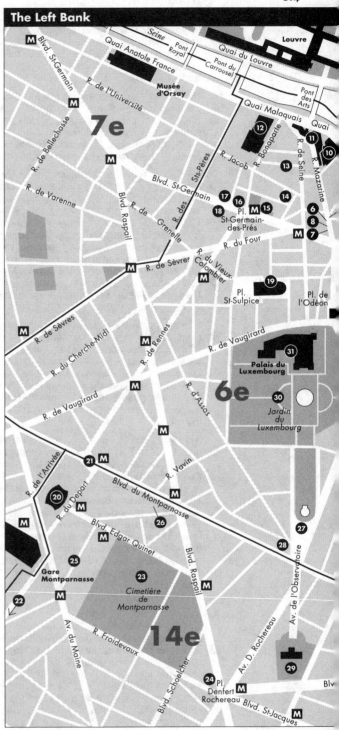

The Left Bank

R. St-Honoré

M **1er**

R. du Pont Neuf

Blvd. Sébastopol

R. du Temple

R. des Archives

R. des Francs-Bourgeois

R. de Turenne

M

M

4e

M

Hôtel de Ville

R. de Rivoli

Pont au Change

R. Fr. Miron

R. St-Antoine

Pont Neuf

de Conti

Quai des Grands Augustins

Pont St-Michel

Blvd. du Palais

M

Ile de la Cité

Conciergerie

Louis Philippe Pont

M

Quai des Célestins

R. de l'Ave Maria

R. St-Paul

9

5

R. St-André des Arts

2

M

1

Pl. St-Michel

Notre Dame

Sq. R. Viviani

R. St-Louis en l'Ile

Pont Marie

Ile St-Louis

Blvd. Henri IV

3 **4**

Blvd. St-Germain

M

38

M

39

Quai de Montebello

Pont St-Louis

Pont de la Tournelle

de Sully

Pont

Seine

32

37

R. St-Jacques

M

Pl. **40** Maubert

R. Bièvre

Blvd. St-Germain

Quai St-Bernard

Pl. de la Sorbonne

33

36

R. des Ecoles

R. Monge

Lemoine

44

R. Cujas

35

R. Soufflot

34

R. du Cardinal-

M

M

43

Jardin des Plantes

M

Blvd. St-Michel

R. Gay Lussac

5e

41

R. R. Rollin

R. Monge

42

M

R. Lhomond

R. Mouffetard

Pl. Monge

Pl. du Puits-de-l' Ermite

R. Daubenton

R. Buffon

Gare d'Austerlitz

R. Claude Bernard

M

Blvd. de l'Hôpital

M

R. St-Jacques

Blvd. de Port Royal

Blvd. St-Marcel

M

13e

M

N

J. Arago

Av. des Gobelins

0 ——— 440 yards

0 ——— 400 meters

neighbors. You may still find jazz played here, but the club is a shadow of its former self.

The next street that shoots out of the Carrefour (moving counterclockwise) is rue Mazarine. Here stands the **Hôtel des Monnaies,** the national mint. Louis XVI transferred the Royal Mint to this imposing mansion in the late 18th century. Although the mint was moved to Pessac, near Bordeaux, in 1973, weights and measures, medals, and limited-edition coins are still made here. In June 1988, an enlarged **Musée Monétaire** opened so that the vast collection of coins, documents, engravings, and paintings could be displayed. The workshops are on the second floor. On Tuesday and Friday afternoons you'll catch the coin and medal craftsmen at work; their ateliers overlook the Seine. *11 quai de Conti. Admission: 20 frs adults, 15 frs students and senior citizens. 15 frs Sun. Open Tues., Thurs.–Sun. 1–6, Wed. 1–9.*

Next door is the **Institut de France.** With its distinctive dome and commanding position over the quai at the foot of the Pont des Arts, it is not only one of France's most revered cultural institutions but also one of the Left Bank's most impressive waterside sights. The Tour de Nesle, which formed part of Philippe-Auguste's wall fortifications along the Seine, used to stand here, and, in its time, it had many royal occupants, including Henry V of England. The French novelist Alexandre Dumas (1824–1895) featured the stormy history of the Tour de Nesle—during which the lovers of a number of French queens were tossed from its windows—in a melodrama of the same name. In 1661, the wealthy Cardinal Mazarin left 2 million French pounds in his will for construction of a college here that would be dedicated to educating students from the provinces of Piedmont, Alsace, Artois, and Roussillon, all of which had been annexed to France during the years of his ministry. Mazarin's coat of arms is sculpted on the dome, and the public library in the east wing, which holds over 350,000 volumes, still bears his name. At the beginning of the 19th century, Napoléon stipulated that the Institut de France be transferred here from the Louvre. The **Académie Française,** the oldest of the five academies that comprise the Institut de France, was created by Cardinal Richelieu in 1635. Its first major task was to edit the French dictionary; today, among other functions, it is still charged with safeguarding the purity of the French language. Election to its ranks is the highest literary honor in the land, subject to approval by the French head of state, and there may only be 40 "immortal" members at any one time. The appointment of historian and authoress Marguerite Yourcenar to the Académie in 1986 broke the centuries-old tradition of the academy as a bastion of male-only linguistic and literary rule. The Institut also embraces the Académie des Beaux-Arts; the Académie des Sciences; the Académie des Inscriptions et Belles Lettres; and the Académie des Sciences Morales et Politiques. *Guided visits are reserved for cultural associations only.*

Just west along the waterfront, on quai Malaquais, stands the **Ecole Nationale des Beaux-Arts,** whose students can usually be seen painting and sketching on the nearby quais and bridges. The school—today the breeding ground for France's most prominent painters, sculptors, and architects—was once the site of a convent, founded in 1608 by Marguerite de Valois, the first wife of Henri IV. During the Revolution, the convent was turned into a depot for works of art salvaged from the monuments that were under threat of destruction by impassioned mobs. Only the church and cloister remained, however, when the Beaux-Arts school was established in 1816. Allow yourself time to wander into the courtyard and galleries of the school to see the casts and copies of the statues that were once stored here, or stop in at one of the temporary exhibitions of professors' and students' works. *14 rue Bonaparte. Open daily 1–7.*

⓭ Tiny **rue Visconti,** running east–west off rue Bonaparte (across from the entrance to the Beaux-Arts), has a lot of history packed into its short length. In the 16th century, it was known as Paris's Little Geneva—named after Europe's foremost Protestant city—because of the Protestant ghetto that formed here. Racine, one of France's greatest playwrights and tragic poets, lived at no. 24 until his death in 1699. Balzac set up a printing shop at no. 17 in 1826, and the fiery Romantic artist Eugène Delacroix (1798–1863) worked here from 1836 to 1844.

Swing right at the next corner onto the pretty rue Jacob, where both Wagner and Stendhal once lived. Follow rue Jacob across rue des Sts-Pères, where it changes to rue de l'Université. You are now in the Carré Rive Gauche, the Left Bank's concentrated quarter-mile of art dealers and galleries.

Return on rue Jacob until you are almost back to rue de Seine. Take the rue de Fürstemberg to the quiet place Fürstemberg, bedecked with white globe lamps and catalpa trees. Here is **⓮** **Atelier Delacroix,** Delacroix's former studio, containing only a paltry collection of sketches and drawings by the artist; the garden at the rear of the studio is almost as interesting. Nonetheless, those who feel the need to pay homage to France's greatest Romantic painter will want to make the pilgrimage. *Place Fürstemberg. Admission: 12 frs adults, 7 frs ages 18–25 and over 60, 7 frs on Sun. Open Wed.–Mon. 9:45–5:15.*

⓯ **St-Germain-des-Prés,** Paris's oldest church, began as a shelter for a relic of the True Cross brought back from Spain in AD 542. Behind it, rue de l'Abbaye runs alongside the former Abbey palace, dating from AD 990 and once part of a powerful Benedictine abbey. The chancel was enlarged and the church then consecrated by Pope Alexander III in 1163. Interesting interior details include the colorful 19th-century frescoes in the nave by Hippolyte Flandrin, a pupil of the classical painter Ingres, depicting vivid scenes from the Old Testament. The church stages superb organ concerts and recitals; programs are displayed outside and in the weekly periodicals *Officiel des Spectacles* and *Pariscope. Open weekdays 8–7:30; weekends 8–9.*

Across the cobbled place St-Germain-des-Prés stands the celebrated **Les Deux Magots** café, named after the grotesque Chinese figures, or *magots,* inside. It still thrives on its post-World War II reputation as one of the Left Bank's prime meeting places for the intelligentsia. Though the Deux Magots remains crowded day and night, these days, you're more likely to rub shoulders with tourists than with philosophers. Yet those in search of the mysterious glamour of the Left Bank can do no better than to station themselves at one of the sidewalk tables—or at a window table on a wintry day—to watch the passing parade.

In the postwar years, Jean-Paul Sartre and Simone de Beauvoir would meet "the family" two doors down at the **Café de Flore** on boulevard St-Germain. "The family" was de Beauvoir's name for their close-knit group, which included fellowgraduates from the prestigious Ecole Normale Supérieure and writers from Gaston Gallimard's publishing house in the nearby rue Sébastien-Bottin. Today the Flore has become more of a gay hangout, but, along with the Deux Magots and the pricey **Brasserie Lipp** across the street, where politicians and showbiz types come to wine and dine (after being "passed" by the doorman), it is a scenic spot that never lacks for action. In case you're in need of a sideshow, you'll also be able to see the street musicians—as likely to be playing Bolivian reed pipes or Scottish bagpipes or an old-style pump accordion—as well as acrobats and fire-eaters who perform in front of the church.

A large part of the area south of boulevard St-Germain, around rue de Grenelle and rue des Saints-Pères, has undergone enormous change but is still home to publishing houses, bookstores, and galleries.

For contrast, take rue du Vieux-Colombier through the Carrefour de La Croix Rouge to place St-Sulpice. This newly renovated square is ringed with cafés, and Yves St-Laurent's famous Rive Gauche store is at no. 6. Looming over the square is the enormous 17th-century church of **St-Sulpice.** The 18th-century facade was never finished, and its unequal towers add a playful touch to an otherwise sober design. The interior is baldly impersonal, however, despite the magnificent Delacroix frescoes—notably Jacob wrestling with the angel—in the first chapel on your right. If you now pick up the long rue de Rennes and follow it south, you'll soon arrive in the heart of Montparnasse.

Montparnasse

With the growth of Paris as a business and tourist capital, commercialization seems to have filled any area where departing residents and businesses have created a vacuum. Nowhere else is this more true than in and around the vaulting, concrete space and starkly functionalist buildings that have come to rule Montparnasse. Seeing it now, it is difficult to believe that in the years after World War I, Montparnasse replaced Montmartre as *the* place in which Parisian artists came to live.

The opening of the 59-story **Tour Maine-Montparnasse** in 1973 forever changed the face of this painters' and poets' haunt. (The name Montparnasse itself came from some 17th-century students, who christened the area after Mount Parnassus, the home of Apollo, leader of the Muses.) The tower was part of a vast redevelopment plan that aimed to make the area one of Paris's premier business and shopping districts. Fifty-two floors of the tower are taken up by offices, while a vast commercial complex, including a Galeries Lafayette department store, spreads over the first floor. Although it is uninspiring by day, it becomes a neon-lit beacon for the area at night. As Europe's tallest high rise, it affords stupendous views of Paris; on a clear day, you can see for 30 miles. (There's a snack bar and cafeteria on the 56th floor; if you go to the top-floor bar for drinks, the ride up is free.) It also claims to have the fastest elevator in Europe! *Admission: 40 frs adults, 30 frs students and senior citi-*

Spend your
vacation
touring
castles.
Not train
stations.

Vacation Cars. Vacation Prices. Wherever your destination
in Europe, there is sure to be one of more than 1,000 Budget locations nearby.
Budget offers considerable values on a wide variety of quality cars, and if
you book before you leave the U.S., you'll save even more with a special
rate package from the Budget World Travel Plan.℠ For information and
reservations, contact your travel consultant or call Budget in the U.S. at
800-472-3325. Or, while traveling abroad, call a Budget reservation center.

THE SMART MONEY IS ON BUDGET.®

We feature Ford and other fine cars.   *A system of corporate and licensee owned locations.*

zens, 22 frs children 5–14. Open daily 9:30 AM–10:30 PM, weekdays 10 AM–9:30 PM in winter.

㉑ Immediately north of the tower is **place du 18 Juin 1940,** part of what was once the old Montparnasse train station and a significant spot in Parisian World War II history. It is named for the date of the radio speech Charles de Gaulle made, from London, urging the French to continue resisting the Germans after the fall of the country to Nazi Germany in May 1940. In August 1944, the German military governor, Dietrich von Choltitz, surrendered to the Allies here, ignoring Hitler's orders to destroy the city as he withdrew; the French General Philippe Leclerc subsequently used it as his headquarters.

Behind the older train station, Gare Montparnasse, you'll see the huge new train terminal that serves Chartres, Versailles, and the west of France. Since 1990, the high-speed *TGV Atlantique* leaves here for Brittany (Rennes and Nantes) and the southwest (Bordeaux, via Tours, Poitiers, and Angoulême). South of this station is one of the oddest residential complexes to appear in this era of architectural experimentation. The
㉒ **Amphithéâtre,** built by Ricardo Boffil, is eye-catching but stark and lacking in human dimension.

㉓ The **Cimetière de Montparnasse** (Montparnasse cemetery) contains many of the quarter's most illustrious residents, buried only a stone's throw away from where they worked and played. It is not at all a picturesque cemetery (with the exception of the old windmill in the corner, which used to be a student tavern) but seeing the names of some of its inhabitants—Baudelaire, Maupassant, Saint-Saëns, and the industrialist André Citroën—may make the visit worthwhile. Nearby, at place Denfert-Rochereau, is the entrance to an extensive complex of
㉔ **catacombs** (*denfert* is a corruption of the word for hell, *enfer*). The catacombs are stocked with the bones of millions of skeletons that were moved here in 1785 from the area's charnel houses. *Admission: 16 frs adults, 10 frs students and senior citizens. Open Tues.–Fri. 2–4, weekends 9–11 and 2–4.*

Montparnasse's bohemian aura has dwindled to almost nothing, yet the area hops at night as *the* place in Paris to find movies of every description, many of them shown in their original language. Theaters and theater-cafés abound, too, especially
㉕ along seedy **rue de la Gaîté.** The Gaîté-Montparnasse, Le Théâtre Montparnasse, and Le Grand Edgar are among the most popular. Up boulevard du Montparnasse and across from the Vavin métro station are two of the better-known gathering
㉖ places of Montparnasse's heyday, the **Dôme** and **La Coupole** brasseries. La Coupole opened in 1927 as a bar/restaurant/dance hall and soon became a home away from home for some of the area's most famous residents, such as Apollinaire, Max Jacob, Cocteau, Satie, Stravinsky, and the ubiquitous Hemingway. It may not be quite the same mecca these days, but it still pulls in a classy crowd.

Across the boulevard, rue Vavin leads past two more celebrated Montparnasse cafés, the **Sélect** and the **Rotonde,** to the Jardin du Luxembourg. But stay on boulevard du Montparnasse for the intersection with boulevard St-Michel, where the
㉗ verdant **avenue de l'Observatoire** begins its long sweep up to the Luxembourg gardens. Here you'll find perhaps the most fa-
㉘ mous bastion of the Left Bank café culture, the **Closerie des**

Lilas. Now a pricey bar/restaurant, the Closerie remains a staple on all literary tours of Paris not least because of the commemorative plaques fastened onto the bar, marking the places where renowned personages sat. Baudelaire, Verlaine, Hemingway, and Apollinaire are just a few of the names. Although the lilacs *(lilas)* have gone from the terrace, it is still a pretty place, opening onto the luxuriant green of the surrounding parkland, and as crowded in the summer as it ever was in the '30s.

㉙ The vista from the Closerie includes the **Paris Observatory** (to the right), built in 1667 by Louis XIV. Its four facades were built to align with the four cardinal points—north, south, east, and west—and its southern wall is the determining point for Paris's official latitude, 48° 50′11″N. French time was based on this Paris meridian until 1911, when the country decided to adopt the international Greenwich Meridian.

A tree-lined alley leads along the avenue de l'Observatoire to the gardens, but before the entrance, you'll pass Davioud's **Fontaine de l'Observatoire** (Observatory Fountain), built in 1873 and decked with four statues representing the four quarters of the globe. Look north from here and you'll have a captivating view of Montmartre and Sacré-Coeur, with the gardens in the foreground.

Palais du Luxembourg

㉚ From avenue de l'Observatoire walk up to the **Jardin du Luxembourg** (the Luxembourg Gardens), one of the city's few large parks. Its fountains, ponds, trim hedges, precisely planted rows of trees, and gravel walks are typical of the French fondness for formal gardens. At the far end is the **Palais du Luxembourg,** **㉛** gray and imposing, built, like the park, for Maria de' Medici, widow of Henri IV, at the beginning of the 17th century. Maria was born and raised in Florence's Pitti Palace, and, having languished in the Louvre after the death of her husband, she was eager to build herself a new palace, somewhere she could recapture something of the lively, carefree atmosphere of her childhood. In 1612, she bought the Paris mansion of the duke of Luxembourg, tore it down, and built her palace. It was not completed until 1627, and Maria was to live there for no more than five years. In 1632, Cardinal Richelieu had her expelled from France, and she saw out her declining years in Cologne, Germany, dying there almost penniless in 1642. The palace remained royal property until the Revolution, when the state took it over and used it as a prison. Danton, the painter David, and Thomas Paine were all detained here. Today, it is the site of the French Senate and is not open to the public.

㉜ The **Théâtre National de l'Odéon,** set at the north end of the Luxembourg Gardens, was established in 1792 to house the Comédiens Français troupe. The massive structure you see today replaced the original theater, which was destroyed by fire in 1807. Since World War II, it has specialized in 20th-century productions. It was the base for Jean-Louis Barrault's and Madeleine Renaud's theater company, the Théâtre de France, until they fell out of favor with the authorities for their alleged role in spurring on the student revolutionaries in May 1968. Today, the Théâtre de l'Odéon is the French home of the Theater of Europe and stages some excellent productions by major foreign companies.

The Sorbonne and the Latin Quarter

If you follow rue de Vaugirard (the longest street in Paris) one block east to boulevard St-Michel, you will soon be at the **place de la Sorbonne,** the hub of the Latin Quarter and nerve center of the student population that has always held such sway over Left Bank life. The square is dominated by the Eglise de la Sorbonne, whose outstanding exterior features are its cupola and 10 Corinthian columns. Inside is the white marble tomb of Cardinal Richelieu. (The church is open to the public only during exhibitions and cultural events.) The university buildings of La Sorbonne spread out around the church from rue Cujas down to the visitor's entrance on rue des Ecoles.

33 The **Sorbonne** is the oldest university in Paris—indeed, one of the oldest in Europe—and has for centuries been one of France's principal institutions of higher learning. It is named after Robert de Sorbon, a medieval canon who founded a theological college here in 1253 for 16 students. By the 17th century, the church and university buildings were becoming dilapidated, so Cardinal Richelieu undertook to have them restored; the present-day Sorbonne campus is largely a result of that restoration. Despite changes in the neighborhood, the maze of amphitheaters, lecture rooms, and laboratories, and the surrounding courtyards and narrow streets, still have a hallowed air. For a glimpse of a more recent relic of Sorbonne history, look for Puvis de Chavannes's painting *Sacred Wood* in the main lecture hall, a major meeting point during the tumultuous student upheavals of 1968, and now a university landmark.

Behind the Sorbonne, bordering its eastern reach, is the rue St-Jacques. The street climbs toward the rue Soufflot, named **34** to honor the man who built the vast, domed **Panthéon,** set atop place du Panthéon. One of Paris's most physically overwhelming sites—it was commissioned by Louis XV as a mark of gratitude for his recovery from a grave illness in 1744—the Panthéon is now a seldom-used church, with little of interest except for Puvis de Chavannes's monumental frescoes and the crypt, which holds the remains of Voltaire, Zola, and Rousseau. In 1789—the year the church was completed—its windows were blocked by order of the Revolutionary Constituent Assembly, and they have remained that way ever since, adding to its sepulchral gloom. The dome, which weighs about 10,000 tons, is best appreciated from a distance. *Admission: 25 frs, 14 frs ages 18–25, 6 frs children 7–17. Open daily 10–5:30.*

Diagonally across from the Panthéon on the corner of rue Clo- **35** vis and rue Cujas stands the striking **St-Etienne-du-Mont.** This mainly 16th-century church's ornate facade combines Gothic, Baroque, and Renaissance elements. Inside, the fretted rood screen is the only one of its kind in Paris. Note the uneven-floored chapel behind the choir, which can be reached via a cloister containing some exquisite stained glass dating from the 17th century.

Up rue St-Jacques again and across from the Sorbonne are the **36** **Lycée Louis-le-Grand** (Molière, Voltaire, and Robespierre studied here) and the elite **Collège de France,** whose grounds continue around the corner onto rue des Ecoles. In 1530, François I created this school as the College of Three Languages, which taught High Latin, Greek, and Hebrew, and any subjects eschewed by academics at the Sorbonne. Diagonally across from the college, on the other side of rue des Ecoles, is the **square Paul-Painlevé**; behind it lies the entrance to the inimitable Hôtel et Musée de Cluny.

Built on the site of the city's enormous old Roman baths, the ③⑦ **Musée de Cluny** is housed in a 15th-century mansion that originally belonged to monks of Cluny Abbey in Burgundy. The remains of the baths that can still be seen are what survived a sacking by Barbarians in the 4th century. But the real reason people come to the Cluny is for its tapestry collection. The most famous series of all is the graceful *Lady and the Unicorn, or Dame à la Licorne*, woven in the 15th or 16th century, probably in the southern Netherlands. And if the tapestries themselves aren't enough at which to marvel, there is also an exhibition of decorative arts from the Middle Ages, a vaulted chapel, and a deep, cloistered courtyard with mullioned windows, set off by the *Boatmen's Pillar*, Paris's oldest sculpture, at its center. *Admission: 17 frs, 9 frs children and Sun. Open Wed.–Mon. 9:30–5:15.*

Above boulevard St-Germain, rue St-Jacques reaches toward the Seine, bringing you past the elegant proportions of the ③⑧ church of **St-Séverin.** Rebuilt in the 16th century and noted for its width and its Flamboyant Gothic style, the church dominates a close-knit Left Bank neighborhood filled with quiet squares and pedestrian streets. In the 11th century, it was the parish church for the entire Left Bank. Louis XIV's cousin, a capricious woman known simply as the Grande Mademoiselle, adopted St-Séverin when she tired of the St-Sulpice church; she then spent vast sums getting Le Brun to modernize the chancel. Note the splendidly deviant spiraling column in the forest of pillars behind the altar. *Open weekdays 11–5:30, Sat. 11–10.*

Running riot around the relative quiet of St-Séverin are streets filled with restaurants of every description, serving everything from souvlaki-to-go to five-course haute cuisine. There is definitely something for every budget here. Rue de la Huchette is the most heavily trafficked of the restaurant streets and especially good for its selection of cheaper Greek food houses and Tunisian patisseries. In the evening, many restaurants put out full window displays of the foods to be offered on that night's menu in order to induce people away from the umbrella-covered terraces of neighboring cafés.

Cross to the other side of rue St-Jacques. In Square René ③⑨ Viviani, which surrounds the church of **St-Julien-le-Pauvre,** stands an acacia tree that is supposed to be the oldest tree in Paris (although it has a rival claim from another acacia at the Jardin des Plantes). This tree-filled square also gives you one of the more spectacular views of Notre Dame. The tiny church here was built at the same time as Notre Dame (1165–1220), on a site where a whole succession of chapels once stood. The church belongs to a Greek Orthodox order today, but was originally named for St. Julian, bishop of Le Mans, who was nicknamed "Le Pauvre" after he gave all his money away.

Behind the church, to the east, are the tiny, elegant streets of the recently renovated **Maubert** district, bordered by quai de Montebello and boulevard St-Germain. Rue de Bièvre, once filled with tanneries, is now guarded at both ends to protect President Mitterrand's private residence.

Between St-Julien-le-Pauvre and place Maubert, two tiny streets—**rue des Anglais** and **rue des Irlandais**—mark the presence of foreign students who have come to study at Paris's academic and theological institutions over the centuries. Very basic board was provided by the small college for Irish students studying to become priests; although it has now been taken over by Polish students, it is still sometimes possible to get accommodation here (for men) if you are one for staying in humble, monklike quarters.

Public meetings and demonstrations have been held in place Maubert ever since the Middle Ages. Nowadays, most gatherings are held inside or in front of the elegantly Art Deco **Palais de la Mutualité,** on the corner of the square, also a venue for jazz, pop, and rock concerts. On Tuesdays, Thursdays, and Saturdays, it is transformed into a colorful outdoor food market.

Head up rue Monge, turn right onto rue du Cardinal-Lemoine, and you'll find yourself at the minute **place de la Contrescarpe.** It doesn't start to swing until after dusk, when its cafés and bars fill up. During the day, the square looks almost provincial, as Parisians flock to the daily market on rue Mouffetard. There are restaurants and cafés of every description on rue Mouffetard, and if you get here at lunchtime, you may want to buy yourself the makings for an alfresco lunch and take it to the unconventional picnic spot provided by the nearby Gallo-Roman ruin of the **Arènes de Lutèce;** it begins on rue Monge, just past the end of rue Rollin. The ancient arena was discovered only in 1869 and has since been excavated and landscaped to reveal parts of the original Roman amphitheater. This site and the remains of the baths at the Cluny constitute the only extant evidence of the powerful Roman city of Lutetia that flourished here in the 3rd century. It is also one of the lesser-known delights of the Left Bank, so you are not likely to find it crowded.

The **Jardin des Plantes** is an enormous swath of greenery containing spacious botanical gardens and a number of natural history museums. It is stocked with plants dating back to the first collections here in the 17th century, and has been enhanced ever since by subsequent generations of devoted French botanists. It claims to shelter Paris's oldest tree, an *acacia robinia,* planted in 1636. There is also a small, old-fashioned zoo here; an alpine garden; an aquarium; a maze; and a number of hothouses. The **Musée Entomologique** is devoted to insects; the **Musée Paléontologique** exhibits fossils and prehistoric animals; the **Musée Minéralogique** houses a stupendous collection of rocks and minerals. *Admission: 12–25 frs. Museums open Wed.–Mon. 9–11:45 and 1–4:45, weekends 2–4:45.*

At the back of the gardens, in place du Puits-de-l'Hermite, you can drink a restorative cup of sweet mint tea in **La Mosquée,** a beautiful white mosque, complete with minaret. Once inside, you'll be convinced that you must be elsewhere than the Left Bank of Paris. The students from the nearby Jussieu and Censier universities pack themselves into the Moslem restaurant here, which serves copious quantities of couscous. The sunken garden and tiled patios are open to the public—the prayer rooms are not—and so are the *hammams*, or Turkish baths. *Baths open daily 11 AM–8 PM; Fri. and Sun. men only; Mon., Wed., Thurs., and Sat. women only. Admission: 15 frs, 65 frs for Turkish baths. Guided tours of mosque Sat.–Thurs. 10–noon and 2–5:30.*

44 In 1988, Paris's large Arab population gained another base: the huge **Institut du Monde Arabe,** which overlooks the Seine on quai St-Bernard, just beyond Université Jussieu. Jean Nouvel's harmonious mixture of Arabic and European styles was greeted with enthusiasm when the center first opened. Note on the building's south side the 240 shutterlike apertures that open and close to regulate light exposure. It contains a sound and image center, a wall of televisions, with Arab programming, a vast library, a documentation center, and fast glass elevators that will take you to the ninth floor for (yet another) memorable view over the Seine and Notre Dame. *23 quai St-Bernard. Admission free. Open Tues.–Sun. 10–6.*

Montmartre

Numbers in the margin correspond to points of interest on the Montmartre map.

On a dramatic rise above the city is Montmartre, site of the Sacré-Coeur basilica and home to a once-thriving artistic community, a heritage recalled today chiefly by the gangs of third-rate painters clustered in the area's most famous square, the place du Tertre. Despite their presence, and the fact that the fabled nightlife of old Montmartre has fizzled down to some glitzy nightclubs and porn shows, Montmartre still exudes a sense of history, a timeless quality infused with that hard-to-define Gallic charm.

The crown atop this urban peak, the Sacré-Coeur is something of an architectural oddity. Its silhouette, viewed from afar at dusk or sunrise, looks more like a mosque than a cathedral. The Sacré-Coeur has been called everything from ugly to sublime; try to see it from as many perspectives as you can before drawing your own conclusion.

Seeing Montmartre means negotiating a lot of steep streets and flights of steps. If the prospect of trudging up and down them is daunting, you can tour parts of Montmartre by public transportation, aboard the Promotrain or the Montmartrobus. The Promotrain offers daily 40-minute guided tours of Montmartre between 10 AM and midnight. The cost is 25 francs for adults, 15 francs for children under 12, and departures are from outside the Moulin Rouge on place Blanche. The Montmartrobus is a regular city bus that runs around Montmartre for the price of a métro ticket. It departs from place Pigalle. If you're visiting only Sacré-Coeur, take the funicular that runs up the hill to the church near Anvers métro station.

Exploring Montmartre

1 Begin your tour at **place Blanche,** site of the Moulin Rouge. Place Blanche—White Square—takes its name from the clouds of chalky dust churned up by the windmills that once dotted

Montmartre

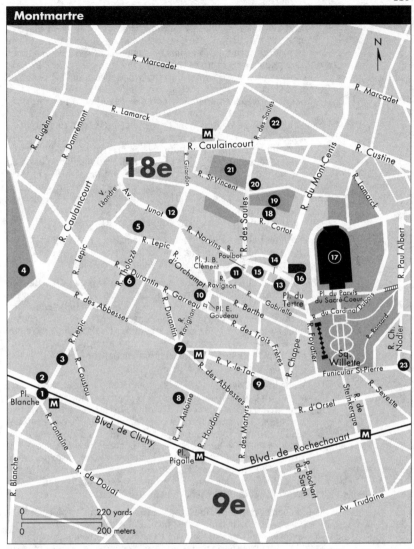

Basilique du Sacré-Coeur, **17**

Bateau-Lavoir, **10**

Chapelle du Martyre, **9**

Cimetière de Montmartre, **4**

Cité Internationale des Arts, **12**

Espace Dali, **15**

La Mère Catherine, **14**

Lapin Agile, **20**

Marché St-Pierre, **23**

Moulin de la Galette, **5**

Moulin de Paris, **11**

Moulin Rouge, **2**

Musée d'Art Juif, **22**

Musée du Vieux Montmartre, **18**

Place Blanche, **1**

Place des Abbesses, **7**

Place du Tertre, **13**

Rue Lepic, **3**

St-Pierre de Montmartre, **16**

St-Vincent Cemetery, **21**

Studio 28, **6**

Théâtre Libre, **8**

Vineyard, **19**

Montmartre (or *La Butte*, meaning "mound" or "hillock"). They were set up here not just because the hill was a good place to catch the wind—at over 300 feet, it's the highest point in the city—but because Montmartre was covered with wheat fields and quarries right up to the end of the 19th century. The carts carrying away the wheat and crushed stone trundled across place Blanche, turning the square white as they passed. Today, only two of the original 20 windmills are intact. A number have been converted to other uses, none more famous than the ❷ **Moulin Rouge,** or Red Windmill, built in 1885 and turned into a dance hall in 1900. It was a genuinely wild place in its early days, immortalized by Toulouse-Lautrec in his boldly simple posters and paintings. The place is still trading shamelessly on the notion of Paris as a city of sin: If you fancy a Vegas-style night out, with computerized light shows and troupes of bare-breasted girls sporting feather headdresses, this is the place to go. The cancan, by the way—still a regular feature here—was considerably more raunchy when Lautrec was around.

For a taste of something more authentically French, walk past ❸ the Moulin Rouge, up **rue Lepic,** site of one of the most colorful and tempting food markets in Paris (closed Mon.).

❹ Turn left onto rue des Abbesses and walk along to **Cimetière de Montmartre** (Montmartre cemetery). It's by no means as romantic or as large as the better known Père Lachaise cemetery in the east of the city, but it contains the graves of many prominent French men and women, including the 18th-century painters Greuze and Fragonard; Degas; and Adolphe Sax, inventor of the saxophone. The Russian ballet dancer Nijinsky is also buried here.

Walk back along rue des Abbesses. Rue Tholozé, the second street on the left, was once a path over the hill, the oldest in ❺ Montmartre. It leads to the **Moulin de la Galette,** one of the two remaining windmills in Montmartre, which has been unroman- ❻ tically rebuilt. To reach it, you pass **Studio 28.** This seems to be no more than a generic little movie theater, but when opened in 1928, it was the first purposely built *art et essai,* or experimental theater, in the world. Over the years, the movies of directors like Jean Cocteau, François Truffaut, and Orson Welles have often been shown here before their official premieres.

❼ Return to rue des Abbesses, turn left, and walk to **place des Abbesses.** The little square is typical of the kind of picturesque and slightly countrified style that has made Montmartre famous. The entrance to the métro station, a curving, sensuous mass of delicate iron, is one of a handful of original Art Nouveau stations left in Paris. The austere, redbrick **church of St-Jean l'Evangéliste** (1904) is worth a look, too. It was one of the first concrete buildings in France; the brick had to be added later to soothe offended locals. The **café St-Jean,** next to it, is a popular local meeting place, crowded on weekends.

There are two competing attractions just off the square. Theater buffs should head down the tiny rue André-Antoine. At no. ❽ 37, you'll see what was originally the **Théâtre Libre,** or Free Theater, founded in 1887 by André Antoine and immensely influential in popularizing the work of iconoclastic young playwrights such as Ibsen and Strindberg. The other attraction is **rue Yvonne-le-Tac,** scene of a vital event in Montmartre's early history and linked to the disputed story of how this quarter got its name. Some say the name Montmartre comes from the Roman temple to Mercury that was once here, called the Mound of Mercury or *Mons Mercurii*. Others contend that it was an adaptation of *Mons Martyrum*, a name inspired by the burial here of Paris's first bishop, St-Denis. The popular version of his martyrdom is that he was beheaded by the Romans in AD 250, but arose to carry his severed head from rue Yvonne-le-Tac to a place 4 miles to the north, an area now known as St-Denis. He is commemorated by the 19th-century **Chapelle du Martyre** at no. 9, built over the spot where he is said to have been executed. It was in the crypt of the original chapel here that St. Ignatius of Loyola founded the Jesuit order in 1540, a decisive step in the efforts of the Catholic Church to reassert its authority in the face of the Protestant Reformation. A final twist on the name controversy is that Montmartre briefly came to be known as Mont-Marat during the French Revolution. Marat was a leading Revolutionary figure who was obliged to spend most of the day in the tub, the result of a disfiguring and severe skin condition. It was in his bath that Charlotte Corday, a fanatical opponent of the Revolutionary government, stabbed him to death.

From rue Yvonne-le-Tac, retrace your steps through place des Abbesses. Take rue Ravignan on the right, climbing to the summit via place Emile-Goudeau, an enchanting little cobbled square. Your goal is the **Bateau-Lavoir**, or Boat Wash House, at its northern edge. Montmartre poet Max Jacob coined the name for the old building on this site, which burned down in 1970. First of all, he said, it resembled a boat. Second, the warren of artists' studios within was always cluttered and paint-splattered, and looked to be in perpetual need of a good hosing down. The new building also contains art studios, but, if you didn't know its history, you'd probably walk right past it; it is the epitome of poured concrete drabness.

It was in the original Bateau-Lavoir that painters Picasso and Braque, early this century, made their first bold stabs at the concept of Cubism—a move that paved the way for abstract painting. The poet Apollinaire, who also kept a Bateau-Lavoir studio, helped Cubism gain acceptance with his book, *Les Peintures du Cubisme* (1913), which set the seal on the movement's historical significance.

Continue up the hill to place Jean-Baptiste Clément. The Italian painter and sculptor Modigliani (1884–1920) had a studio here at no. 7. Some have claimed he was the greatest Italian artist of the 20th century, the man who fused the genius of the Italian Renaissance with the modernity of Cézanne and Picasso. He claimed that he would drink himself to death—he eventually did—and chose the right part of town to do it in. This was one of the wildest areas of Montmartre. Its bistros and cabarets have mostly gone now, though, and only the **Moulin de Paris** still reflects a glimmer of the old atmosphere. Look for the octagonal tower at the north end of the square; it's all that's left of Montmartre's first water tower, built around 1840 to boost the area's feeble water supply.

Rue Norvins, formerly rue des Moulins, runs behind and parallel to the north end of the square. Turn left along it to reach stylish avenue Junot, site of the **Cité Internationale des Arts** (International Residence of the Arts), where the city authorities rent out studios to artists from all over the world. Retrace your steps to rue Norvins and continue east past the bars and tourist shops, until you reach place du Tertre.

⑬ Place du Tertre (*tertre* means hillock) regains its village atmosphere only in the winter, when the somber buildings gather in the grays of the Parisian light and the plane tree branches sketch traceries against the sky. At any other time of year, you'll have to fight your way through the crowds to the southern end of the square and the breathtaking view over the city. The real drawback is the swarm of artists clamoring to dash off your portrait. If you're in the mood, however. . . . Most are licensed to be there, and, like taxi drivers, their prices are officially fixed. But there is no shortage of con men, sketch pads in hand, who will charge whatever they think they can get away with. If one produces a picture of you without having first asked, you're under no obligation to buy it, though that's not to say you won't have to argue your case. It's best just to walk away.

⑭ La Mère Catherine, the restaurant at the northern end of the square, has an honored place in French culinary history. It was a favorite with the Russian cossacks who occupied Paris in 1814 after Napoléon had been exiled to the island of Elba. Little did they know that when they banged on the tables and shouted *"bistro,"* the Russian word for "quick," they were inventing a new breed of French restaurant. For a restaurant catering almost entirely to the tourist trade, La Mère Catherine is surprisingly good but its prices are high.

⑮ Around the corner on rue Poulbot, the **Espace Dalí** houses more than 300 works by Salvador Dalí, who once kept a studio in the area. The museum's atmosphere is meant to approximate the surreal experience, with black walls, low lighting, and a new-agey musical score—punctuated by recordings of Dalí's own voice. If you're interested in seeing some of Dalí's less familiar works, including a series of sculptures and bronzes, a visit will prove worthwhile. Those unmoved by this eccentric genius and showman may want to skip this stop in favor of strolling the place du Tertre. *11 rue Poulbot, tel. 42–64–40–10. Admission: 35 frs adults, 25 frs children. Open daily 10–7; until 8 in summer.*

It was in place du Tertre in March 1871 that one of the most destructively violent episodes in French history began, one that colored French political life for generations. Despite popular images of later-19th-century France—and Paris especially—as carefree and prosperous, for much of this period the country was desperately divided into two camps: an ever more vocal and militant underclass, motivated by resentment of what they considered an elitist government, and a reactionary and fearful bourgeoisie and ruling class. It was a conflict that went back at least as far as the French Revolution at the end of the 18th century, and one that twice flared into outbreaks of civil war and rebellion, in 1832 and 1848, as the country oscillated between republican and imperial forms of government. In 1870, France, under the leadership of an opportunistic but feeble Napoléon III (nephew of the great Napoléon), was drawn into a disastrous war with Bismarck's Prussia, which was rapidly growing into one of the most formidable military powers in Europe. (Soon after, Prussia was to dominate a newly united and aggressive Germany.) In September that year, Prussia invaded France, surrounded Paris, and laid siege to it. After four months of appalling suffering—during which time the Louvre became a munitions factory, the Gare de Lyon was converted into a cannon foundry, and the two elephants in the zoo, Castor and Pollux, were eaten by starving Parisians—the new government under French statesman Adolphe Thiers capitulated. Although mass starvation seemed imminent, fears that Thiers would restore an imperial rather than a republican government caused Parisians to refuse to surrender their arms to him. Thiers then ordered that the guns at Montmartre be captured by loyal government forces. Insurgents responded by shooting the two generals ordered to retake the guns. Almost immediately, barricades were thrown up across the city streets, and the fighting began in earnest. The antimonarchists formed the Commune, which for three heady months ruled Paris. In May, from his base at Versailles, Thiers ordered the city retaken. Estimates as to the numbers killed in the fighting vary greatly. Some say 4,000 Communards lost their lives; others claim 20,000. No one, however, doubts that upward of 10,000 Communards were executed by government troops after the collapse of the Commune.

In expiation for this bloodshed, the French government decided, in 1873 (after the downfall of Thiers), to build the basilica of the Sacré-Coeur. It was to be a sort of national guilt offering. ⑯ Before visiting this landmark, walk to the church of **St-Pierre de Montmartre** at the east side of place du Tertre. It's one of the oldest churches in the city, built in the 12th century as the abbey church of a substantial Benedictine monastery. It's been remodeled on a number of occasions down through the years, and the 18th-century facade, built by Louis XIV, contrasts uncomfortably with the mostly medieval interior. Its setting is awkward, too: The bulk of the Sacré-Coeur looms directly behind it.

⑰ The **Basilique du Sacré-Coeur,** begun in 1873 and completed in 1910 (though not consecrated until 1919), symbolized the return of relative self-confidence to later-19th-century Paris after the turmoil of the Commune. Even so, the building was to some extent a reflection of political divisions within the country. It was largely financed by French Catholics fearful of an anticlerical backlash and determined to make a grand statement on behalf of the Church. Stylistically, the Sacré-Coeur borrows elements from Romanesque and Byzantine models, fusing them under its distinctive Oriental dome. Although it was built on a grand scale, the effect is strangely disjointed and unsettling, rather as if the building had been designed by an architect of railway stations, with a pronounced taste for exoticism. (The architect, Abadie, died in 1884, long before the church was finished.) The gloomy, cavernous interior is worth visiting for its golden mosaics; climb to the top of the dome for the view over Paris.

More of Montmartre beckons north and west of the Sacré-Coeur. Take rue du Mont-Cenis down to rue Cortot, site of the ⑱ **Musée du Vieux Montmartre.** Like the Bateau-Lavoir, the building that is now the museum sheltered an illustrious group of painters, writers, and assorted cabaret artists in its heyday toward the end of the 19th century. Foremost among them were Renoir—he painted the *Moulin de la Galette,* an archetypical Parisian scene of sun-drenched revels, while he lived here—and Maurice Utrillo, Montmartre painter par excellence. Utrillo was encouraged to paint by his mother, Suzanne Valadon, a regular model of Renoir's and a considerable painter in her own right. Utrillo's life was anything but happy, despite the considerable success his paintings enjoyed. He was an alcoholic continually in trouble with the police, and he spent most of his declining years in hospitals. Having taken the gray, crumbling streets of Montmartre as his subject matter, he discovered that he worked more effectively from postcards than from the streets themselves. For all that, his best works—almost all produced before 1916; he died in 1955—evoke the atmosphere of old Montmartre hauntingly. Look carefully at the pictures in the museum here and you can see the plaster and sand he mixed with his paints to help convey the decaying buildings of the area. Almost the best thing about the museum, however, is the view over the tiny **vineyard** on neighboring rue des Saules, the only vineyard in Paris, which still produces a symbolic 125 gallons of wine every year. It's hardly vintage stuff, but there are predictably bacchanalian celebrations during the October harvest. *Musée du Vieux Montmartre, 12 rue Cortot. Admission: 25 frs adults, 15 frs students and senior citizens. Open Tues.– Sun. 11–5:30.*

There's an equally famous Montmartre landmark on the corner of rue St-Vincent, just down the road: the **Lapin Agile.** It's a bar-cabaret and originally one of the raunchiest haunts in Montmartre. Today, it manages against all odds to preserve at least something of its earlier flavor, unlike the Moulin Rouge. It got its curious name—it means the Nimble Rabbit—when the owner, André Gill, hung a sign outside (you can see it now in the Musée du Vieux Montmartre) of a laughing rabbit jumping out of a saucepan clutching a wine bottle. In those days, the place was still tamely called La Campagne (The Countryside). Once the sign went up, locals rebaptized the place Lapin à Gill, which, translated, means rabbit, Gill-style. When in 1886 it was sold to cabaret singer Jules Jouy, he called it the Lapin Agile, which has the same pronunciation in French as Lapin à Gill. In 1903, the premises were bought by the most celebrated cabaret entrepreneur of them all, Aristide Bruand, portrayed by Toulouse-Lautrec in a series of famous posters.

Behind the Lapin Agile is the **St-Vincent Cemetery;** the entrance is off little rue Lucien-Gaulard. It's a tiny graveyard, but serious students of Montmartre might want to visit to see Utrillo's burial place.

Continue north on rue des Saules, across busy rue Caulaincourt, and you come to the **Musée d'Art Juif,** the Museum of Jewish Art. It contains devotional items, models of synagogues, and works by Pissarro and Marc Chagall. *42 rue des Saules. Admission: 20 frs adults, 15 frs students and children. Open Sun.–Thurs. 3–6.*

There are several routes you can take back over Montmartre's hill. Luxurious avenue Junot, from which you'll see the villa Léandre, one of Montmartre's most charming side streets, makes for a picturesque return from the area around the cemetery and the museum. Alternatively, you can turn east onto rue Lamarck, past several good restaurants, to circle around the quieter side of the Sacré-Coeur basilica. If you then take the little stairpath named after Utrillo down to rue Paul Albert, you'll come upon the **Marché St-Pierre** (St. Pierre Market), the perfect place to rummage for old clothes and fabrics. Prices are low. *Open Tues.–Sun. 8–1.*

Take rue de Steinkerque, opposite the foot of the Sacré-Coeur gardens, then turn right onto boulevard de Rochechouart and continue down to **Place Pigalle** to complete your tour of the essential Montmartre. Despite the area's reputation as a tawdry red-light district, a number of trendy clubs have opened here. If you choose to visit at night, however, be aware that dubious characters and lewd sex shows still prevail.

On the Fringe

The Bois de Boulogne

Class and style have been associated with "Le Bois," as it is known, ever since it was landscaped into an upper-class playground by Baron Haussmann in the 1850s at the request of Napoléon III. This sprawling, 2,200-acre wood, crisscrossed by broad, leafy roads, lies just west of Paris, surrounded by the wealthy residential districts of Neuilly, Auteuil, and Passy. Here you will discover rowers, joggers, strollers, riders, lovers, hookers, *pétanque*-players, and picnickers. Horse races at Longchamp and Auteuil are high up the social calendar and recreate something of a Belle Epoque atmosphere. The French Open tennis tournament at the beautiful Roland Garros Stadium in late May is another occasion when Parisian style and elegance are on full display. The manifold attractions of these woods include cafés, restaurants, lakes, gardens, and waterfalls. Rowboats are available at the two largest lakes, the Lac Inférieur and Lac Supérieur. A cheap and frequent ferry crosses to the idyllic island in the middle of the Lac Inférieur.

Buses traverse the Bois de Boulogne during the day (service 244 from Porte Maillot), but the métro goes only to the fringe: Alight at Porte Dauphine (east), Les Sablons (north), or Porte d'Auteuil (south). Porte Dauphine is one of the few stations still to possess an original Art Nouveau iron-and-glass entrance canopy, designed by métro architect Hector Guimard. It stands at the bottom of avenue Foch, connecting the Bois to the Champs-Elysées. It used to be known as the avenue de l'Impératrice in honor of the Empress Eugénie (wife of Napoléon III) and is Paris's grandest boulevard—for both its sheer size (330 yards wide) and its high-priced real estate.

One of the best ways of getting around the Bois is by bicycle. Bikes can be rented on Wednesdays and on weekends from Le Relais du Bois restaurant, Route de Suresnes (tel. 45–27–54–65). The cost is 25 francs an hour or 90 francs a day.

A word of warning: The Bois becomes a distinctly adult playground after dark, when walking, and even driving, are not advisable; the Bois's night population can be dauntingly aggressive.

Besides being a charming place to stroll or picnic, the Bois de Boulogne boasts several individual attractions worth a visit in their own right:

Parc de Bagatelle. This is a beautiful floral park with irises, roses, tulips, and water lilies among the showpieces; it is at its freshest and most colorful between April and June. The velvet green lawns and majestic 18th-century buildings (often host to art exhibitions) are fronted by a terrace with views toward the Seine—an attractive sight at any time of year. *Entrance: Route de Sèvres à Neuilly, or off Allée de Longchamp (Bus 244 or Métro: Pont de Neuilly). Admission: 6 frs adults, 3 frs children to park, 35 frs adults, 25 frs children to château buildings. Open 8:30 AM–8 PM.*

Jardin d'Acclimatation. This delightful children's amusement park on the northern edge of the Bois de Boulogne has plenty to enchant adults as well. There are boat trips along an "enchanted river," a zoo with a refreshing mix of exotic and familiar animals, a miniature railway, a high-towered folly, and various fairground stalls to keep young and old entertained. The zoo and amusement park can be reached via the miniature railway—a surefire hit with children—that runs from Porte Maillot (Wed. and weekends from 1:30; 4 frs). Many of the attractions (though not the zoo, which is spread out through the park) have separate entry fees, notably the child-oriented **Musée en Herbe** (13 frs; 11 frs excluding garden; 20 frs with workshop). There are plenty of open-air cafés for a refreshing break. *Blvd. des Sablons (Métro: Les Sablons). Admission: 9 frs adults, 4 frs children. Open Sun.–Fri. 10–6, Sat. 2–6.*

Musée des Arts et Traditions Populaires. This museum, situated right alongside the Jardin d'Acclimatation in an ugly modern building, contains an impressive variety of artifacts related principally to preindustrial rural life. Many exhibits have buttons to press and knobs to twirl; however, there are no descriptions in English. The museum is a favorite destination for school field trips, so avoid weekday afternoons, except Wednesdays, when the children are not in school. *6 route du Mahatma-Gandhi (Métro: Les Sablons). Admission: 23 frs adults, 15 frs children and Sun. Open Wed.–Mon. 10–5:15.*

Pré Catalan. This pleasant, well-tended area in the heart of the Bois de Boulogne includes one of Paris's largest trees: a copper beech over 200 years old. The "Shakespeare Garden" contains flowers, herbs, and trees mentioned in Shakespearean plays. *Route de la Grande Cascade (Bus 244 or Métro: Porte Dauphine). Guided tours at 11, 1:30, 3, 5, and 5:30.*

The Bois de Vincennes

Situated to the southeast of Paris, sandwiched between the unexciting suburb of Charenton and the working-class district of Fontenay-sous-Bois, the Bois de Vincennes is often considered a poor man's Bois de Boulogne. Although the east of Paris has less to attract visitors than the west, the comparison is largely unfair. The Bois de Vincennes is no more difficult to get to (bus 46; métro to Porte Dorée) and has equally illustrious origins. It, too, was landscaped under Napoléon III—a park having been created here by Louis XV as early as 1731.

Also like the Bois de Boulogne, the Bois de Vincennes has several lakes, notably Lac Daumesnil, with two islands, and Lac des Minimes, with three. Rowboats can be hired at both. There is also a zoo, a cinder-track racecourse (Hippodrome de Vincennes), a castle, an extensive flower garden, and several cafés. The Foire du Trône, in spring, is one big fun fair. Bikes can be rented from Château de Vincennes métro station (tel. 47–66–55–92). The cost is 20 francs an hour or 80 francs a day.

Château de Vincennes. On the northern edge of the Bois is the historic Château de Vincennes, France's medieval Versailles, an imposing, high-walled castle surrounded by a dry moat and dominated by a 170-foot keep through which guided tours are offered. The sprawling castle grounds also contain a replica (1379–1552) of the Sainte-Chapelle on the Ile de la Cité, and two elegant, classical wings designed by Louis Le Vau in the mid-17th century (now used for naval/military administration, and closed to the public). *Av. de Paris, Vincennes (Métro: Château de Vincennes). Admission: 25 frs adults, 14 frs students and senior citizens. Open daily 10–6; 10–4 in winter. Guided tours of chapel every 45 minutes.*

Musée de l'Art Africain et des Arts Océaniques. This museum, housed in a building erected for the Colonial Exhibition of 1931, is devoted to African and Oceanic Art and features head-dresses, bronzes, jewelry, masks, statues, and pottery from former French colonies in Africa and the South Seas. There is also a tropical aquarium. *293 av. Daumesnil (Métro: Porte Dorée). Admission: 23 frs adults, 15 frs children and on Sun. Open Wed.–Mon. 10–5:30, weekends 10–6.*

Parc Floral. The 70-acre Vincennes flower garden includes a lake and water garden and is renowned for its seasonal displays of blooms. The "exotarium" contains tropical fish and reptiles. *Route de la Pyramide, Vincennes (Métro: Château de Vincennes). Admission: 5 frs, children under 6 free. Open daily 9:30–8, 9:30–5 in winter.*

Zoo. Some 600 mammals and 200 species of bird can be seen at Vincennes Zoo, the largest in France. One of the most striking features is an artificial rock 236 feet high, inhabited by wild mountain sheep. *53 av. de St-Maurice (Métro: Porte Dorée). Admission: 35 frs adults, 20 frs children. Open Apr.–Oct., daily 9–6; Nov.–Mar., daily 9–5:30.*

Père Lachaise Cemetery

This largest, most interesting, and most prestigious of Paris cemeteries dates back to the start of the 19th century. Situated on the eastern fringe of Paris, it is a veritable necropolis whose tombs compete in grandiosity, originality, and often, alas, dilapidation. Cobbled avenues, steep slopes, and lush vegetation contribute to a powerful atmosphere. The cemetery was the site of the Paris Commune's final battle on May 28, 1871, when the rebel troops were rounded up, lined against the **Mur des Federes** (Federalist's Wall; now in the southeast corner of the cemetery), and shot. Named after the Jesuit father—Louis XIV's confessor—who led the reconstruction of the Jesuit Rest House completed here in 1682, the cemetery houses the tombs of the French author Colette; the composer Chopin; the playwright Molière; the writers Honoré Balzac, Marcel Proust, Paul Eluard, and Oscar Wilde; the popular French actress Simone Signoret and her husband, singer-actor Yves Montand; and Edith Piaf. Perhaps the most noticeable shrine is to rock star Jim Morrison: Lyrics scribbled on tombstones will lead you to the gravesite, where dozens of hippie faithfuls sit in silent homage to the songwriter. Get hold of a map at the entrance—and remember that Père Lachaise is an easy place to get lost in. *Rue des Rondeaux (Métro: Gambetta, Père Lachaise). Open daily 8–6, 8–dusk in winter.*

St-Denis

Although today St-Denis is a pretty seedy, downmarket north-ern suburb, its history—exemplified by its huge green-roof ca-thedral—is illustrious. The **Basilique de St-Denis** can be reached by métro from Paris and is worth visiting for several reasons. It was here, under dynamic prelate Abbé Suger, that Gothic architecture (typified by pointed arches and rib vaults) arguably made its first appearance. Suger's writings also show the medieval fascination with the bright, shiny colors that ap-pear in stained glass. The kings of France soon chose St-Denis as their final resting place, and their richly sculpted tombs—along with what remains of Suger's church—can be seen in the choir area at the east end of the church. The vast 13th-century nave is a brilliant example of structural logic. Its elements—columns, capitals, and vaults—are a model of architectural harmony. The facade retains the rounded arches of the Roman-esque style that preceded Gothic and is set off by a small rose window, reputedly the earliest in France. There was originally a left tower, with spire, as well as a right one; there is currently talk of reconstructing it. *Métro: St-Denis–Basilique. Admis-sion to choir: 24 frs adults, 13 frs students and senior citizens. Open daily 10–7, 10–5 in winter.*

La Villette

The so-called **Cité des Sciences et de l'Industrie** is housed in the vast **Parc de la Villette,** created in the mid-1980s on the site of a former *abattoir* (slaughterhouse) in the unfashionable out-skirts of northeast Paris. The sprawling complex includes a sci-ence and industry museum; planetarium; curved-screen cinema; an "inventorium," or children's play area; a concert hall (the Zénith—a major rock venue); and the huge iron-and-glass Grande Halle, used for concerts and exhibitions.

The **museum** tries to do for science and industry what the look-alike Pompidou Center does for modern art. It is a brave at-tempt to make technology seem fun and easy. The visual displays are bright and thought-provoking, while dozens of "try-it-yourself" contraptions make the visitor feel more par-ticipant than onlooker. It's fascinating stuff and, perhaps, a forerunner of the museums of tomorrow—despite the huge, echoing main hall that is unpleasantly like a high-tech factory, and the lines (especially during school holidays), which can be absurdly long. *Métro: Porte de la Villette. Admission: 45 frs adults, 35 frs children (planetarium 15 frs extra). Open Tues.–Sun. 10–6.*

The **Géode** cinema, facing the museum building across the un-ruffled sheen of a broad moat, looks like a huge silver golf ball: It's actually made of polished steel. Thanks to its enormous, 180-degree-curved screen, it has swiftly become a cult movie venue. As its capacity is limited, we suggest you materialize in the morning or early afternoon to be sure of a same-day ticket. *Admission: 50 frs (joint ticket with museum 85 frs adults, 75 frs children). Screenings Tues.–Sun. 10–9.*

The futuristic outlines of the Géode and Science Museum shim-mer in the canals that crisscross the Parc de la Villette, princi-pally the barge-bearing Canal de l'Ourcq on its way from Paris to St-Denis. The whole area is ambitiously landscaped—there are sweeping lawns, a children's playground, canopied walkways, and weird, brightly painted pavilions—and is at last beginning to take shape, although a massive musical academy by the Porte de Pantin entrance will need several years of additional construction before completion.

The former slaughterhouse—the **Grande Halle**—is a magnificent structure that provides an intelligent link with the site's historic past: Its transformation into an exhibition-cum-concert center has been carried out as ingeniously as that of the former Gare (now Musée) d'Orsay. It is an intriguing sight at night, too, when strips of red neon along the roof and facade flicker on and off like a beating heart.

Off the Beaten Track

Académie de la Bière

Beer and *moules-frites* (mussels cooked in white wine and served with french fries) is more a Belgian than a French specialty, yet it's readily available in Paris, as if to underline the gastronomic as well as linguistic ties between the two neighbors. A good place to sample this satisfying combination is the friendly, unpretentious Académie de la Bière, near Montparnasse, the nearest Paris comes to the atmosphere of a British pub, with a cozy, wood-benched interior and pavement terrace for lazy summer evenings. There is a choice of 200 beers from numerous countries (several on draft), plus various snacks. *88 bis blvd. de Port-Royal, 5e, tel. 43-54-66-65. Open 6 PM–2 AM; closed Sun. RER: Port-Royal.*

Buttes-Chaumont

This is an immensely picturesque park in the downbeat 19th Arrondissement of northeast Paris. It boasts a lake, waterfall, and cliff-top folly or "belvedere." Until town planner Baron Haussmann got his hands on it in the 1860s, the area was a garbage dump and quarry—hence the steep slopes. *Rue Botzaris. Métro: Buttes-Chaumont, Botzaris.*

Canal St-Martin

Place de la République is the gateway to east Paris, a largely residential area often underestimated by tourists. One of its highlights is the Canal St-Martin, which starts just south of the Bastille but really comes into its own during the mile-long stretch north of République, across the 10th Arrondissement. With its quiet banks, locks, and footbridges, the Canal St-Martin has an unexpected flavor of Amsterdam—and is much loved by novelists and film directors. (Simenon's famous inspector Maigret solved many a mystery along its deceptively sleepy banks.) Major development has transformed the northern end of the canal, around the place de Stalingrad and its 18th-century rotunda, and there are boat trips along the once-industrial Bassin de la Villette to the nearby Parc de la Villette. *Métro: Jacques-Bonsergent, Colonel-Fabien, or Jaurès.*

Les Catacombes

The catacombs consist of an extensive underground labyrinth built by the Romans, tunneling under much of the Left Bank and into the near suburbs. They were subsequently used to store bones from disused graveyards; then, during World War II, they became the headquarters of the French Resistance. You are well advised to take a flashlight with you. *1 pl. Denfert-Rochereau. Admission: 16 frs, 10 frs students and senior citizens. Open Tues.–Fri. 2–4, weekends 9–11 and 2–4. Guided tours on Wed. at 2:45; 20 frs extra. Métro and RER: Denfert-Rochereau.*

The Métro

Many visitors spend considerable time on the cheap and practical métro system without realizing it is a considerable attraction in its own right. For a start, it is not strictly a "subway" or "underground," inasmuch as it ventures out of its tunnels at several points to offer a delightful rooftop tour of the city. Part of **Line 2** (Dauphine–Nation) is above ground, yielding views of the Sacré-Coeur and the Canal St-Martin. Nearly all of **Line 6** (Nation–Etoile) is above ground and gives terrific views of the Invalides and Eiffel Tower. There is a charming glimpse of Notre Dame, Ile de la Cité, and Ile St-Louis as **Line 5** crosses the Seine between quai de la Rapée and Gare d'Austerlitz, continuing past the fine 17th-century Hôpital de la Salpêtrière.

A number of métro stations are attractions in themselves—the **Louvre** and **Varenne** stations are well known for their museumlike feeling, **Cluny-Sorbonne** and **Pasteur** for their imaginative use of mosaics. The entrance canopies to **Porte Dauphine** and **Abbesses** stations are the best remaining examples of the florid, interlacing Art Nouveau ironwork created by Hector Guimard at the start of the century.

Nation Quarter

The towering, early 19th-century statue-topped columns on the majestic **place de la Nation** stand sentinel at the Gates of Paris, the eastern sector's equivalent of the Arc de Triomphe; the bustling but unpretentious Cours de Vincennes provides a down-to-earth echo of the Champs-Elysées. Place de la Nation (originally known as place du Trône, but Throne Square was far too monarchical a title to survive the Revolution) was the scene of over 1,300 executions at the guillotine in 1794. Most of these unfortunates were buried around the corner (via rue Fabre d'Eglantine) in the **Cimetière de Picpus,** a peaceful convent cemetery containing the grave of General Lafayette, identified by its U.S. flag. *35 rue Picpus. Open Tues.–Sun. 2–6, 2–4 in winter; closed Mon. Métro: Nation, Picpus.*

4 Shopping for Bargains

By Corinne LaBalme

Corinne LaBalme is a Paris-based freelance writer and a contributing editor to United Airlines' Hemispheres.

Window-shopping is one of Paris's great spectator sports. Tastefully displayed wares—luscious cream-filled éclairs, lacy lingerie, rare artwork, gleaming copper pots—entice the eye and awaken the imagination. And shopping is one of the city's greatest pastimes, a chance to mix with Parisians and feel the heartbeat of the country. Who can understand the magic of the country's home cuisine until they've watched a French family shopping for Sunday lunch in an open-air market? Or resist the thrill of seeing a Chanel evening gown displayed in its own glossy Paris boutique—where even the doorknobs are shaped like Chanel Number 5 crystal perfume stoppers?

Happily, shopping in Paris is not confined to Cartier watches, Baccarat chandeliers, silk-lined Dior gloves, or the fanciest floors of department stores. That's only part of the Parisian experience. Paris shopping is also about the sprawling flea markets on the outskirts of town, the bargain stores on the Alesia, and the china showroom district on the rue de Paradis. In the chapter that follows, we provide a mix of the cheap and the chic.

Perfume and designer clothing are undoubtedly the most coveted Parisian souvenirs, but bargains are distressingly elusive even on haute couture's home turf. Foreign visitors, always subject to fluctuating exchange rates, are advised to know prices in their own country before arrival. A Pierre Cardin tie or a Lalique bottle of *L'Air du Temps* may possibly be cheaper at the mall back home . . . although it won't be as much fun to buy.

Agatha, **4, 14**
Au Bon Marché, **12**
Cacharel Stock, **23**
Chipie Stock, **22**
Dominique
Morlotti, **11**
Dorothée bis Stock, **21**
FNAC, **15**
Galeries Lafayette, **17**
Guerlain, **5**
Kenzo, **7**
La Bagagerie, **8**
Le Monde en
Marche, **2**
Le Mouton à Cinq
Pattes, **13**
Marie Papier, **19**
Poilâne, **9**
Shakespeare and
Company, **1**
Sonia Rykiel, **6**
Souleido, **3**
SR Stock, **20**
Tati, **16**
Tea and Tattered
Pages, **18**
YSL Rive Gauche, **10**

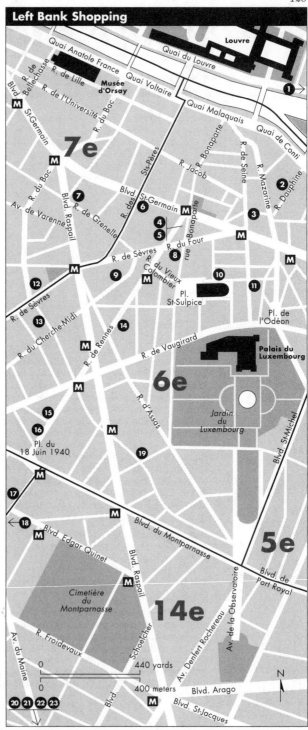

Left Bank Shopping

Storefronts announcing *troc* or *dépot-vente* can be treasure troves. These are Parisian swap shops, and we've included a few that have especially fine designer clothing. *Brocante* is another bargain byword, usually referring to secondhand furniture and trinkets. (The best troc and brocante shops usually close for vacation from late July into August.) Bargain hunters should watch for the word *soldes* (sale). Sales are generally held in July and January, but the relatively meager markdowns (10%–15%) may disappoint international visitors.

Paris is highly cosmopolitan, with numerous outlets for Burberry raincoats, Benetton sweaters, and Levi's jeans. We've concentrated our listings on characteristically French products.

Credit Cards Even stores that will accept currency other than francs will generally give you a lower rate of exchange than in banks or exchange offices. You're better off using credit cards, which are more widely used in France than in the United States. Even the corner newsstand or flea market salesperson is likely to honor plastic. VISA is the most common and preferred card, followed closely by MasterCard/EuroCard. American Express, Diners Club, and Access are accepted in the larger international stores.

Duty-Free Shopping Visitors from outside the European Community, ages 15 and over, whose stay in France and/or the EC is less than six months can benefit from VAT (Value Added Tax) reimbursements, known in France as TVA or *détaxe*. To qualify, non-EC residents must spend at least 2,000F in a single store. Refunds vary from 13% to 18.6% and are mailed to you by check or credited to your charge card. The major department stores have simplified the process with special détaxe desks where the *bordereaux* (export sales invoices) are prepared. Most high-profile shops with international clients have détaxe forms, but stores are not required to do this paperwork. If the discount is extremely important to you, ask if it is available before making your purchase. Invoices and bordereaux forms must be presented to French customs upon leaving the country. The items purchased should also be available for inspection.

Mailing Purchases Home Smaller shops are reluctant to mail purchases overseas, in case the goods get lost. Mailing goods yourself is possible—all French post offices sell self-sealing mailing boxes—but postage is costly. Remember that if you are claiming a Value Added Tax deduction (*see above*), you should have the goods with you when you leave the country.

Shopping Areas

Avenue Montaigne It won't cost you a sou to look in the showcase windows lining this gracious boulevard, home to are the honor roll of haute couture: Chanel, Dior, Nina Ricci, Christian Lacroix, Emanuel Ungaro, Céline, Valentino, Per Spook, Escada, Thierry Mugler, Hanae Mori. Yves St-Laurent's salon is located nearby, at 5 av. Marceau.

Left Bank Browsing through the antiques shops, bookstores, and art galleries of St-Germain-des-Prés, Paris's intellectual core, is window-shopping at its most varied. High fashion arrived here in the '70s, when YSL opened Rive Gauche boutiques for men and women on the place St-Sulpice. The area around rue de

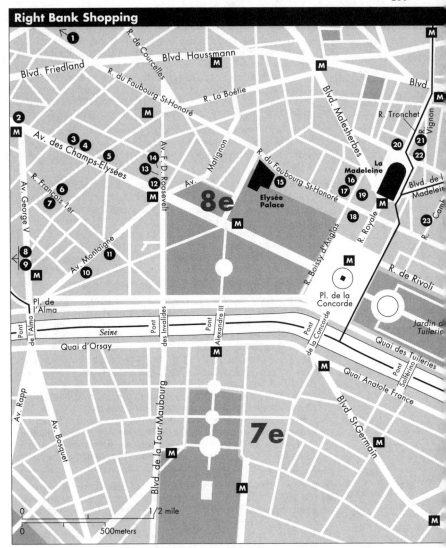

Right Bank Shopping

8e

7e

0 ———————————— 1/2 mile

0 ——————— 500meters

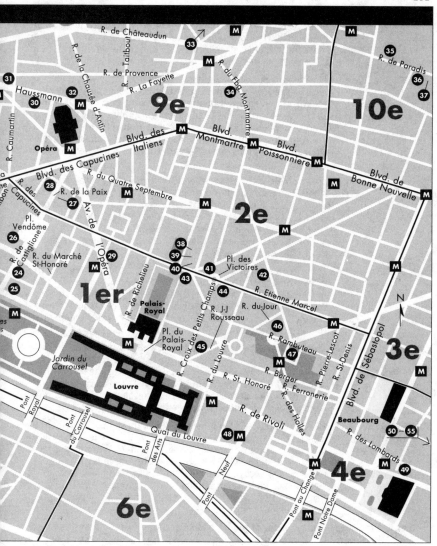

La Maison du
Chocolate, **1, 7**
La Samaritaine, **48**
La Tisanière, **36**
Le Monde
du Bagage, **40**
Lolita bis, **51**
Lolita Lempicka, **50**
Marché St-Pierre, **33**
Marks & Spencer, **30**
Mendès, **42**

Michel Swiss, **27, 29**
Natalys, **54**
Réciproque, **8**
Sonia Rykiel, **15**
Suzette Idier, **53**
Victoire, **41**
Virgin Megastore, **5**
W.H. Smith, **25**

Grenelle and rue Sts Pères is known for intimate designer boutiques (Sonia Rykiel, Claude Montana) and shoe shops (Maud Frizon, Charles Jourdan, Stéphane Kélian, and Carel). Among these fashionable storefronts you'll find **Le Mouton à Cinq Pattes,** selling designer clothes at bargain prices.

Le Marais The elegant mansions and tiny kosher-food stores that characterized the low-lying area between the Beaubourg and place des Vosges were overtaken by New Wave fashion and trendy gift shops in the 1980s. Avant-garde designers Azzedine Alaia, Lolita Lempicka, Issey Miyake, and Romeo Gigli have boutiques within a few blocks of the stately Picasso and Carnavalet museums. Shopping for offbeat decorative household items is excellent here.

Les Halles The narrow pedestrian streets on the former site of Paris's wholesale food market are lined with fast-food joints, sex shops, jeans outlets, and garish souvenir stands. Street artists claim the plaza in front of the Pompidou Center, and prostitutes rule the nearby rue St-Dénis. In the middle of the action, the **Forum des Halles**—a multilevel underground shopping mall— caters to a noisy teenage clientele.

Opéra to Madeleine Three major department stores—Au Printemps, Galeries Lafayette, and the British Marks & Spencer (*see* Department Stores, *below*)—are clustered behind Paris's ornate 19th-century opera house. The place de la Madeleine is home to two luxurious food stores, Fauchon and Hédiard, plus a 75-shop mall, Les Trois Quartiers.

Montparnasse The bohemian mecca for artists and writers in the '20s and '30s, Montparnasse is better known for bars and restaurants than shops. A recently built commercial center near the train station boasts a Galeries Lafayette outlet but is too charmless to attract many tourists. The rue d'Alésia on the southern fringe of Montparnasse is known for discount clothing shops.

Place Vendôme and the Rue de la Paix Here's where Holly Golightly would eat breakfast. The magnificent 17th-century place Vendôme, and the rue de la Paix leading north from Vendôme, have attracted the world's most elegant jewelers: Cartier, Boucheron, Buccellati, Van Cleef and Arpel, Répossi, Mellerio, Mauboussin, and Mikimoto. This super-posh pedestrian square was repaved with silver-gray granite in 1992, and is a must-see even for those with no intention of serious shopping here.

Rue du Faubourg St-Honoré The presence of the Elysée Palace and the official residences of the American and British ambassadors mean this chic shopping and residential street is well patrolled by the police. The Paris branch of Sotheby's and renowned antiques galleries such as Didier Aaron and Odermatt-Cazeau add artistic flavor. Boutiques include Hermès, Lanvin, Karl Lagerfeld, Reveillon Furs, Louis Feraud, and Christian Lacroix.

Trocadéro–Victor Hugo This aristocratic and conservative neighborhood in the 16th Arrondissement attracts predictably classic retailers, most of whom are centered around the place Victor Hugo. Bargain hunters know that the secondhand shops in this wealthy area offer exceptionally fine goods. **Réciproque** (123 rue de la Pompe) is one of the biggest and best, with three storefronts of nearly new designer fashions and gifts for both men and women.

Champs-Elysées Cafés and movie theaters keep the once-chic Champs-Elysées active 24 hours a day, but the invasion of exchange banks, car showrooms, and fast-food chains has lowered the tone. Four glitzy 20th-century arcade malls (Galérie du Lido, Le Rond-Point, Le Claridge, and Elysées 26) capture most of the retail action.

Department Stores

Paris's top department stores offer both convenience and chic. Some are open until 10 PM one weekday evening, and all six major stores listed below have multilingual guides, international welcome desks, détaxe offices, and restaurants.

Opéra Area **Au Printemps** (64 blvd. Haussmann, 9e, tel. 42–82–50–00) is a glittery three-store complex that includes "La Maison," for housewares and furniture; "La Mode," for ladies and children; and "Brummel," a six-floor emporium devoted to menswear. Flo Prestige, the celebrated Parisian brasserie chain, caters the in-house restaurants. *Open Mon.–Sat. 9:30–7.*

Galeries Lafayette (40 blvd. Haussmann, 9e, tel. 42–82–34–56) is equally elegant, and it spices up its Parisian aura with periodic exhibits featuring crafts from exotic countries. Be sure and look up while in the main store: The glorious Belle Epoque stained-glass dome is a Parisian landmark. Stylish private-label fashions (Briefing and Jodphur) offer good value. *Open Mon–Sat. 9:30–6:45. Another branch is at Centre Commercial Montparnasse, 15e, tel. 45–38–52–87.*

Marks & Spencer (35 blvd. Haussmann, 9e, tel. 47–42–42–91) is a British store chiefly noted for its moderately priced sportswear and its excellent English grocery and take-out food service. *Open Mon.–Sat. 9:30–7, Tues. 10–7.*

Louvre–Pont Neuf Area **La Samaritaine** (19 rue de la Monnaie, 1er, tel. 40–41–20–20), a sprawling four-store complex, is rapidly shedding its fusty, grandmotherly image. Especially good for kitchen supplies, housewares, and furniture, it's famous for its rooftop snackbar that offers a marvelous view of Notre Dame. *Open Mon.–Sat. 9:30–7, Thurs. 9:30–10.*

Hôtel de Ville/Marais area **Bazar de l'Hôtel de Ville** (52–64 rue de Rivoli, 4e, tel. 42–74–90–00), affectionately called BHV, houses an enormous basement hardware store that sells everything from doorknobs to cement mixers! The fashion offerings are minimal, but BHV is noteworthy for quality household goods, home decor materials, and office supplies. *Open Mon.–Sat. 9:30–7, Wed. 9:30–10.*

Left Bank **Au Bon Marché** (22 rue de Sèvres, 7e, tel. 44–39–80–00), founded in 1852, is chiefly known for linens, table settings, and high-quality furniture. La Grande Epicerie, a grocery store and deli here, is a gourmet's delight, and the sleek restaurant was designed by jet-set decorator Andrée Putman. The basement is a treasure trove for books, records, and arty gifts. *Open Mon.–Fri. 9:30–6:30, Sat. 9:30–7.*

Budget Most Parisians dash into their neighborhood **Monoprix** or **Prisunic** stores—with branches throughout the city—at least once a week. These handy shops stock inexpensive cosmetics, toothpaste, groceries, toys, typing paper, bathmats—and are better bets than the city's overpriced pharmacies. Clothing often represents good value: Noted designers like Elisabeth de

Senneville occasionally create special low-price lines for these stores.

Tati stores are known for bargain-basement prices, although goods are not always top quality. One of the largest is at 140 rue de Rennes, 6e.

Specialty Shops

Bags and Luggage **La Bagagerie** (41 rue du Four, 6e, tel. 45–48–85–88; also 11 rue Fbg. St-Honoré, 8e, tel. 47–42–79–13, and 12 rue Tronchet, 8e, tel. 42–65–03–40) features brightly colored bags and belts with youthful style and moderate prices.
Le Monde du Bagage (4 rue des Petits Champs, 2e, tel. 42–86–90–45) features crushable-but-chic, leather-trimmed canvas carry-alls and knapsacks.

English-Language Books An eternal Parisian pastime is strolling by the open-air book-stalls along the Seine.

W.H. Smith (248 rue de Rivoli, 1er, tel. 44–77–88–89) carries an excellent range of travel and language books, cookbooks, and fiction for adults and children. **Brentano's** (37 av. de l'Opéra, 2e, tel. 42–61–52–50) is another well-stocked general bookstore.
Village Voice (6 rue Princesse, 6e, tel. 46–33–36–47), known for its selection of contemporary authors, hosts regular literary readings.
Shakespeare and Company (5 rue de la Brulerie, 5e, no phone) is a sentimental Left Bank favorite, specializing in expatriate literature.
Tea and Tattered Pages (24 rue Mayet, 6e, tel. 40–65–94–35) sells cheap, secondhand English tomes.

Clothing (Women's)
Classic Chic You may stumble upon a sale or pick up an affordable bauble at the following:

Chanel (42 av. Montaigne, 8e, tel. 47–23–74–12, and 29 rue Cambon, 1er) has undergone a radical transformation under Karl Lagerfeld, who has added leather 'n' chains to classic suits and accessories.
Christian Dior (30 av. Montaigne, 8e, tel. 40–73–54–44) is a pearl gray palace selling ladies' and menswear, perfumes, jewelry, lingerie, furs, leather goods, porcelain, and gifts.
Givenchy Boutique (8 av. Georges V, 8e, tel. 47–20–81–31) presents slightly more affordable versions of the designer's elegant ready-to-wear.

Trendsetters **Jean-Paul Gaultier** (6 rue Vivienne, 2e, tel. 42–86–05–05), Madonna's clothier, specializes in outrageously attention-getting garments for men and women.
Lolita Lempicka (13 bis rue Pavée, 4e, tel. 42–74–50–48) serves up sharp suits and whimsical silk dresses. Lolita bis, a lower-priced junior line, is sold in a shop across the street.
Victoire (12 pl. des Victoires, 2e, tel. 42–61–09–02) is a discreet boutique that taps into new trends.

Chic and Casual **Agnes b.** (3 and 6 rue du Jour, 1er, tel. 45–08–49–89) has knitwear separates that are wardrobe basics for young Parisians.
Sonia Rykiel (175 blvd. St-Germain, 6e, tel. 49–54–60–60 and 79 rue Fbg. St-Honoré, 8e, tel. 42–65–20–81) singlehandedly made cotton velour into a recognized fashion statement.
Suzette Idier (9 rue de Birague, 4e, tel. 42–77–72–52) runs an

intimate, pocket-size boutique chockful of superb "little black dresses," elegant daywear, and all the latest Paris accessories.

Clothing (Men's) **Brummel** (Au Printemps department store, 64 blvd. Haussmann, 9e, tel. 42–82–50–00) is Paris's menswear fashion leader: six floors of suits, sportswear, underwear, coats, ties, and accessories in all price ranges.

Dominique Morlotti (25 rue St-Sulpice, 6e, tel. 43–54–89–89) offers an easygoing approach to menswear. Moderately priced designer separates have that debonair Parisian flair.

Kenzo (3 pl. des Victoires, 2e, tel. 40–39–72–03, and 17 blvd. Raspail, 7e, tel. 45–49–33–75) brings exuberant color and fantasy to his menswear collections. Move on if you're looking for a classic three-piece suit.

Clothing (Children) **Natalys** (32 rue St-Antoine, 4e, tel. 48–87–77–42, and 92 av. des Champs-Elysées, 8e, tel. 43–59–17–65) is a major French chain selling clothing, toys, furniture, and accessories for newborns and grade-school children.

Clothing (Resale) **Réciproque** (95, 101, and 123 rue de la Pompe, 16e, tel. 47–04–30–28 [women's] and 47–27–93–52 [menswear]) is Paris's most exclusive swap shop. Anyone hoping to sell designer cast-offs here must make an appointment weeks in advance (no appointment is necessary to buy). There's not much in the way of service or space, but savings are significant: 4,200 frs for a brocade Nina Ricci dinner suit, 300 frs for Camille Unglick shoes. Closed Mondays and from the end of July through August.

Catherine Baril (14–16–25 rue de la Tour, 16e, tel. 45–20–95–21), smaller than Réciproque and even more exclusive, has one-of-a-kind haute couture in addition to designer ready-to-wear.

Clothing (Discount) This street in the 14th Arrondissement is lined with stock
Rue d'Alésia shops selling last season's items at a discount. Be forewarned: Dressing rooms are not always provided.

SR Store (64 rue d'Alésia, 14e, tel. 43–95–06–13) slices 50% off last year's prices for Sonia Rykiel fashions for men, women, and children, and still manages to hold 20%–30% sales in January and July.

Cacharel Stock (114 rue d'Alésia, 14e, tel. 45–42–53–04) offers impressive savings for men's, women's, and children's clothing (plus even bigger markdown sales racks on the second floor).

Chipie Stock (82 rue d'Alésia, 14e, tel. 45–42–07–52) has jeans and sweaters for the whole family.

Dorothée bis Stock (74 rue d'Alésia, 14e, tel. 45–42–17–11) practices multiple markdowns on selected gowns and sportswear.

Central Paris **Mendès** (65 rue Montmartre, 2e, tel. 42–36–83–32), the manufacturer of Yves St-Laurent's Rive Gauche and Variations lines for women, sells last season's clothes at half price.

Le Mouton à Cing Pattes (8/10/18 rue St-Placide, 6e, tel. 45–48–86–26) is a refreshing eyesore with designer clothes crammed into bargain bins.

Fabrics **Marché Saint Pierre** (2 rue Charles Nodier, 18e, tel. 46–06–92–25), a raucous, four-floor warehouse in Montmartre, supplied designers like Kenzo in its salad days. It offers cheap end-of-bolt specials, upholstery, and wall fabrics.

Food   **Poilâne** (8 rue du Cherche-Midi, 6e, tel. 45–48–42–59) pro-
Bread   duces the most famous bread in the world. The chewy sour-
            dough loaves are sold in hundreds of Paris restaurants and
            shops and are airmailed to U.S. and Tokyo restaurants every
            day.

Candy and **A la Mère de Famille** (35 rue du Fbg. Montmarte, 9e, tel. 47–
Chocolate 70–83–69) is an enchanting shop specializing in old-fashioned
            bonbons, sugar candy, and more.
            Jadis et Gourmande (49 bis av. Franklin Roosevelt, 8e, tel. 42–
            25–06–04; 27 rue Boissy d'Anglas, 8e, tel. 42–65–23–23; and 88
            blvd. de Port-Royal, 5e, tel. 43–26–17–75) personalizes choco-
            late bars with names and initials.
            La Maison du Chocolat (52 rue François 1er, 8e, tel. 47–23–38–
            25) is heaven for cocoa purists. Take home chocolates, ice
            cream, and other treats, or meet a friend in the tearoom for sin-
            fully rich hot chocolate and chocolate-mousse *frappés* (cold
            drinks). Take-out only at 8 rue de la Madeleine, 9e, tel. 47–42–
            86–52 and 225 rue Fbg. St-Honoré, 8e, tel. 42–27–39–44.

Gourmet Shops **Fauchon** (26–28–30 pl. de la Madeleine, 8e, tel. 47–42–60–11)
            and **Hédiard** (21 pl. de la Madeleine, 8e, tel. 42–66–44–36) sell
            prestigious house brands of paté, mustard, honey, and jellies,
            plus sumptuous produce from around the world. The **Galeries
            Lafayette Gourmet shop** (40 blvd. Haussmann, 9e, tel. 42–82–
            34–56) is equally chic, but less intimidating. The Grande
            Epicerie, on the ground floor of **Au Bon Marché** (22 rue de Sè-
            vres, 7e, tel. 44–39–80–00), has an excellent array of fine
            French foodstuffs.

Jewelry Most of the big names are based near the place Vendôme. De-
            signer costume and semiprecious jewelry is sold in most of the
            av. Montaigne and rue du Faubourg St-Honoré boutiques.

            Cartier (7 and 23 pl. Vendôme, 1er, tel. 42–61–55–55) has two
            less formal "Les Must" boutiques, which carry lighters, pens,
            watches, key-chains, and other gift items.

Costume **Agatha** (97 rue de Rennes, 6e, tel. 45–48–81–30; 45 rue Bona-
            parte, 6e, tel. 46–33–20–00; and 12–14 av. Champs-Elysées,
            8e, tel. 43–59–68–68) has trendy but moderately priced sea-
            sonal collections.

Lingerie **Chantal Thomass** (1 rue Vivienne, 1er, tel. 40–15–02–36) sets
            the right mood for her trademark black-lace hosiery, satin cor-
            sets, and feather-trimmed negligees in this plush, pink velvet
            boutique that resembles a Victorian bordello.
            Natari (7 pl. Vendôme, 1er, tel. 42–96–22–94) seduces all, with
            selections for every pocketbook. Movie-star lingerie and pei-
            gnoir sets come in pure silk or washable synthetic versions.

Music/Records **FNAC** (Forum des Halles, 1er, tel. 40–41–40–00; 26 av. Ternes,
            17e, tel. 44–09–18–00; and 136 rue de Rennes, 6e, tel. 49–54–
            30–00) is a high-profile French chain selling music; photo, TV,
            and audio equipment; and books.
            Virgin Megastore (52–60 av. des Champs-Elysées, 8e, tel. 40–
            74–06–48) has acres of CDs and tapes—everything from classic
            to rap—plus a book division.

Perfumes **Annick Goutal** (14 rue de Castiglione, 1er, tel. 42–60–52–82) is
            a gilt-and-ivory cream puff selling this exclusive signature per-
            fume line.
            Guerlain (68 av. des Champs Elysées, 8e, tel. 47–89–71–84,
            and 47 rue Bonaparte, 6e, tel. 43–26–71–19) boutiques are the

only authorized Paris outlets for legendary perfumes like Shalimar, Jicky, Vol de Nuit, Mitsouko, and Chamade.

Discount **Michel Swiss** (16 rue de la Paix, 2nd fl., 2e, tel. 42–61–61–11, and 24 av. de l'Opéra, 1er, tel. 47–03–49–11) offers large savings on perfumes and fashion accessories. Service is not helpful; know what you want before flagging a salesperson.

Scarves **Hermès** (24 rue Fbg. St-Honoré, 8e, tel. 40–17–47–17). These all-silk *carrés* are legendary not only for their brilliant colors and intimate designs, but also for their sky-high prices. But scarves are half-price at the annual October sale (when the faithful line up the night before).
Souleiado (78 rue de Seine, 6e, tel. 43–54–62–25, and 83 av. Paul Doumer, 16e, tel. 42–24–99–34) uses traditional Provençal patterns for cotton scarves, quilted bags, and linens.

Stationery **Marie Papier** (26 rue Vavin, 6e, tel. 43–26–46–44) sells an extraordinary variety of colored writing paper and notebooks.

Tableware **Au Bain Marie** (8 rue Boissy d'Anglas, 8e, tel. 42–66–59–74) is an enchanted kingdom for amateur and professional cooks. Come here for crockery, porcelain, and a world-class collection of cookbooks.
Geneviève Lethu (28 rue St-Antoine, 4e, tel. 42–74–21–25) is a homey, casual shop selling tea services, potpourri mixtures, and table linens for your real or imagined country house.

Discount The **rue de Paradis** in the 10th Arrondissement is lined with china and crystal showrooms. Shoppers with style numbers, pocket calculators, and comparison prices from home often profit from serious savings on fine Limoges porcelain.

La Tisanière (21 rue de Paradis, 10e, tel. 47–70–22–80) sells china "seconds."
Arts-Céramiques (15 rue de Paradis, 10e, tel. 48–24–83–70) has special promotional sales in its back room.

Silver **Jean-Pierre de Castro** (17 rue des Francs-Bourgeois, 4e, tel. 42–72–04–00) is a dusty secondhand shop selling old-fashioned silver settings by the kilo-weight. The inexpensive bracelets made of Victorian silver spoons and forks make marvelous gifts.

Toys **Le Monde en Marche** (34 rue Dauphine, 6e, tel. 43–26–66–53) specializes in unusual, old-fashioned wooden toys.

Shopping Arcades

The various shopping arcades, or *passages*, scattered around Paris offer a pleasant shopping alternative. Especially noteworthy are those dating back to the 19th century, most of which have been splendidly restored. Their arching glass roofs, mosaic or marble flooring, and brass lamps are now set off to full advantage.

Most arcades are conveniently located in the central 1st and 2nd arrondissements on the Right Bank. A favorite is **Galerie Vivienne** (4 rue des Petits-Champs, 2e) between the Stock Exchange (Bourse) and the Palais-Royal. It has a range of interesting shops and an excellent tearoom and is home to **Cave Legrand,** a quality wine shop. **Galerie Véro-Dodat** (19 rue Jean-Jacques Rousseau, 1er) has painted ceilings and slender copper pillars. You'll find an arcade called **Passage des Pavillons** at 6 rue de Beaujolais, 1er, near the Palais-Royal gardens; and **Passage des Princes** at 97 rue de Richelieu, 2e. **Passage des Panoramas** (11 blvd. Montmartre, 2e) is the oldest of them all, opened in 1800. Across the Grands Boulevards is **Passage Jouffroy** (12 blvd. Montmartre, 9e), with shops selling toys, perfumes, original cosmetics, and dried flowers: Try **Pain d'Epices** (no. 29) and **Au Bonheur des Dames** (no. 39).

Markets

Food Markets Paris's open-air food markets are among the city's most colorful attractions. Every *quartier* (district) has one, although many are open only a few days each week. Sunday morning, till 1 PM, is usually a good time to go; Monday is the day these markets are likely to be closed. The local markets usually concentrate on food, but they always have a few brightly colored flower stalls. The variety of cheeses is astounding.

Many of the better-known markets are located in areas you'd visit for sightseeing; good choices are on **rue de Buci**, 6e (open daily); **rue Mouffetard**, 5e; and **rue Lepic** in Montmartre (the latter two best on weekends). The **Marché d'Aligre** (open Sat., Sun., and Mon. mornings) is a bit farther out, beyond the Bastille on rue d'Aligre in the 12th Arrondissement, but you won't see many tourists in this less affluent area of town, and Parisians from all over the city know it and love it. The prices come tumbling down as the morning draws to a close.

Flower and Bird Markets Paris's main flower market is located right in the heart of the city on Ile de la Cité, between Notre Dame and the Palais de Justice. It's open every day except Sunday, when a bird market takes its place, and Monday, when it's closed. Birds and a host of other animals are also sold in the shops and stalls on the quai de la Mégisserie on the Right Bank. Other colorful flower markets are held beside the Madeleine church, 8e, on place des Ternes, 17e, down the road from the Arc de Triomphe. Both are open daily except Monday.

The Stamp Market Philatelists should head for Paris's unique stamp market on avenue Marigny and avenue Gabriel, overlooking the gardens at the bottom of the Champs-Elysées. *Open Thurs., Sat., Sun., and public holidays.*

Flea Markets The **Marché aux Puces** on Paris's northern boundary (Métro: Porte de Clignancourt) still attracts the crowds, but its once unbeatable prices are now a feature of the past. This century-old labyrinth of alleyways packed with antiques dealers' booths and junk stalls now spreads for over a square mile. But be warned—if there's one place in Paris where you need to know how to barter, this is it! For lunch, stop for mussels and fries in one of the rough-and-ready cafés. *Open Sat., Sun., and Mon.*

There are other, less impressive flea markets on the southern and eastern slopes of the city—at **porte de Montreuil** and **porte de Vanves**—but they have a depressing amount of real junk and are best avoided, except by obsessive bargain hunters.

5 Where to Eat on a Budget

By Robert Noah

Robert Noah is the founder of Paris en Cuisine, a company that offers food-related tours in Paris and elsewhere in France, and the editor of its English-language newsletter on French food.

Paris's restaurants are notorious for their sky-high prices as well as their wonderful food. Where else can you spend almost $40 for a bowl of chicken soup? But less expensive meals in Paris are not only possible, they're often preferable. The memory of a crusty cassoulet and carafe of wine from a cozy neighborhood spot may linger long after the rarified flavors of haute cuisine have faded. These days, even Parisians themselves, perhaps reacting to a sluggish economy and uncertain times, are filling less expensive restaurants in record numbers, and a trend toward simpler, more budget-conscious bistros shows no sign of abating. The reviews that follow provide a selection of affordable dining places—from new and trendy offshoots of expensive, star-chef properties to aging corner restaurants faithfully serving regulars for half a century. In addition, we have included a fair number of wine bars, café-type spots, and other establishments where a quick snack or one-course meal are possible. Because space is at a premium, our selection is limited to places with primarily French rather than ethnic dishes.

Restaurant Types What's the difference between a bistro and a brasserie? Can you order food at a café? Do you go to a restaurant for just a snack? The following definitions should help.

A **restaurant** traditionally serves a three-course (first, main, and dessert) meal at both lunch and dinner. Don't expect to grab a quick snack. In general, restaurants are what you choose when you want a complete meal and when you have the time to linger over it. Wine is typically drunk with restaurant meals. Hours are fairly consistent; *see* Mealtimes, *below*.

Many say **bistros** served the world's first fast food. After the fall of Napoléon, the Russian soldiers who occupied Paris were known to bang on zinc-topped café bars, crying "bistrot"—"hurry" in Russian. In the past, bistros were simple places with minimum decor and service. Although many nowadays are quite upscale, with beautiful interiors and chic clientele, most remain simple establishments serving straightforward, frequently gutsy cooking, with plenty of variety meats and long-simmered dishes such as *pot-au-feu* and veal *blanquette*.

Brasseries—ideal places for quick, one-dish meals—originated when Alsatians fleeing German occupiers after the Franco-Prussian War came to Paris and opened restaurants serving specialties from home. Pork-based dishes, *choucroute* or *choueroute garni* (sauerkraut and sausages), and beer (brasserie also means brewery) were—and still are—mainstays here. The typical brasserie is convivial and keeps late hours. Some are open 24 hours—a good thing to know, since many restaurants stop serving at 10:30 PM.

Like bistros and brasseries, **cafés** come in confusing variety. Usually informal neighborhood hangouts, cafés may also be veritable showplaces attracting chic, well-heeled crowds. At most cafés, regulars congregate at the bar, where coffee and drinks are cheaper than at tables. At lunch, tables are set and a limited menu is served. Sandwiches, usually with *jambon* (ham), *fromage* (cheese, often Gruyere or Camembert), or *mixte* (ham and cheese) are served throughout the day. Cafés are for lingering, for people-watching, and for daydreaming.

Wine bars, or *bistrots à vins*, are a newer phenomenon. These informal places serve very limited menus, often no more than open-faced sandwiches (*tartines*) and selections of cheeses and cold cuts (*charcuterie*). Owners concentrate on their wine lists, which often include less well known, regional selections, many of them available by the glass. Like today's bistros and brasseries, some wine bars are very fancy indeed, with costly wine lists and full menus. Most remain friendly and unassuming, good places for sampling wines you might otherwise never try.

If you're not very hungry or want to eat at an odd hour, consider one of Paris's many **charcuteries.** Today's charcuterie is virtually a restaurant (though without waiter service), and the pâtés and meat products that once filled the shelves have moved over to make room for prepared salads, quiches, breads, and desserts. Choose what appeals to you most and take it to one of the city's green spaces for your own *déjeuner sur l'herbe*. Or you can put together your picnic by visiting a number of shops, including **boulangeries** (bakeries), **pâtisseries** (pastry shops), and **fromageries** (cheese shops).

Mealtimes Generally, Paris restaurants are open from noon to about 2, and from 7:30 or 8 to 10 or 10:30. Brasseries have longer hours and often serve all day and late into the evening; some are open 24 hours. The iconoclastic wine bars do as they want, frequently serving hot food only through lunch and cold assortments of charcuterie and cheese until a late afternoon or early evening close.

We have included days closed in all our listings, including yearly vacations when known. Assume a restaurant is open seven days a week, year-round, unless otherwise indicated. Surpris-

We can wire money to every major city in Europe almost as fast as you can say, "Zut alors! J'ai perdu mes valises".

How fast? We can send money in 10 minutes or less, to 13,500 locations in over 68 countries worldwide. That's faster than any other international money transfer service. And when you're *sans* luggage, every minute counts.

MoneyGram from American Express® is available throughout Europe. For more information please contact your local American Express Travel Service Office or call: 44-71-839-7541 in England; 33-1-47777000 in France; or 49-69-21050 in Germany. In the U.S. call 1-800-MONEYGRAM.

MoneyGram™

INTERNATIONAL MONEY TRANSFERS.

Ten-minute delivery subject to local agent hours of operation. Local send/receive facilities may also vary. ©1993 First Data Corporation.

519 M.P.H.

190 M.P.H.

75 M.P.H.

0 M.P.H.

WE LET YOU SEE EUROPE AT YOUR OWN PACE.

Regardless of your personal speed limits, Rail Europe offers everything to get you over, around and through anywhere you want in Europe. For more information, call your travel agent or **1-800-4-EURAIL**.

ingly, many prestigious restaurants close on Saturday as well as Sunday. July and August are the most common months for annual closings, but Paris in August is no longer the wasteland it used to be, and many restaurants now close for a few weeks in winter instead. The past couple of years have been hard for many Paris restaurants, and management may hesitate to announce vacation dates too far in advance or suddenly decide not to close after all. We suggest you call ahead.

Because most restaurants are open for only a few set hours for lunch and dinner, and because meals are much longer affairs here than they are in the United States, we strongly advise you to make reservations. Most wine bars do not take reservations; reservations are also unnecessary for brasserie and café meals at odd hours. In the reviews below, we have indicated where reservations are advised or required (and when booking weeks or months in advance is necessary), and where reservations are not accepted. If you want nonsmoking, make this clear when you reserve. Though the law requires all restaurants to provide a nonsmoking area, this is sometimes limited to a very few tables.

Menus All establishments must post their menus outside, so study them carefully before deciding to enter. Most restaurants offer two basic types of menu: à la carte and fixed price (prix fixe, or *un menu*). The prix-fixe menu will usually offer the best value, though choices are limited. Most menus begin with a first-course section, often subdivided into cold and hot starters, followed by fish and poultry, then meat; it's rare today that anyone orders something from all three. However, outside of brasseries, wine bars, and other simple places, it's inappropriate to order just one dish, as you'll understand when you see the waiter's expression. In general, consider the season when ordering. Daily specials are usually based on what's freshest in the market that day.

Following are a number of menu items that appear frequently on French menus and throughout the reviews that follow. *See also* our Menu Guide at the end of the book for additional guidance.

bavarois—usually, a dessert of whipped cream, custard, and gelatin; it can also be savory, made with vegetables or fish.
blanquette—a stew—often veal—with a white-sauce base.
bouef à la Bourguignonne—a beef stew cooked in red wine, with onions, mushrooms, and bacon.
boeuf à la ficelle—pieces of beef tied with string and simmered in stock.
bouef à la mode—a refined beef stew.
boudin blanc—sausage made with white meat.
boudin noir—sausage made with pig's blood.
brandade—creamy cod purée, sometimes incorporating potato purée and garlic.
charcuterie—a selection of cold, pork-based products such as sausages, pâtés, and terrines.
choucroute—hearty dish of sauerkraut, usually accompanied by sausage, pork, and sometimes duck; also called *choucroute garnie*.
clafoutis—a hearty, flanlike tart with a base of seasonal fruit.
confit—meat (often duck), cooked in fat and preserved.
coq au vin—a classic preparation of chicken cooked in red wine and garnished with pearl onions, mushrooms, and bacon.

daube—beef stew.

fondant—traditionally, a shiny glaze used to decorate cakes and other desserts. Today, the word has a number of meanings, including flourless cake.

fricassée—any of several kinds of stews and braised dishes.

langoustine—a type of crustacean, similar to crawfish but smaller.

mille-feuille—a classic dessert composed of alternate layers of puff pastry and pastry cream (Napoléon in English).

navarin—a kind of stew, frequently made with lamb.

pastilla—originally a flaky pastry used in Moroccan cuisine. Today's French chefs use it to encase a variety of foods.

profiterole—a small cream puff with a savory or sweet filling (often ice cream).

quenelle—a dumpling, usually of fish or poultry.

ragoût—a kind of stew.

rillettes—potted, minced meat, often pork or goose.

sabayon—traditionally, an egg-and-wine-based dessert; also a savory preparation based on an egg-and-wine mixture.

Wine The wine that suits your meal is the wine you like. The traditional rule of white with fish and red with meat no longer applies. If the restaurant has a *sommelier*, let him help you. Most sommeliers are knowledgeable about their lists, and will suggest what is appropriate after you've made your tastes and budget known. In addition to the wine list, informal restaurants will have a *vin de la maison* (house wine) that is less expensive. Simpler spots will have wines *en carafe* or *en pichet*. Except for wine bars and brasseries, most restaurants do not sell wine by the glass. If you'd like something before the meal, consider ordering your wine for the meal ahead of time, or sample a typical French *apéritif*.

Dress Code Perhaps surprisingly, casual dress is acceptable at all but the fanciest restaurants. Use your judgment, of course, and remember that casual to the French does not mean without style. When in doubt, leave the blue jeans behind. In the reviews below, we have indicated where a jacket and tie are advised or required, and where casual attire is appropriate.

Prices The restaurants reviewed below are grouped in three price ranges: Under 250F, Under 175F, and Under 100F. Generally these prices are for a first, main, and cheese or dessert course. Sometimes, however, our selections are over budget if you order à la carte; in these cases you must order the prix-fixe menu to stay within our price category. This is indicated when appropriate. A few of our selections are affordable only at lunch, and usually with a prix-fixe menu only; this is also indicated in the review. All prices include tax and tip (*service compris* or *prix nets*). No additional tip is expected, though pocket change left on the table in simple places, or an additional 5% of the bill in better restaurants, is appreciated.

The following credit card abbreviations are used: AE, American Express; DC, Diners Club; MC, MasterCard; and V, Visa.

Highly recommended restaurants are indicated by a ★.

1st Arrondissement (Louvre)
See Right Bank Dining map

Under 250F **Gaya.** Come here for seafood in all its guises, from marinated anchovies to fish soup—much of it with a Mediterranean accent. The colorful Portuguese azulejos on the ground floor are delightful; upstairs is less attractive. *17 rue Duphot, Métro: Madeleine, tel. 42–60–43–03. Reservations advised. Dress: casual. AE, DC, MC, V. Closed Sun. and Mon.*

★ **Pharamond.** A Halles landmark since its founding in 1870. No one would dare touch the polychrome tiles and mosaics, mirrors, and handsome woodwork, or the classic bistro menu with Norman specialties such as scallops in cider, grilled meats, *tripes à la mode de Caen,* and souffléed potatoes. *24 rue de la Grande Truanderie, Métro: Les Halles, tel. 42–33–06–72. Reservations advised. Dress: casual. AE, DC, MC, V. Closed Sun., Mon. lunch, and mid-July–mid-Aug.*

Under 175F **Le Petit Bourbon.** The cheaper of this charming restaurant's
★ two fixed-price menus is in this price category. On both menus, first and main courses such as mushroom terrine with shellfish sauce, stuffed rabbit medallions, and chocolate soup transcend the ordinary. The intimate dining room has exposed stone walls, cream colors, and pretty paintings of the Midi region. *15 rue du Roule, Métro: Louvre, tel. 40–26–08–93. Reservations advised. Dress: casual. MC, V. Closed Sun., Mon.*

Le Petit Machon. This is an authentic version of the uniquely Lyonnais bistro, the *machon.* Bring a big appetite, for the long menu offers such robust choices as stuffed pig's foot, duck terrine, braised ham shank, and veal flank with shallots. Wines are overpriced, so stick to a *pichet* of the Coteaux du Lyonnais or Beaujolais. Arrive early or book well in advance: The Machon gets very busy after 9 PM. *158 rue St-Honoré, Métro: Louvre, tel. 42–60–23–37. Reservations advised. Dress: casual. AE, DC, MC, V. Closed Sun.*

Les Cartes Postales. In this small, plain restaurant near the Opéra, the Japanese chef/owner adds a touch of the East to his very French cuisine for such winning combinations as crab *galette* with grapefruit vinaigrette, hot foie gras with spices, and roast duck fillet with orange and ginger. The cheapest menu keeps this within budget; à la carte is more expensive. Too bad the service is not more agreeable. *7 rue Gomboust, Métro: Pyramides, tel. 42–61–02–93. Reservations advised. Dress: casual. MC, V. Closed Sat. lunch, Sun.*

Under 100F **A La Cloche des Halles.** Get here by 12:30 PM if you want to lunch at this small and popular wine bar in the Les Halles neighborhood. Forgive the tacky decor and enjoy quiche (the only hot dish) and the assortments of high-quality cheeses and charcuterie. Wines, served by the glass or bottle, include some good Beaujolais. The simple menu is served until closing at 10 PM. *28 rue Coquillière, Métro: Les Halles, tel. 42–36–93–89. No reservations. Dress: casual. No credit cards. Closed Sun.*

★ **Juvenile's.** The little brother of the fashionable Willi's Wine Bar, just around the corner, is a friendly, unpretentious place. It serves various hot dishes and some copious salads, including the house chicken salad, which makes an excellent light meal when accompanied by lentils or an assortment of tapas. The wine list is impressive and the waitstaff, young and agreeable. *47 rue de Richelieu, Métro: Palais-Royal, tel. 42–97–46–49. Reservations advised. Dress: casual. MC, V. Closed Sun.*

Right Bank Dining

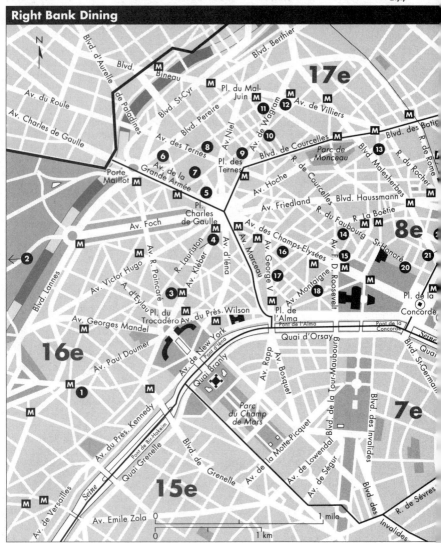

A. Beauvilliers, **28**	Bistrot de l'Etoile Lauriston, **4**	Chez Jenny, **48**	La Butte Chaillot, **3**
A La Cloche des Halles, **40**	Bistrot des Deux Théâtres, **27**	Chez Philippe/ Pyrénées-Cévennes, **47**	La Ferme St. Hubert, **21**
A La Courtille, **45**	Bofinger, **58**	Fauchon Cafeteria, **25**	La Fermette Marbeuf, **17**
Al Goldenberg, **10**	Brasserie Flo, **44**	Fouquet's Café, **57**	La Galoche d'Aurillac, **56**
Astier, **49**	Café Flo, **22**	Gaya, **24**	La Niçoise, **8**
Aux Négotiants, **29**	Café Runtz, **33**	Jacques Mélac, **52**	La Rôtisserie d'Armaillé, **7**
Baracane, **59**	Chartier, **31**	Julien, **43**	La Table d'Anvers, **30**
Benoît, **62**	Chez Georges, **6**	Juvenile's, **35**	
Berry's, **13**	Chez Géraud, **1**	La Boutique à Sandwiches, **14**	

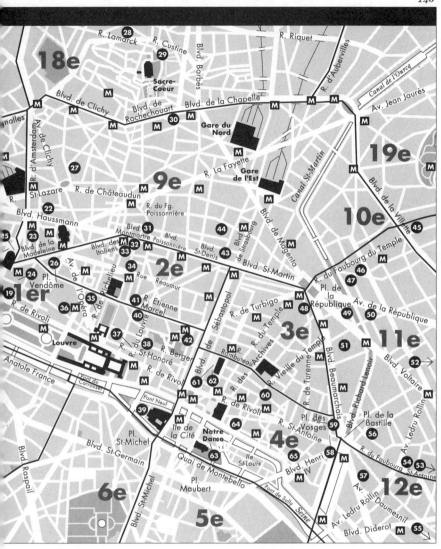

La Taverne
Henri IV, **39**

L'Auberge du
Bonheur, **2**

Le Bistrot d'a Côté
Faubert, **11**

Le Bistrot du
17ème, **12**

Le Clown Bar, **51**

Le Drouot, **32**

Le Graindorge, **5**

Le Grizzli, **61**

Le Maraîcher, **65**

Le Passage, **54**

Le Petit Bourbon, **38**

Le Petit Machon, **37**

Le Roi du
Pot-au-Feu, **23**

Le Rubis, **36**

Le Vaudeville, **34**

Le Vieux Bistrot, **63**

Le Villaret, **50**

Les Amognes, **53**

Les Cartes
Postales, **26**

Les Fernandises, **46**

Lescure, **19**

L'Espace, **20**

L'Huitrier, **9**

Lina's, **41**

L'Oulette, **55**

Miravile, **60**

Pharamond, **42**

Savy, **18**

Sébillon, **16**

Trumilou, **64**

Yvan, **15**

Left Bank Dining

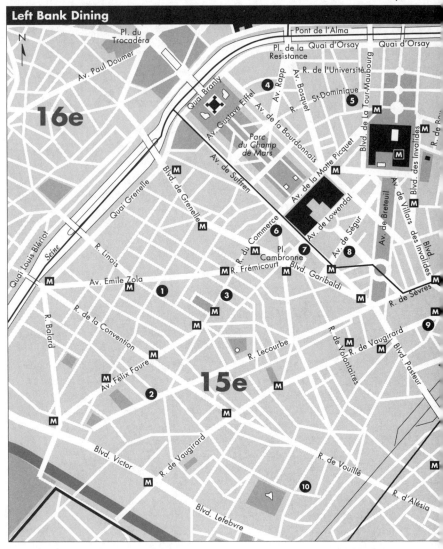

Au Pied de Fouet, **14**
Au Sauvignon, **23**
Aux Charpentiers, **30**
Aux Fins
Gourmets, **11**
Bistrot de la Gare, **16**
Campagne et
Provence, **35**
Chez Germaine, **13**

Chez Pento, **39**
Chez René, **36**
Chez Toutoune, **34**
Contre-Allée, **21**
Entre-Siècle, **7**
La Cagouille, **17**
La Coupole, **19**
La Rôtisserie
d'En Face, **31**

L'Armoise, **1**
L'Arpège, **12**
Le Barrail, **9**
Le Bistrot de
Breteuil, **8**
Le Bistrot
du Dôme, **20**
Le Café du
Commerce, **3**

Le Clos Morillons, **10**
Le Pavillon
Montsouris, **22**
Le Petit Navire, **38**
Le Petit Plat, **33**
Le Petit St-Benoît, **25**
Le Petit Zinc, **27**
Le Sancerre, **4**
Le Télégraphe, **15**
Le Vin des Rues, **18**

L'Ecaille de PCB, **29**
Lipp, **24**
Moissonnier, **37**
Morot-Gaudry, **6**
Pierre Vedal, **2**
Polidor, **32**
Restaurant des
Beaux-Arts, **26**
Thoumieux, **5**
Vagenende, **28**

Le Rubis. This humble, neighborhood wine bar enjoys tremendous popularity with everyone from executives to laborers. One or two hearty plats du jour, such as *petit salé* (salted, slow-cooked pork ribs) with lentils and boudin noir plus omelets, cheeses, and charcuterie assortments, make up the menu here. There's an eclectic selection of adequate wines by the glass or bottle. *10 rue du Marché St-Honoré, Métro: Tuileries, tel. 42–61–03–34. No reservations. Dress: casual. No credit cards. Closed Sat. eve., Sun., and mid-Aug.*

Lescure. Hidden away down short rue Mondovi next to place de la Concorde, this very old restaurant with a largely foreign clientele offers good bistro cuisine: pâté *en croûte*, poached haddock, beef bourguignon. The tiny, rustic dining room is cozy; a few tables are set on the sidewalk in nice weather. *7 rue de Mondovi, Métro: Concorde, tel. 42–60–18–91. MC, V. Closed Sat. eve., Sun., and Aug.*

La Taverne Henri IV. This informal wine bar near the Pont Neuf, on the tip of the Ile de la Cîté, is an excellent choice for a quick lunch or snack. No full meals are served, but a selection of open-faced sandwiches on Poilâne bread (from the celebrated bakery), cheese and charcuterie plates, and varied wines by the glass or bottle make for a satisfying meal. *13 pl. du Pont Neuf, Métro: Pont Neuf, tel. 43–54–27–90. No reservations. Dress: casual. No credit cards. Closed Sat., Sun., and Aug.*

2nd Arrondissement (Stock Exchange)
See Right Bank Dining map

Under 250F **Le Vaudeville.** Like the other six Parisian brasseries of Jean-Paul Bucher, the Vaudeville has history and a good-looking clientele (many of them from the stock exchange across the street). Go for the fixed-price lunch menu or the after-11 PM Faim de Nuit menu, cheaper still. Shellfish, house smoked salmon, and desserts are particularly fine. You can enjoy the handsome 1930s decor and joyful din until 2 AM daily. *29 rue Vivienne, Métro: Bourse, tel. 40–20–04–62. Reservations advised. Dress: casual. AE, DC, MC, V.*

Under 175F **Café Runtz.** Next to the Salle Favart in a neighborhood once
★ full of theaters, this friendly bistro with rich *boiseries* (woodwork) and photos of customers from the entertainment industry serves up an Alsatian feel and cuisine. Tasty, hearty dishes include Gruyère salad, onion tart, choucroute, and fresh fruit tarts. Order a *pichet* of Riesling or other Alsatian wine. *16 rue Favart, Métro: Richelieu-Drouot, tel. 42–96–69–86. Reservations advised. Dress: casual. AE, MC, V. Closed weekends and Aug.*

Under 100F **Le Drouot.** Forever popular with bachelors on a budget, students, and tourists, this gigantic restaurant in a building near the famous Drouot auction house has a very long menu of classic French dishes. You can get everything from celery *rémoulade* (a tart, mayonnaise-based sauce) to pâté, roast veal with spinach, and ice cream. *103 rue de Richelieu, Métro: Richelieu-Drouot, tel. 47–42–69–06. Reservations advised. Dress: Casual. No credit cards.*

Lina's. The immediate popularity of this sandwich boutique spawned four more in Paris, including one in the Galeries Lafayette department store. The original, near the place des Victoires, prepares some 20 different sandwiches, including smoked salmon, turkey with bacon, and shrimp/avocado. A sandwich, brownie or piece of pecan pie, and a beer make a meal. You must stand to eat, or order take-out for a picnic. Open 9 AM–6 PM. *50 rue Etienne Marcel, Métro: Halles, tel. 42-21-16-14. No reservations. MC, V. Closed Sun.*

3rd Arrondissement (Le Marais/Beaubourg)
See Right Bank Dining map

Inexpensive **Chez Jenny.** Order the filling choucroute Jenny and a carafe of
★ Alsatian wine, then sit back and watch the bustle at this large Alsatian brasserie decorated with museum-quality marquetry and woodwork. Waitresses in regional costume wend their way through many salons on two levels, serving forth hearty fare. Though the clientele is not the chic crowd of some other brasseries, everyone's having just as much fun. *39 blvd. du Temple, Métro: République, tel. 42-74-75-75. Reservations advised. Dress: casual. AE, DC, MC, V.*

4th Arrondissement (Le Marais/Ile St-Louis)
See Right Bank Dining map

Under 250F **Bofinger.** Founded in 1864, this may be Paris's oldest brasserie. It's also one of the prettiest, with its authentic Belle Epoque decor, white linen tablecloths, black leather banquettes, and beautiful stained-glass dome (ask to be seated on the main floor). The menu offers excellent shellfish and choucroute (including a lighter version with fish), and there's a large selection of Alsatian beers. Only steps from the place de la Bastille, and open until 1 AM, Bofinger is a good post-opera rendezvous. *5 rue de la Bastille, Métro: Bastille, tel. 42-27-87-82. Reservations advised. Dress: casual. AE, DC, MC, V.*

★ **Le Grizzli.** It's said this turn-of-the-century bistro was one of the last to have dancing bears as entertainment—thus the name. Today's owner gets many of his ingredients—especially the wonderful ham and cheeses—from his native Auvergne. Several dishes are cooked on hot slate, including salmon and lamb. There's an interesting selection of wines from Southwest France. *7 rue St. Martin, Métro: Châtelet, tel. 48-87-77-56. Reservations advised. Dress: casual. MC, V. Closed Sun., Mon. lunch.*

Le Maraîcher. With its exposed stone walls and wood beams, this intimate little restaurant on a quiet street in the Marais is very *vieux Paris*. The young owner worked at the renowned Lucas-Carton, which may account for the table settings and service, which are surprisingly refined considering the reasonable prices. Freshness and seasonality are hallmarks of such dishes as sweetbreads with ginger, rabbit medallions with cabbage, and fresh fig crêpes. *5 rue Beautreillis, Métro: Sully-Morland, tel. 42-71-42-49. Reservations advised. Dress: casual. MC, V. Closed Sat. lunch, Sun., late July-early Aug.*

Le Vieux Bistrot. Forgive the corny name and touristy location next to Notre Dame. This really *is* generations old, and its menu is full of bistro classics such as blanquette of veal, beef fillet with marrow, and giant éclairs. Decor is nondescript, but the frequently fancy crowd doesn't seem to notice. *14 rue du Cloître-Notre-Dame, Métro: Hôtel de Ville, tel. 43-54-18-95. Reservations advised. Dress: casual. MC, V.*

★ **Miravile.** This latest Miravile—the third for successful young owners Gilles and Muriel Epié—has California-style decor and a Provençal-inspired menu. Mr. Epié's celery *remoulade* with foie gras, and chocolate mille-feuille exemplify his full-flavored style. The restaurant is quite expensive if you order à la carte, but the special lunch menu is within our price range. This spot is popular with staff members from the adjacent Hôtel de Ville (city hall). *72 quai de l'Hôtel de Ville, Métro: Pont-Marie, tel. 42–74–72–22. Reservations advised. Dress: casual. MC, V. Closed Sat. lunch, Sun.*

Under 100F
★

Baracane. This is one of the best values in the Marais district. The owner oversees the menu, full of the robust specialties of his native Southwest France, including rabbit confit, braised oxtail with foie gras, and pear poached in wine and cassis. A reasonable dinner menu and cheaper menu at lunch keep the Baracane solidly within this price range. *38 rue des Tournelles, Métro: Bastille, tel. 42–71–43–33. Reservations advised. Dress: casual. MC, V. Closed Sat. lunch, Sun.*

Trumilou. Popular with students, artist types, and others on a budget, the Trumilou serves unremarkable bistro cuisine such as leg of lamb and apple tart. But the homely nondecor is somehow homey, and the friendly staff remains friendly despite the crowd. The location facing the Seine and the Ile St-Louis is especially pleasant in nice weather, when you can sit on a narrow terrace under the trees. *84 quai de l'Hôtel de Ville, Métro: Pont-Marie, tel. 42–77–63–98. Reservations accepted. Dress: casual. MC, V. Closed Mon.*

5th Arrondissement (Latin Quarter)
See Left Bank Dining map

Under 175F

Campagne et Provence. The talented young owners of the Miravile (*see* 4th Arrondissement, *above*) also run this small establishment on the quai across from Notre Dame. Fresh, colorful, Provençal-inspired cuisine includes vegetables stuffed with cod brandade and ratatouille omelets. The list of reasonably priced regional wines helps keep prices down. *25 quai de la Tournelle, Métro: Maubert-Mutualité, tel. 43–54–05–17. Reservations advised. Dress: casual. MC, V. Closed Sat. lunch, Sun.*

Chez Pento. Few Paris locations are more touristy than that of this simple neighborhood restaurant near the Panthéon. But it offers quality and good value, with one remarkably low-priced prix-fixe menu. The limited choices here include both classic bistro fare such as *petit salé* of duck with lentils and steak of the day, and more original dishes, such as guinea hen marinated in lime. The bistro setting includes modern posters, moleskin banquettes, and bare tabletops. *9 rue Cujas, Métro: St-Michel, tel. 43–26–81–54. Reservations advised. Dress: casual. V. Closed Sat. lunch, Sun.*

Moissonnier. M. and Mme. Moissonnier are always present to greet their faithful habitués. The Lyonnais cuisine includes *saladiers Lyonnais* (assorted cold salads), pike quenelles, eggs in a *meurette* (red wine) sauce, and, to drink, a variety of Beaujolais. With its homey decor, this is the perfect place to experience a typical French Sunday lunch. Ask to be seated in the ground-floor dining room. *28 rue des Fossés-St-Bernard, Métro: Cardinal Lemoine, tel. 43–29–87–65. Reservations advised. Dress: casual. MC, V. Closed Sun. eve., Mon., Aug.*

Le Petit Navire. Attentive Mme. Cousty takes care of the series of intimate dining rooms in this charming neighborhood restau-

rant, while her husband prepares mostly fish dishes with the taste of the Mediterranean: *tapenade* (anchovy and black olive spread), fish soup, and sea bass grilled with fennel. You must order carefully to keep your meal in this price category. *14 rue des Fossés-St-Bernard, Métro: Cardinal-Lemoine, tel. 43–54–22–52. Reservations advised. Dress: casual. AE, DC, MC, V. Closed Sun., Mon., mid-Aug., mid-Feb., and Christmas week.*
Chez René. This reliable address at the eastern end of the blvd. St-Germain has satisfied three generations of Parisians, who count on finding Burgundian dishes such as boeuf à la Bourguignonne and coq au vin, and the wines of the Maconnais and Beaujolais. The dining rooms are cozy. *14 blvd. St-Germain, Métro: Cardinal Lemoine, tel. 43–54–30–23. Reservations advised. Dress: casual. MC, V. Closed Sat., Sun., Aug.*

★ **Le Petit Plat.** Only 10 tables fill this tiny Latin Quarter restaurant half a block from the Seine near Odéon. There's virtually no decor, but plenty of delicious home-style food: *nage* (poaching broth) of mussels and cockles, lentil salad, onion soup, grilled steak, and duck confit with a potato *galette* (cake). Sample something from the original list of good regional wines at low prices. This spot has been discovered by the locals, so be sure and book in advance. *3 rue des Grands Degrés, Métro: Maubert-Mutualité, tel. 40–46–85–34. Reservations advised. Dress: casual. MC, V. Closed Mon., Tues. lunch.*
Chez Toutoune. This brightly lit, noisy Latin Quarter address is within budget if you stick to the prix-fixe menu. The enterprising, blond *patronne* prepares a flavorful cuisine rooted in home cooking, but with a touch of fantasy: lentil salad with crab, *charlotte* of lamb, and snow eggs with pink pralines. Reservations are not always honored and service can be slow, but Toutoune is fun and good quality. *5 rue de Pontoise, Métro: Maubert-Mutualité, tel. 43–26–56–81. Reservations advised. Dress: casual. AE, MC, V. Closed Sun., Mon. lunch, Aug.*

6th Arrondissement (Luxembourg)
See Left Bank Dining map

Under 250F **L'Ecaille de PCB.** A la carte prices are high at this enjoyable St-Germain-des-Prés fish restaurant, but the special prix-fixe lunch justifies its inclusion here. It's always full of Parisians enjoying well-prepared, very fresh fish such as anchovy salad, sardine rillettes, and whole sea bass stuffed with fennel. There are a few meat dishes also. Book well ahead, especially at lunch. *5 rue Mabillon, Métro: Mabillon, tel. 43–26–73–70. Reservations advised. Dress: casual. AE, MC, V. Closed Sat. lunch and Sun.*
Lipp. At this classic Left Bank brasserie, politicians, entertainers, rubber-necking tourists, and everyone else vie for tables, especially in the ground-floor dining room. Food is classic brasserie-style, too: herring in cream, choucroute, and millefeuille. The pretty decor is straight from the 1920s, and the ceramics are landmarked. *151 blvd. St-Germain, Métro: St-Germain-des-Prés, tel. 45–48–53–91. No reservations; expect lines. Dress: jacket and tie required. AE, DC, MC, V. Closed mid-July–mid-Aug.*
Le Petit Zinc. It's hard to believe the extravagant fin-de-siècle-style decor is new. The kitchen does a creditable job with shellfish, veal liver, and duck confit. Careful ordering will keep your meal under 250 francs. Le Muniche, next door, has the same

owners and a lively atmosphere. *11 rue St. Benoît, Métro: St-Germain-des-Prés, tel. 46–33–51–66. Reservations strongly advised. Dress: casual. AE, DC, MC, V.*

La Rôtisserie d'En Face. A long rotisserie is part of the attractive country-elegant decor at this bistro created by renowned chef Jacques Cagna. The cuisine includes roast chicken with mashed potatoes, grilled salmon with spinach, and chocolate éclairs. The menu is fixed-price only, and it's cheaper at lunch. Dinner is two set seatings only. *2 rue Christine, Métro: Odéon, tel. 43–26–40–98. MC, V. Closed Sat. lunch, Sun.*

Under 175F **Aux Charpentiers.** This old, large neighborhood bistro in St-Germain-des-Prés is eternally popular with students, locals, and tourists. Enjoy the homemade preparations of foie gras, cod *aïoli* (garlic mayonnaise) with vegetables, boeuf à la mode, and chocolate mousse. The atmosphere is boisterous. *10 rue Mabillon, Métro: Mabillon, tel. 43–26–30–05. Reservations advised. Dress: casual. AE, DC, MC, V. Closed Sun.*

Bistrot de la Gare. Of the many Bistrots de la Gare all over Paris, all with the same menu and prices, this one stands out for its authentic Belle Epoque decor and its location, in the thick of things in Montparnasse. To the usual bistro fare add such international choices as carpaccio of beef with basil (all you can eat), Scandinavian plate (various kinds of smoked fish), and steak. Sidewalk tables are set on busy blvd. du Montparnasse in good weather. Service until 1 AM. *59 blvd. du Montparnasse, Métro: Montparnasse, tel. 45–48–38–01. Reservations advised. Dress: casual. MC, V.*

Restaurant des Beaux-Arts. This two-level restaurant with various cozy dining rooms is across the street from the Ecole des Beaux-Arts. Students and anyone on a budget will appreciate the low-priced, honest bistro cuisine, including frog's legs with garlic, lamb stew, and Mont-Blanc (chestnut cream). Service is attentive. *11 rue des Beaux-Arts, Métro: St-Germain-des-Prés, tel. 43–26–92–64. Reservations advised. Dress: casual. No credit cards.*

Vagenende. This is a kind of poor man's Maxim's, with an equally gorgeous, landmarked Belle Epoque interior, but without the pretense. Classic dishes include the house foie gras, sea trout with red-wine sauce, pot-au-feu, and *baba au rhum* (rum-soaked cake). Service can be inept when the large restaurant is full. Prix-fixe menus keep meals in this price range; à la carte is higher. Service until 1 AM. *142 blvd. St-Germain, Métro: Odéon, tel. 43–26–68–18. Reservations advised. Dress: casual. AE, MC, V.*

Under 100F **Le Petit St-Benoît.** This bare-bones bistro has been nurturing
★ poor students and travelers for more than 125 years. Classics of the *cuisine bougeoise* are served by frequently sassy waitresses in a communal atmosphere. Try veal roast, blanquette, or *hachis Parmentier* (ground beef-and-mashed-potato pie). *4 rue St-Benoît, Métro: St-Germain-des-Prés, tel. 42–60–27–92. Reservations advised. Dress: casual. No credit cards. Closed weekends.*

Polidor. It represents a disappearing breed: the honest, neighborhood bistro serving uncomplicated food at rock-bottom prices. A mix of locals, students, and tourists tuck into such time-honored dishes as hard-boiled egg with mayonnaise, guinea hen with cabbage, and tarte Tatin. Service is downright motherly. *41 rue Monsieur-le-Prince, Métro: Odéon, tel. 43–*

26–95–34. Reservations advised. Dress: casual. No credit cards.

7th Arrondissment (Invalides)
See Left Bank Dining map

Under 175F **Aux Fins Gourmets.** What would the far western end of the
★ blvd. St-Germain be without this comforting bistro? Solid
country dishes prevail: *pipérade* (mixture of eggs, peppers, onions, tomatoes, and garlic), duck confit, and cassoulet. Pastries
come from the excellent shop Peltier. In warm weather, dinner
or lunch on the sidewalk terrace, under the shady plane trees,
is a delight. *213 blvd. St-Germain, Métro: Bac, tel. 42–22–06–
57. Reservations advised. Dress: casual. No credit cards.
Closed Sun., Mon. lunch, Aug.*

Le Bistrot de Breteuil. A few years ago this neighborhood
brasserie was redecorated and given a fixed-price menu that's
appreciated even by the affluent neighborhood residents who
come here. Choices are not commonplace at this price and
might include foie gras, snails with hazelnuts, or rack of lamb.
It's very pleasant to dine at one of the tables under the trees on
the calm place de Breteuil. *3 pl. de Breteuil, Métro: Duroc, tel.
45–67–07–27. Reservations advised, especially for Sat. dinner
and Sun. lunch. Dress: casual. MC, V.*

★ **Le Sancerre.** Family-run for several generations, this low-key
spot near the Invalide is a showcase for the wines of Sancerre—
white, red, and rosé—available by the glass or bottle. The
menu is quite limited: salads, quiche, omelets, and the tasty
Chavignol goat cheese from the Sancerre. The wood-paneled
dining room is inviting. *25 av. Rapp, Métro: Ecole-Militaire,
tel. 45–51–75–91. Reservations advised. Dress: casual. MC,
V. Closed Sat. eve. and Sun.*

Le Télégraphe. This cavernous restaurant near the Musée
d'Orsay was once a residence for female postal workers. Today's occupants are youngish, fashionable inhabitants of the
wealthy neighborhood, who like the reasonable fixed-price
menu (à la carte is more). Although the cuisine is fine
(cassoulette of oysters, *sauté* of beef, chocolate surprise), people come here for the atmosphere. *41 rue de Lille, Métro: Bac,
tel. 40–15–06–65. Reservations advised. Dress: casual. AE, V.*

Under 100F **Au Pied de Fouet.** As much a home as a restaurant for some people, the very simple Au Pied de Fouet has no decor to mention
and serves plain home-cooked food (lentil salad, veal
blanquette, tarts) with absolutely no pretense. It's noisy, always crowded, and inexpensive. *45 rue de Babylone, Métro:
Vaneau, tel. 47–05–12–27. No reservations. Dress: casual. No
credit cards. Closed Sat. eve., Sun., Aug., Christmas week,
and Easter.*

★ **Au Sauvignon.** A young, modish, intellectual crowd fills this
tiny wine bar, where you'll find the usual limited menu of
tartines, or open-faced sandwiches, on the famous Poilâne loaf,
topped with good-quality charcuterie, cheese, or both. The colorful murals will amuse you, but it's even more fun to people-
watch from one of the tables set on the narrow sidewalk. *80 rue
des Saints Pères, Métro: Sèvres-Babylone, tel. 45–48–04–69.
No reservations. Dress: casual. No credit cards. Closed Sat.
eve., Sun., Aug., Christmas week, and Easter.*

Chez Germaine. New owners have not fooled with this popular
little restaurant, with its woodwork, collection of paintings,

and warm welcome. The menu also remains faithful to the bistro tradition, with dishes such as leeks *en vinaigrette*, sauté of rabbit, grilled boudin, and rice pudding. Here's remarkable value in an expensive area. *30 rue Pierre Leroux, Métro: Vaneau, tel. 42-73-28-34. Reservations advised. Dress: casual. No credit cards. Closed Sat. dinner, Sun.*

Thoumieux. Virtually everything at this third-generation restaurant is made on the premises, including foie gras, rillettes, duck confit, cassoulet, and the homey desserts. The red velour banquettes, mellow yellow walls, and bustling waiters in long, white aprons are delightfully Parisian. *79 rue St-Dominique, Métro: Invalides, tel. 47-05-49-75. Reservations advised. Dress: casual. MC, V.*

8th Arrondissement (Champs-Elysées)
See Right Bank Dining map

Under 250F **La Fermette Marbeuf.** It's a favorite haunt of French TV and
★ movie stars, who like the spectacular Belle Epoque mosaics, tiles, and stained glass (discovered by accident when the restaurant was being redecorated), and appreciate the solid, updated classic cuisine. Try *gâteau* of chicken livers and sweetbreads, lamb navarin with vegetables, and bitter chocolate fondant. Prices here are exceptional, considering the quality of the food, the surroundings, and the neighborhood. The Fermette becomes animated late, around 9. *5 rue Marbeuf, Métro: Franklin Roosevelt, tel. 47-20-63-53. Reservations advised. Dress: casual but elegant. AE, DC, MC, V.*

Savy. This 60-year-old restaurant still wears an honest, homey face, despite its rarefied avenue Montaigne location. Expect 1950s decor and substantial cuisine, with specialties of central France such as stuffed cabbage, roast lamb shoulder, and prune tart. *23 rue Bayard, Métro: Champs-Elysées-Clemenceau, tel. 47-23-46-98. MC, V. Reservations advised. Dress: casual. Closed weekends and Aug.*

Sébillon. The original Sébillon has nurtured chic residents of the fashionable suburb of Neuilly for generations, and this elegant, polished new branch off the Champs-Elysées should do as well. The menu is similar, with lobster salad, lots of shellfish, and—its great specialty—roast leg of lamb sliced at table and served in unlimited quantity. Service is notably friendly. *66 rue Pierre Charron, Métro: Franklin Roosevelt, tel. 43-59-28-15. Reservations advised. Dress: casual chic. AE, DC, MC, V.*

Yvan. This very "in" spot near the Champs-Elysées is full of entertainment personalities who are not above appreciating the modest prices and friendly service. Yvan, the young Belgian chef, serves a cuisine that is a mix of classic and modern with Belgian influences. Sample scallops-and-salmon with potato crêpes, sole waterzoi, and Granny Smith apple compote. Stick to one of the fixed-price menus to stay within budget. It's open until midnight. *1 bis rue Jean Mermoz, Métro: Franklin Roosevelt, tel. 43-59-18-40. Reservations advised. Dress: casual. AE, DC, MC, V. Closed Sat. lunch, Sun.*

Under 175F **L'Espace.** Pierre Cardin's L'Espace has unappealing decor but excellent prices. Bypass the à la carte menu in favor of the savory and dessert buffets, which are huge and varied. Eating on the big terrace in the gardens of the Champs-Elysées is delightful in nice weather. *1-3 av. Gabriel, Métro: Concorde, tel.*

42–66–17–30. Reservations advised. Dress: casual. AE, DC, MC, V. Closed Sat. lunch and Sun. dinner Apr.–Sept.; lunch only Sept.–Apr.

Under 100F **Berry's.** This tiny annex next door to the more expensive Le Grenadin, near the Parc Monceau, is a bargain. Talented chef-owner Patrick Cirotte prepares dishes of his native Berry region (veal simmered in red wine) and serves local wines, including fine Sancerres. Decor is lean and modern, the atmosphere young and upbeat. It's open until 1 AM. *46 rue de Naples, Métro: Villiers, tel. 40–75–01–56. Reservations advised. Dress: casual. AE, MC, V. Closed Sun.*

Fauchon Cafétéria. The basement-level cafeteria of this world-renowned luxury food emporium provides the perfect opportunity to sample some of Fauchon's savory and sweet creations. There are a few stools and tables, but at peak hours you will have to stand. If you just want a snack, go for coffee and a pastry at tea time. Service is from 8:15 AM to 7 PM. *30 pl. de la Madeleine, Métro: Madeleine, tel. 47–42–60–11. No reservations. Dress: casual. AE, DC, V. Closed Sun.*

La Boutique à Sandwiches. This long, bright delicatessen-style spot on the congested rue du Colisée serves surprisingly good food until the wee hours, making it a hardy stop after a film on the Champs. You'll find good sandwiches, various kinds of herring, Welsh rarebit, and all-you-can-eat raclette. *12 rue du Colisée, Métro: Franklin Roosevelt, tel. 43–59–56–69. Reservations advised. Dress: casual. MC, V. Closed Sun., Aug.*

La Ferme St. Hubert. Reserve ahead for lunch, as this unpretentious spot serving primarily cheese dishes is mobbed then. The owner has a cheese shop next door—one of the best in the city—and from its shelves come the main ingredients for fondue, raclette, and the best *croque Hubert* (toasted cheese sandwich) in Paris. The house wines are decent, and the location is convenient to the fancy food shop, Fauchon, on the place de la Madeleine. *21 rue Vignon, Métro: Madeleine, tel. 47–42–79–20. Reservations essential at lunch, advised at dinner. Dress: casual. AE, DC, MC, V. Closed Mon. dinner and Sun.*

9th Arrondissement (Opéra)
See Right Bank Dining map

Under 250F **La Table d'Anvers.** One of the best restaurants near Montmar-
★ tre, it is expensive at dinner but serves a reasonably priced lunch menu. The cuisine has Italian and Provençal touches in dishes like gnocchi of langoustines and *girolles* (wild mushrooms), saddle of rabbit with polenta, and *croustillant* of asparagus with crab. The Table's desserts, such as strawberry tart with rhubarb, are among the best in Paris. *2 pl. d'Anvers, Métro: Anvers, tel. 48–78–35–21. Reservations advised. Dress: casual but elegant. AE, MC, V. Closed Sat. lunch, Sun., mid-Aug.*

Under 175F **Bistrot des Deux Théâtres.** Quality is high and prices are low in this well-run restaurant in the Pigalle/Clichy area. The prix-fixe menu includes apéritif, first and main courses, a cheese or dessert course, half a bottle of wine, and coffee. The food is far from banal; try salad of foie gras, seafood navarin, and apple tart flambéed with Calvados. *18 rue Blanche, Métro: Trinité, tel. 45–26–41–43. Reservations advised. Dress: casual. MC, V.*

Le Roi du Pot-Au-Feu. Definitely a cold-weather address, for this old neighborhood favorite serves only *pot-au-feu:* a rich bouillon in which assorted cuts of beef and vegetables have simmered. Resign yourself to nondecor and occasionally curt service, and dig in. It's convenient to the fancy food shops on the place de la Madeleine and to the big department stores. *34 rue Vignon, Métro: Havre-Caumartin, tel. 47–42–37–10. Reservations advised. Dress: casual. MC, V. Closed Sun., July, and Aug.*

Under 100F　**Café Flo.** Under the same management as the Brasserie Flo in the 10th arrondissement (*see below*), this is located on the 6th floor of the Printemps department store, under its magnificent glass dome. Dinner is not served, but from 9:30 AM to 7 PM you can order anything from a dessert to a full meal. Recommended dishes include salmon/crab terrine, tomato/mozzarella salad, pepper steak, and apple *feuilleté* (baked in puff pastry). A la carte prices are over budget for a full meal, so order a single dish or the fixed-price menu. *Printemps Haussmann, 64 blvd. Haussmann, Métro: Chaussée-d'Antin, tel. 42–82–50–53. No reservations. Dress: casual. MC, V. No dinner. Closed Sun.*

Chartier. This cavernous turn-of-the-century restaurant enjoys a huge following among the budget-minded, including students, solitary bachelors, and tourists. You may find yourself sharing a table with strangers as you study the long, old-fashioned menu of such favorites as hard-boiled eggs with mayonnaise, pâté, and roast veal with spinach. *7 rue du Faubourg-Montmartre, Métro: rue Montmartre, tel. 47–70–86–29. No reservations. Dress: casual. No credit cards.*

10th Arrondissement (République)
See Right Bank Dining map

Under 175F　**Brasserie Flo.** This, the first of brasserie king Jean-Paul Bucher's seven Paris addresses, is hard to find down its passageway near the Gare de l'Est, but worth the effort. The rich wood- and stained-glass interior is typically Alsatian, the service enthusiastic, and the brasserie standards such as shellfish, steak tartare, and choucroute tasty. Order one of the carafes of Alsatian wine. An à la carte meal is outside our price range, but two lunch menus are under 175F, as is the after-11 PM Faim de Nuit menu. *7 cour des Petites Ecuries, Métro: Château d'Eau, tel. 47–70–13–59. Reservations advised. Dress: casual but elegant. AE, DC, MC, V. Closed Christmas eve.*

Julien. Another Bucher brasserie (*see above*), this one has dazzling Belle Epoque decor and good prices. Go for the cheaper prix-fixe lunch menu or the late-night fixed-price menu. Brasserie fare includes smoked salmon, foie gras, cassoulet, and good sherbets. The crowd is ebullient and lots of fun. *16 rue du Faubourg St-Denis, Métro: Strasbourg-St-Denis, tel. 47–70–12–06. Reservations advised. Dress: casual but elegant. AE, DC, MC, V. Closed Christmas eve.*

11th Arrondissement (Bastille)
See Right Bank Dining map

Under 250F　**Chez Philippe/Pyrénées-Cévennes.** Old-timers still refer to this
★　comfortable bistro by its original name—Pyrénées-Cévennes —while others know it as Chez Philippe. The eclectic menu combines the cooking of Burgundy, central France—even Spain—in such dishes as snails in garlic butter, cassoulet, and

paella. An attentive staff bustles amid cozy surroundings, with beamed ceiling and polished copper. *106 rue de la Folie-Méricourt, Métro: République, tel. 43-57-33-78. Reservations advised. Dress casual. MC, V. Closed weekends, Aug.*

Under 175F **Astier.** You'll find remarkable value at this pleasant restaurant, where the prix-fixe menu (there's no à la carte) includes first and main courses, cheese (excellent), and dessert. Among high-quality dishes, try mussel soup with saffron, fricassée of beef cheeks, and plum clafoutis. Service can be rushed, but the enthusiastic crowd does not seem to mind. Study the excellent wine list, which has some surprising buys. *44 rue Jean-Pierre Timbaud, Métro: République, tel. 43-57-16-35. Reservations advised. Dress: casual. MC, V. Closed weekends, Aug.*

La Galoche d'Aurillac. This venerable bistro in the up-and-coming Bastille area is located down the sinister-seeming rue de Lappe, now lined with bars, restaurants, and clubs. Hearty cuisine derives from the Auvergne region of central France, and many of the ingredients come direct from home. Enjoy charcuteries, *tripoux* (mutton tripe), Cantal cheese, and walnut tart amid rustic decor. *41 rue de Lappe, Métro: Bastille, tel. 47-00-77-15. Reservations advised. Dress: casual. No credit cards. Closed Sun., Aug.*

Le Passage. The friendly Passage is located in the rather obscure Passage de la Bonne Graine, not far from the place de la Bastille. Though it bills itself as a wine bar, it has a full menu, including five styles of *andouillettes* (chitterling sausage), sometimes a succulent hot duck and cabbage terrine, and giant chocolate éclairs. The wine list is excellent. *18 Passage de la Bonne Graine (enter by 108 ave. Ledru-Rollin), Métro: Ledru-Rollin, tel. 47-00-73-30. Reservations advised. Dress: casual. AE, DC, MC, V. Closed Sat. lunch, Sun.*

Le Villaret. The owner of this newcomer once ran the excellent Astier (*see above*), and his experience shows. Menu choices are often interesting, always well prepared. Try salmon tart, hot foie gras salad, duck confit, and seasonal fruit clafoutis. Decor, with exposed stone and half-timbering, combines traditional and modern styles. The restaurant does not serve lunch, but makes up for that by serving dinner until 1 AM. *13 rue Ternaux, Métro: Parmentier, tel. 43-57-89-76. Reservations advised. Dress: casual. MC, V. Closed lunch, Sun.*

Les Amognes. Chef Thierry Coué is a most talented cook and deserves better than this ordinary-looking restaurant near the place de la Nation. But never mind, the menu is full of good things, such as mussel soup with the special lentils of Le Puy, cod fritters with fried basil, roast pigeon, and pineapple soup. Stick with fixed-price or you'll be over budget. *243 rue du Faubourg-St-Antoine, Métro: Faidhzevz-Chaligny, tel. 43-72-73-05. Reservations advised. Dress: casual. MC, V. Closed Sun. dinner, Mon. and Aug.*

★ **Les Fernandises.** You'll find the Normandy-inspired cuisine and homey service as at the owner's Chez Fernand next door, but with a special lunch menu and another at dinner that make it considerably cheaper. Look for mackerel rillettes, duck prepared various ways, skate with Camembert, and Camembert ripened in five different styles. *17 rue Fontaine-au-Roi, Métro: République, tel. 43-57-46-25. Reservations advised. Dress: casual. V. Closed Sun., Mon., and Aug.*

Under 100F **Jacques Mélac.** There's robust cuisine to match the noisy camaraderie at this popular wine bar–restaurant, owned by mustachioed Jacques Mélac. Charcuterie, a salad of preserved duck gizzards, braised beef, and cheeses from central France make good choices here. M. Mélac has his own miniature vineyard out the front door and hosts a jolly party at harvest time. *42 rue Léon Frot, Métro: Charonne, tel. 43-70-59-27. Reservations advised. Dress: casual. MC, V. Closed weekends Aug.; dinner Tues-Fri. to 8:30 only.*

Le Clown Bar. This friendly neighborhood wine bar is well named: Clown themes dominate the colorful landmarked mosaics, posters, and *objets;* and customers once came from the Cirque d'Hiver next door. Cuisine is simple bistro: eggs *en meurette* (red wine sauce), hot sausage with pistachios, and chocolate cake. Varied wines are available by the glass or bottle. Service is until 1 AM. Closing hours were expected to change, so call ahead. *114 rue Amelot, Métro: Filles-du-Calvaire, tel. 43-55-87-35. Reservations advised. Dress: casual. No credit cards. Closed Sun., Aug., and some Sat. lunches.*

12th Arrondissement (Gare de Lyon)
See Right Bank Dining map

Under 175F   **Fouquet's Café.** This eastern branch of the famous Champs-Elysées café/restaurant is part of the new Opéra building on the place de la Bastille. The long, curving dining room is a handsome example of clean, modern design, and the brasserie menu is varied. Try snails, soup of the day, grilled salmon, and rib roast with béarnaise sauce; there's a long list of desserts. The café opens at 7:30 AM and serves breakfast, lunch, tea, and dinner until midnight. *130 rue de Lyon, Métro: Bastille, tel. 43-42-18-18. Reservations advised. Dress: casual. AE, DC, V. Closed Sat. lunch and dinner.*

L'Oulette. Chef-owner Baudis once ran his restaurant from a smaller location in the 4th, but success encouraged him to open this larger, fancier spot, with lean, modern decor. Although something indefinable was lost in the move, the cuisine of Baudis's native Southwest France is as good as ever. Recommended dishes include *émincé* (thin slices) of duck with coriander and fresh figs, fresh cod with celeriac and walnuts, and *pain d'épices* (spice cake). À la carte meals will exceed our price range. The restaurant, in the rebuilt Bercy district, is a bit hard to find. *15 pl. Lachambeaudie, Métro: Dugommier, tel. 40-02-02-12. Reservations advised. Dress: casual. MC, V. Closed Sat. lunch, Sun., Aug.*

14th Arrondissement (Montparnasse)
See Left Bank Dining map

Under 250F   **Le Pavillon Montsouris.** This bucolic building on the edge of
★   Parc Montsouris was recently restored, and the pretty pastel interior and large terrace facing the park make for a charming spot on a sunny day. A multichoice, prix-fixe menu is a real bargain, and dishes prepared by the bright, young chef here are fresh and interesting. Try mussel soup with langoustines, *hachis Parmentier* (a kind of rich man's shepherd's pie) with foie gras and duck, and mango clafoutis. Service can slow down during peak times; go when you have time for a leisurely meal. *20 rue Gazan, Métro: RER Cité-Universitaire, tel. 45-88-38-52. Reservations advised. Dress: casual. DC, MC, V.*

Under 175F **Contre-Allée.** This large, simply decorated restaurant is popular with a Left Bank crowd of students and professor-types. The interesting menu includes original choices, such as squid salad with mussels and roast cod with parmesan. Homemade fresh pasta accompanies many dishes. A sidewalk terrace enlivens shady Denfert-Rochereau. The restaurant serves until 11:30 PM. *83 av. Denfert-Rochereau, Métro: Denfert-Rochereau, tel. 43–54–99–86. Reservations advised. Dress: casual. AE, DC, MC, V. Closed Sat. lunch.*

★ **La Cagouille.** One of the best fish restaurants in Paris, this expensive spot has a prix-fixe lunch menu that allows you to experience chef Gérard Allemandou's magical cuisine. Few sauces or adornments mask the fresh, clean flavors of fish, from elegant sole and turbot to more pedestrian sardines and mackerel. Besides his excellent wine list, La Cagouille has the finest collection of Cognacs in the city. This vast, modern space is on the somewhat sterile place Brancusi, with a large terrace for warm-weather dining. *10–12 pl. Brancusi, Métro: Gaité, tel. 43–22–09–01. Reservations advised. Dress: casual but elegant. AE, MC, V.*

La Coupole. This world-renowned, cavernous address in Montparnasse practically defines the term brasserie. Everyone from Left Bank intellectuals (Jean-Paul Sartre and Simone de Beauvoir were regulars) to bourgeois grandmothers come here. New owner Jean-Paul Bucher (of the Flo group of brasseries) had the sense to leave well enough alone when he restored it, simply polishing and cleaning the famous murals. Expect the usual brasserie menu, including perhaps the largest shellfish presentation in Paris, choucroute, and a big choice of desserts. The buffet breakfast from 7:30 to 10:30 daily is an excellent value. *102 blvd. du Montparnasse, Métro: Vavin, tel. 43–20–14–20. Reservations advised. Dress: casual. AE, DC, MC, V.*

Le Bistrot du Dôme. This cheery yellow fish bistro in Montparnasse belongs to the fancy and expensive Dôme, and benefits from that elegant brasserie's excellent sources of fish. The many seafood dishes are always very fresh and simply presented. Decor includes colorful tiles and pretty Italian glass light fixtures. Jovial service and a limited but affordable wine list add to the enjoyment. *1 rue Delambre, Métro: Vavin, tel. 43–35–32–00. Reservations advised. Dress: casual. MC, V.*

Under 100F **Le Vin des Rues.** The abrupt owner of this Lyon-style restaurant does things his way, meaning dinner is only twice a week, and you should arrive at 9 PM. Patrons comply in order to eat well-prepared food in the Lyonnais tradition: *saladiers Lyonnais* (assorted cold meat and vegetable salads), house terrine, pike quenelles, and daube of beef cheek. You'll find it a convivial place. *21 rue Boulard, Métro: Denfert-Rochereau, tel. 43–22–19–78. Reservations advised, especially in the evening. Dress: casual. No credit cards. Closed Sun., Mon., Aug., and Easter week. No dinner except Wed. and Fri.*

15th Arrondissement (Front de Seine)
See Left Bank Dining map

Under 250F **Entre-Siècle.** Chef Olivier Simon is from northern France and is a true believer in that region's cooking. The flavorful, original cuisine here makes frequent use of beer, such as in eel *au vert* (in a spinach and sorrel sauce), trout in a beer aspic—even beer-based sabayon. Overseeing the dining room is Mme. Simon, who will help you design a menu of regional specialties. About a dozen carefully chosen beers are offered, along with wines. Prix-fixe menus are a good value at both lunch and dinner. *29 av. de Lowendal, Métro: Ségur, tel. 47-83-51-22. Reservations advised. Dress: casual but elegant. AE, MC, V. Closed Sat. lunch, Sun., Aug.*

★ **Morot-Gaudry.** Located on top of a building near the Ecole Militaire, this popular place offers the luxury of well-spaced tables and an unusual outlook over Paris. Chef-owner Jean-Pierre Morot-Gaudry prepares a personalized cuisine that's a combination of classic and modern. Recommended are scallops with Jerusalem artichokes, veal blanquette, and chocolate mille-feuille with wild raspberries. The menu marries a different wine with each dish; the prix-fixe menu at lunch puts Morot-Gaudry within this price range. *6 rue de la Cavalerie, Métro: Motte-Picquet, tel. 47-34-62-92. Reservations advised. Dress: casual. AE, MC, V. Closed weekends.*

Pierre Vedel. Burly Pierre Vedel's very Parisian bistro attracts entertainers and other fashionable patrons. M. Vedel's menu changes according to what looks good in the market, but generally includes Mediterranean-inspired dishes such as brandade, poached eggs with tomato sauce, *osso bucco* (braised veal shanks) with lemon, and peach soup with mint. *19 rue Duranton, Métro: Boucicaut, tel. 45-58-43-17. Reservations advised. Dress: casual chic. MC, V. Closed weekends.*

Under 175F **L'Armoise.** There's excellent value-for-money in this quiet neighborhood restaurant near the Front de Seine development. Chef-owner Georges Outhier prepares one of the best veal livers in Paris, along with such treats as a delicious duck breast with honey and sea trout with spice butter. Madame Outhier is an attentive hostess in the salmon-pink dining rooms. *67 rue des Entrepreneurs, Métro: Charles Michel, tel. 45-79-03-31. Reservations advised. Dress: casual. MC, V. Closed Sat. lunch, Sun. mid-Feb., Aug.*

Le Barrail. A favorite with staff from nearby *Le Monde*, this good neighborhood spot is in the under-175F range with the special lunch menu, or under 250F for a prix-fixe dinner. Impeccable ingredients go into such dishes as mushroom terrine, lobster with pepper risotto, and the increasingly hard-to-find potatoes Dauphine (potatoes mashed with pâté à choux and deep-fried). *17 rue Falguière, Métro: Pasteur, tel. 43-22-42-61. Reservations advised. Dress: casual. AE, MC, V. Closed weekends, early Aug.*

Le Clos Morillons. The chef here has made many trips to the Far East, and his cuisine incorporates such Oriental flavorings as sesame and ginger. But the menu is unmistakably French, with its delicious terrine of potato with foie gras, roast guinea fowl, and the all-chocolate dessert (several kinds of chocolate desserts on one plate). Added pluses are the professional service in the quiet dining room, an interesting wine list emphasizing Loire wines, and fixed-price menus at lunch and dinner that put the Clos in the under-175F range at lunch and under 250F at dinner. *50 rue Morillons, Métro: Convention, tel. 48-28-04-37. Reservations advised. Dress: casual. MC, V. Closed Sat. lunch, Sun.*

Under 100F **Le Café du Commerce.** The vast, two-story Commerce on the animated street of the same name offers reasonable prices and a friendly neighborhood ambience. Nothing unusual in the cuisine: celery rémoulade, skate with capers, pot-au-feu, and chocolate mousse. Service until midnight. *51 rue du Commerce, Métro: Commerce, tel. 45-75-03-27. Reservations advised. Dress: casual. AE, DC, MC, V.*

16th Arrondissement (Trocadéro/Bois de Boulogne)
See Right Bank Dining map

Under 250F   **La Butte Chaillot.** This, the latest of star-chef Guy Savoy's fashionable bistros, is the largest and most impressive: A dramatic iron staircase connects two levels, decorated in turquoise and earth colors. Dining here is part theater, as the *à la mode* clientele will attest, but it's not all show: The very good food includes tasty ravioli of Royans (tiny cheese pillows), roast chicken with mashed potatoes, and stuffed veal breast with rosemary. The wine list includes some moderately priced choices. A wide sidewalk terrace fronts tree-shaded av. Kléber. *112 av. Kléber, Métro: Trocadéro, tel. 47-27-88-88. Reservations advised. Dress: casual chic. AE, MC, V.*

Bistrot de l'Etoile Lauriston. Another bistro from Guy Savoy (*see above*), this attractive, subdued establishment features the intelligent yet homey cuisine of chef William Ledeuil. His full-flavored dishes include stuffed, gratinéed zucchini, ravioli with *pistou* and lamb sautéed with rosemary. An upscale crowd includes many Americans. *19 rue Lauriston, Métro: Charles de Gaulle, tel. 40-67-11-16. Reservations advised. Dress: casual. AE, MC, V. Closed Sun.*

Chez Géraud. Cherubic, jolly Géraud Rongier runs this fairly new bistro in the chic Passy district. Dishes such as salad of preserved duck gizzards, roast pigeon with Port sauce, and bitter-chocolate cake exemplify the robust cuisine here. Rongier's knowledge of wine is vast, and his eclectic wine list has everything from great chateaux to little-known regional bottles. Notice the pretty tile mural at the back of the dining room. *31 rue Vital, Métro: Passy, tel. 45-20-33-00. Reservations advised. Dress: casual. MC, V. Closed weekends, Aug.*

Under 175F   **L'Auberge du Bonheur.** Food is not the reason to come to this informal spot behind the Grande Cascade restaurant in the Bois de Boulogne. The attraction, in warm weather, is outdoor dining on the huge gravel terrace, surrounded by chestnut and plane trees, wisteria and bamboo. Order simply: Salads and grilled meats are best. *Allée Longchamp, Métro: Porte Dauphine, tel. 42-24-10-17. Reservations advised. Dress: casual. MC, V. Open daily Apr.–Oct.; lunch only Sun.–Fri. Nov.–Mar.*

17th Arrondissement (Monceau/Clichy)
See Right Bank Dining map

Chez Georges. Open since 1926, this popular brasserie next to the huge Méridien and Concorde-Lafayette hotels prepares a gutsy cuisine for hearty eaters: cabbage soup, hachis Parmentier, rib roast carved tableside, and huge éclairs. It's always packed, with service until 11:30 PM. *273 blvd. Pereure, Métro: Porte Maillot, tel. 45-74-31-00. Reservations advised. Dress: casual. MC, V. Closed Aug.*

La Rôtisserie d'Armaillé. Admire the handsome oak paneling, cranberry and green upholstery, and the very Parisian crowd at star-chef Jacques Cagna's third restaurant. The prix-fixe menu has many tempting choices, among them *tagliatelle* (flat noodles) with shellfish, *pastilla* of guinea hen, and a terrific chocolate cake. Wines are a little pricey. *6 rue d'Armaillé, Métro: Argentine, tel. 42-27-19-20. Reservations advised. Dress: casual. AE, DC, MC, V. Closed Sat. lunch, Sun.*

Le Bistrot d'a Côté Faubert. This, the first of star-chef Michel Rostang's fashionable bistros, is within budget if you order carefully. The food includes modernized, lightened versions of classic bistro favorites, with an added touch of M. Rostang's native Dauphiné region: warm lentil salad with *cervelas* sausage, macaroni gratin with ham, and raspberry clafoutis. This former store is full of odds and ends seemingly salvaged from Grandmother's attic. *10 rue Gustave Flaubert, Métro: Terne, tel. 42-67-05-81. Reservations advised. Dress: casual. AE, MC, V. Closed Sat. lunch, Sun.*

Le Graindorge. Chef-owner Bernard Broux, formerly at the immensely popular Trou Gascon in the 12th Arrondissement, recently opened his own establishment. Here he prepares an original mix of the cuisines of southwest France and of his native Flanders. Try his succulent eel terrine in a delicious herb aspic, pork cheeks with juniper, and caramelized brioche *galette* (pancake). Mme. Broux oversees the pleasant dining rooms, and can help you choose one of the fine beers offered here. À la carte prices are high, but special lunch and dinner menus keep this under budget. *15 rue de l'Arc-de-Triomphe, Métro: Charles De Gaulle/Etoile, tel. 47-54-00-28. Reservations advised. Dress: casual. AE, MC, V. Closed Sat. lunch, Sun.*

Under 175F   **La Niçoise.** Posters of Nice adorn the simple upstairs dining room, and Mediterranean flavors emerge from the kitchen at this enjoyable Niçoise oasis. Try ricotta ravioli with basil, or *petits farcis Niçois* (stuffed vegetables). Moderately priced Provençal wines help keep prices down. *4 rue Pierre Demours, Métro: Ternes, tel. 45-74-42-41. Reservations advised. Dress: casual. AE, DC, MC, V. Closed Sat. lunch, Sun.*

Le Bistrot du 17ème. The fixed-price menu includes aperitif, first and main courses, cheese or dessert course, a half-bottle of wine, and coffee. Choices include foie gras salad, beef carpaccio with basil, and veal liver with cider. Enjoy pleasant, airy surroundings and rapid service, with outdoor eating in nice weather. *108 av. de Villiers, Métro: Pereire, tel. 47-63-32-77. Reservations advised. Dress: casual. MC, V.*

L'Huitrier. Come here if you share the Parisians' craving for oysters. Owner Alain Bunel will describe the different kinds available, and you can follow these with any of several fish specials offered daily. The excellent cheeses are from the outstanding shop of Roger Alléosse. Blond wood and cream colors prevail. *16 rue Saussier-Leroy, Métro: Ternes, tel. 40-54-83-44. Reservations advised. Dress: casual. MC, V.*

Under 100F   **Al Goldenberg.** This almost historic restaurant and takeout place is the closest thing Paris has to a New York deli, with items such as chopped liver, pastrami, smoked fish, and cheesecake. Stock up for a picnic or stop in for a quick, restorative snack. Service is nonstop until nearly midnight. *69 av. Wagram, Métro: Ternes, tel. 42-27-34-79. Reservations advised. Dress: casual. MC, V.*

18th Arrondissement (Montmartre)
See Right Bank Dining map

Under 250F   **A. Beauvilliers.** Ebullient host Edovard Carlier's flower-filled restaurant—the best in Montmartre—is accessible to budget diners with a special lunch menu. (It's too expensive for dinner.) The three dining rooms are filled with the owner's personal collection of paintings and valuable *bibelots*, and a tiny, vine-covered terrace makes for delightful summer dining. Chefs here come and go, but M. Carlier maintains quality, serving both original creations and reinterpreted classics. Recommended are the red mullet *en escabèche* (in a peppery marinade) and foie gras, lobster, and sweetbread *tourte*. The mouth-puckering lemon tart is not to be missed. One drawback: Service can be distant if you are not known. *52 rue Lamarck, Métro: Lamarck-Caulaincourt, tel. 42-54-54-42. Reservations essential. Jacket and tie advised. AE, MC, V. Closed Sun., Mon. lunch, and Sept.*

Under 100F   **Aux Négotiants.** This wine bar in Montmartre has zero decor, but gives a warm welcome to its mix of neighborhood regulars and well-heeled clientele. One or two hot plates are offered daily; otherwise, enjoy the terrines, cheeses, and other simple choices, served with affordable wines by the glass or bottle. *27 rue Lambert, Métro: Château Rouge, tel. 46-06-15-11. No reservations. Dress: casual. No credit cards. Closed weekends; dinner served Tues., Thurs., and Fri. only.*

20th Arrondissement (Père Lachaise)
See Right Bank Dining map

Under 175F   **A La Courtille.** This large wine bar–restaurant with a trendy following has a spectacular view of Paris over the new Parc de Belleville. (Notice the black-and-white photos of the quaint old Belleville neighborhood before the wrecking ball.) The kitchen prepares modernized versions of bistro classics and fresh, light creations such as marinated salmon with dill, roast cod with zucchini, and veal liver. An excellent wine list offers many choices by the glass. There's a large terrace, and service until 11 PM. *1 rue des Envierges, Métro: Pyrénées, tel. 46-36-51-59. Reservations advised. Dress: casual chic. MC, V.*

Splurges

Benoît. Founded in 1912, Benoît retains the feel of a classic bistro—with its frosted glass, lace curtains, polished brass, and a warm welcome—despite its high prices. Try the layered beef tongue–foie gras Lucullus, marinated salmon, cassoulet, or game in season. Patrons debate the merits of the front or back room, but conviviality reigns in both. *20 rue St. Martin, Métro: Châtelet, tel. 42-72-25-76. Reservations required. Dress: casual. No credit cards. Closed Sat., Sun., Aug.*

L'Arpège. This small, striking restaurant one block from the Rodin Museum is currently one of the most talked-about of Paris's restaurants. It features the cuisine of young chef-owner Alain Passard, whose menu is both original (lobster/turnip starter in a sweet-sour vinaigrette, stuffed sweet tomato) and classic (beef Burgundy, pressed duck). With its curving, hand-crafted wood panels and wrought-iron window frames, the decor is unusually minimalist. Service, although young and energetic, sometimes falls behind. *84 rue de Varenne, Métro: Varenne, tel. 45–51–47–33. Reservations advised. Dress: casual but elegant. AE, DC, MC, V. Closed Sat., Sun. lunch, Aug.*

6 The Arts and Nightlife

The Arts

Parisians consider their city a bastion of art and culture, and indeed it is. But surprisingly, much of the theater, opera, music, and ballet here is not on a par with what you'll find in London, New York, or Milan. Mime and contemporary dance performances are often better bets, and they pose no language problems. Smaller fringe theaters also offer good value, and you'll find free church concerts at some of the most beautiful settings in the city.

The music season usually runs from September through June. Theaters stay open during the summer, but many productions are at summer festivals elsewhere in France. The weekly magazines *Pariscope, L'Officiel des Spectacles,* and *7 à Paris* are published every Wednesday and give detailed entertainment listings. The best place to buy tickets is at the venue itself. Otherwise, try your hotel or a travel agency such as **Paris-Vision** (214 rue de Rivoli). Tickets for some events can be bought at the **FNAC** stores—especially Alpha-FNAC (1–5 rue Pierre Lescot, 1e, Forum des Halles, third level down). **Virgin Megastore** (52 av. des Champs Elysées) sells theater and concert tickets. Half-price tickets for many same-day theater performances are available at the **Kiosque Théâtre** across from 15 place de la Madeleine; expect a line. There's another branch at Châtelet RER station (closed Sun.). **Jeunesse Musicales de France** (20 rue Joffroy l' Asnier, 4e) sells two-week membership cards that enable anyone under 30 to obtain half-price tickets at major theaters. The student organization **COPAR** (39 av. Georges Bernanos, 5e, tel. 42–51–37–13) sells discounted theater tickets.

Theater A number of theaters line the Grands Boulevards between Opéra and République, but there is no Paris equivalent to Broadway or the West End. Shows are mostly in French. Classical drama is performed at the distinguished **Comédie Française** (Palais-Royal, 1er, tel. 40-15-00-15). You can reserve seats in person about two weeks in advance, or turn up an hour beforehand and wait in line for returned tickets.

The intimate **Gymnase** (38 blvd. de Bonne-Nouvelle, 10e, tel. 42-46-79-79) and the homely **Renaissance** (20 blvd. St-Martin, 10e, tel. 42-08-18-50), once home to Belle Epoque star Sarah Bernhardt, rub shoulders along the Grands Boulevards. The rue de la Gaîté near Montparnasse, lined with some of the raunchier Paris theaters since the 19th century, is still home to the stylish, old-fashioned **Gaîté-Montparnasse** (26 rue de la Gaîté, 14e, tel. 43-22-16-18).

The avant-garde is well represented by a number of small, off-beat theaters in the Marais and Bastille neighborhoods, or go a little farther north to Peter Brooks's **Bouffes du Nord** (37, bis blvd. de la Chapelle, 10e, tel. 46-07-34-50), offering wonderful experimental productions.

Ionesco admirers should visit the tiny Left Bank **Théâtre de la Huchette** (23 rue de la Huchette, 5e, tel. 43-26-38-99), where the playwright's short modern plays make a deliberate mess of the French language. In the Latin Quarter, the popular and inexpensive **Nouveau Théâtre Mouffetard** (73 rue Mouffetard, 5e, tel. 43-31-11-99) is great fun.

Many Paris theaters are worthy of a visit based solely on architectural merit and ambience, such as the elegantly restored **Théâtre des Champs-Elysées** (15 av. Montaigne, 8e, tel. 49-52-50-00), a plush Art Deco temple that hosts concerts and ballet as well as plays.

A particularly Parisian form of theater is *Café-Théâtre*—a mixture of satirical sketches and variety show riddled with slapstick humor and viewed in a café setting. It's fun if you have a good grasp of French. We suggest the reasonably priced **Café de la Gare** (41 rue du Temple, 4e, tel. 42-78-52-51).

Concerts Before the new Opéra de la Bastille opened, the **Salle Pleyel** (252 rue du Fbg. St-Honoré, 8e, tel. 45-63-07-96), near the Arc de Triomphe, was Paris's principal home of classical music. The Paris Symphony Orchestra and other leading international orchestras still play here regularly. Paris isn't as richly endowed as New York or London when it comes to orchestral music, but the city compensates with a never-ending stream of inexpensive lunchtime and evening concerts in churches. The candlelit concerts held in the **Sainte-Chapelle** are outstanding—make reservations well in advance. **Notre Dame** is another church where you can combine sightseeing with good listening. Others that offer concerts are **St-Eustache**, near Les Halles; **St-Germain-des-Prés**, on the Left Bank; **St-Louis-en-l'Ile; St-Roch,** north of the Louvre; and the lovely **St-Louis des Invalides.**

Both the **Musée du Louvre** (34 quai du Louvre, 1e, tel. 40-20-51-51) and the **Musée d'Orsay** (1 rue de Bellechasse, 7e, tel. 45-49-48-14) hold concerts, often at lunchtime.

Opera The **Opéra** itself, or **Opéra Garnier** (pl. de l'Opéra, 9e, tel. 47-42-53-71) has alas conceded its role as Paris's main opera house to the **Opéra Bastille** (pl. de la Bastille, tel. 40–01–16–16). The old Opéra now devotes itself to classical dance; French ballet superstar Patrick Dupont is the reigning artistic director. The Opéra Bastille, meanwhile, has had its share of start-up and management problems, and many feel it is not living up to its promise of grand opera at affordable prices. The **Théâtre Musical de Paris,** better known as the Théâtre du Châtelet (2 pl. du Châtelet, 1er, tel. 40–28–28–28) offers opera and ballet for a wider audience, at more reasonable prices.

Dance Apart from the traditional ballets sometimes on the bill at the Opéra (*see above*), the highlights of the Paris dance year are the visits of major foreign troupes, usually to the **Palais des Congrès** at Porte Maillot (tel. 40–68–22–22) or the **Palais des Sports** at the Porte de Versailles (tel. 48–28–40–48).

Movies Parisians are far more addicted to the cinema as an art form than are Londoners or New Yorkers. There are hundreds of movie theaters in the city, and a number of them, especially in principal tourist areas such as the Champs-Elysées and the boulevard des Italiens near the Opéra, run English films. Check the *Officiel du Spectacle* or *Pariscope* for a movie of your choice. Look for the initials "v.o.," which mean *version originale;* i.e., not subtitled or dubbed. Cinema admission runs from 40 francs to 55 francs; there are reduced rates on Wednesdays and, in some cinemas, for morning shows. Most ushers and usherettes expect a franc or two tip.

Real movie buffs should visit the **Pompidou Center,** with lots of classics and obscure films. The **Musée du Cinéma** at the Palais de Chaillot houses a fabulous collection of posters, costumes, set designs, and props from all over the world. The **Cinémathèque Française** at Trocadéro has a reference library and photograph collection as well as an outstanding collection of films. The **Vidéothèque de Paris,** in the Forum des Halles, is a public archive of films and videos on the city of Paris.

The Champs-Elysées bristles with cinemas, but tickets cost more here. A better bet, on the Left Bank, is the Action chain of cinemas, with frequently discounted tickets. These include the **Action Ecoles** (23 rue des Ecoles, 5e), **Action Rive Gauche** (5 rue des Ecoles, 5e), and **Action Christine** (4 rue Christine, 6e). The latter shows offbeat films and reruns; so do the **Studio Galande** (42 rue Galande, 5e), the **Saint-André-des-Arts** (30 rue Saint-André-des-Arts, 6e), and the **Lucernaire Forum** (53 rue Nôtre-Dame-des-Champs, 6e). The Chinese-style **Pagoda** (57 rue de Babylone, 7e) is a national monument, and well worth a visit.

Nightlife

The French are definitely night birds, though these days that means smart, elegant *bars de nuit* rather than frenetic discos. The **Champs-Elysées,** that ubiquitous cabaret land, is making a comeback, though the clientele remains predominantly foreign. The tawdry **Pigalle** and down-at-the-heels **Bastille** areas are trendy these days, and the **Left Bank** boasts a bit of everything. During the week, people are usually home after closing hours at 2 AM, but weekends mean late-night partying.

Cabaret Paris's nightclubs are household names, shunned by wordly Parisians and beloved of foreign tourists, who flock to the shows.

All of them are expensive. Prices can range from 350 francs (simple admission plus one drink) to more than 1,000 francs (dinner plus show). If you must experience it, the **Moulin Rouge** (pl. Blanche, 18e, tel. 46–06–00–19) mingles the cancan and crocodiles in an extravagant spectacle that is a bit less expensive than similar shows.

Bars and Nightclubs The more upscale Paris nightclubs tend to be both expensive (1,000 francs for a bottle of gin or whiskey) and private—in other words, you'll usually need to know someone who's a member in order to get through the door. Bars, where you can linger over a single drink, are cheaper. Literary types will head for **Harry's Bar** (5 rue Daunou, 2e), a cozy, wood-paneled hangout for Americans that's haunted by the ghosts of Ernest Hemingway and F. Scott Fitzgerald. Also highly popular among the nostalgic set are the many hotel bars in the city, including the reasonably priced **Normandy** (7 rue de l'Echelle, 1er) and the **Bélier** at **l'Hôtel** (13 rue des Beaux Arts, 6e).

Other popular spots are **Le Rosebud** (11 bis rue Delambre, 14e) a cult spot for the *jeunesse dorée* (young and fashionable) of the Left Bank; **La Casbah** (18 rue de la Forge Royale, 11e), a bit of Casablanca in the Bastille area; and **le Forum** (4 blvd. Malsherbes, 8e), an archetypical French cocktail bar with one of the best selection of drinks in Paris.

Other fun places for an evening out include:

Caveau des Oubliettes. Listen to Edith Piaf songs in a medieval cellar that was once the dungeons of a prison. It's complete with minstrels, troubadours, and serving wenches—and tourists love it. *11 rue St-Julien-le-Pauvre, 5e. Admission: 130 frs. Open 9 PM–2 AM. Closed Sun.*

Au Lapin Agile. It considers itself the "doyen of cabarets," and Picasso once paid for a meal with one of his paintings. The setting, in Montmartre, is touristy but picturesque. *22 rue des Saules, 18e. Admission: 110 frs. Open 9 PM–2 AM. Closed Mon.*

Jazz Clubs The French take jazz seriously, and Paris is one of the great jazz cities of the world, with plenty of variety, including some fine, distinctive local coloring. For nightly schedules, consult the specialty magazines *Jazz Hot* or *Jazz Magazine*. Remember that nothing gets going till 10 or 11 PM, and that entry prices can vary widely from about 35 francs to over 100 francs.

Start on the Left Bank at the **Caveau de la Huchette** (5 rue de la Huchette, 5e), a smoke-filled shrine to the Dixieland beat. **Le Petit Journal** (71 blvd. St-Michel, 5e), opposite the Luxembourg gardens, serves up good food and traditional jazz. In the 1st Arrondissement, **Au Duc des Lombards** (42 rue des Lombards, 1er) is an ill-lit, romantic venue. The **Slow Club** (130 rue de Rivoli, 1er) plays swing and Dixieland jazz. **New Morning** (7 rue des Petites Ecuries, 10e) is a more expensive but truly premier spot for visiting musicians and French bands.

Rock Clubs Unlike French jazz, French rock is not generally considered to be on par with its American and British cousins. Admission is quite steep—from 80 francs to 100 francs—and nothing gets going until about 11 PM. If you're a dedicated rock fan, try the **Dancing Gibus Club** (18 rue du Fbg. du Temple, 11e), a place of long standing. **Le Bataclan** (50 blvd. Voltaire, 11e) features mostly French punk rock bands. **Le Sunset** (60 rue des Lombards, 1er) is a small, whitewashed cellar with first-rate live music and a clientele that's there to listen.

Discos Discos aren't as hot as they once were here; you'll find more Parisians seeking moody little cocktail bars these days. Still, stalwarts continue to seek the beat. A Paris disco's life is often short and sweet, so don't be surprised if some of those listed here have closed their doors or changed their names. The **Balajo** (9 rue de Lappe, 11e), is a Bastille institution that thumps to sounds old and new. On the same street, the **Chapelle des Lombards** (19 rue de Lappe, 11e) goes for an Afro-Cuban beat. Those with a penchant for Latin rhythms should try the **Trottoirs de Buenos-Aires** (37 rue des Lombards, 1er) for some mambo, samba, and salsa. **Le Tango** (13 rue Au-Maire, 4e) attracts a sensuous dance crowd. **Club Zed** (2 rue des Anglais, 6e) is a prime rock'n'roll venue for all ages.

Pubs The number of Paris bars that woo English-speaking clients with a pub atmosphere and dark beer are becoming increasingly popular with Parisians, too. The **Académie de la Bière** (88 bis blvd. de Port-Royal, 5e) serves more than 100 foreign brews to accompany good french fries and *moules marinière* (mussels cooked in white wine). The **Bar Belge** (75 av. de St-Ouen, 17e) is an authentically noisy Flemish drinking spot, while the **Mayflower** (49 rue Descartes, 5e) is a classy, Left Bank spot, British-style. The **Micro-Brasserie** (106 rue de Richelieu, 2e), just off the Grands Boulevards, brews its own beer. Quaff Guinness in an Irish mode at **Kitty O'Shea** (10 rue des Capucines, 2e) or at the animated **Finnegan's Wake** (42 rue des Boulangers, 5e) in the Latin Quarter. In the Bastille area, pubs are popping up at a rapid rate. The doyen is the seedy but colorful **Café de la Plage** (59 rue de Charonne, 11e).

Gays **Chez Moune** (54 rue Pigalle, 18e) is a cabaret and disco for lesbians. Upscale **Katmandou** (21 rue du Vieux Colombier, 7e) is Paris's best-known lesbian nightclub. Gay men can try the popular **Le BH** (7 rue du Roule, 1e) or **Broad Connection** (3 rue de la Ferronerie, 1er).

All-night Restaurants Chances are that some of your nocturnal forays will have you looking for sustenance at an unlikely hour. If so, you might find it handy to know that the following restaurants stay open round the clock:

Au Pied de Cochon (6 rue Coquillière, 1er, tel. 42–36–11–75), near St-Eustache church in Les Halles, once catered to the all-night workers at the adjacent Paris food market. Today, its Second Empire decor has been restored, and traditional dishes like pig's trotters and chitterling sausage still grace the menu. **Batifol** (29 av. Corentin-Cariou, 19e, tel. 40–36–12–36) serves cheap, authentic bistro food.
The Chicago Pizza Factory (5 rue de Berry, 8e, tel. 45–62–50–23) will satisfy your craving for deep-dish pizza.

For more suggestions, *see* Where to Eat on a Budget, Chapter 5.

7 **Excursions**

Chartres

Although Chartres is chiefly visited for its magnificent Gothic cathedral with world-famous stained-glass windows, the whole town—one of the prettiest in France, with old houses and picturesque streets—is worth leisurely exploration.

Worship on the site of the cathedral goes back to before the Gallo-Roman period; the crypt contains a well that was the focus of Druid ceremonies. The original cult of the fertility goddess merged into that of the Virgin Mary with the arrival of Christianity. In the late 9th century, King Charles the Bold presented Chartres with what was believed to be the tunic of the Virgin. This precious relic attracted hordes of pilgrims, and Chartres swiftly became—and has remained—a prime destination for the faithful. Pilgrims trek to Chartres from Paris on foot to this day.

The noble, soaring spires of Chartres compose one of the most famous sights in Europe. Try to catch a glimpse of them surging out of the vast golden grainfields of the Beauce as you approach from the northeast.

Getting There

There are hourly trains from Paris (Gare Montparnasse) to Chartres (travel time is 50–70 minutes, depending on service), many of which stop at Rambouillet and Maintenon.

Paris Environs

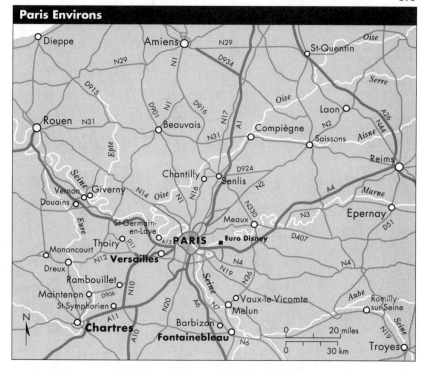

Dieppe · Amiens · N29 · St-Quentin · Oise · N29 · N1 · D934 · Serre · D915 · Oise · Laon · A26 · D901 · N1 · D916 · N17 · Beauvais · A1 · Compiègne · N2 · N44 · Rouen · N31 · Epte · N31 · Soissons · Aisne · Reims · D924 · Chantilly · Senlis · Marne · Seine · Giverny · N14 · Oise · N16 · N2 · A4 · Epernay · Vernon · Douains · N1 · N330 · N3 · D51 · Eure · St-Germain-en-Laye · Meaux · D407 · Monancourt · Thoiry · D11 · A13 · **PARIS** · Euro Disney · Dreux · N12 · **Versailles** · N4 · N4 · Rambouillet · D10 · N19 · N36 · Maintenon · D906 · N20 · A6 · Seine · N7 · Vaux-le-Vicomte · Aube · Romilly-sur-Seine · St-Symphorien · A11 · Melun · **Chartres** · A10 · Barbizon · **Fontainebleau** · N6 · Seine · N19 · Troyes

N

0 · 20 miles
0 · 30 km

Guided Tours

Paris Vision (214 rue de Rivoli, tel. 42–60–31–25) and **Cityrama** (4 pl. des Pyramides, tel. 42–60–30–14) can arrange guided visits to a number of sites in the Paris region. Both feature half-day trips to Chartres on Tuesday and Saturday afternoons (250 frs); and combined excursions to Chartres and Versailles (395 frs) on the same days. Additional trips are scheduled in summer; call for information.

Tourist Information

Office du Tourisme, pl. de la Cathédrale, 28000 Chartres, tel. 16/37–21–50–00.

Exploring

Today's **Chartres cathedral** is the sixth church to occupy the same spot. It dates mainly from the 12th and 13th centuries, having been erected after the previous, 11th-century building burned down in 1194. A well-chronicled outburst of religious fervor followed the discovery that the Virgin's relic had miraculously survived unsinged. Reconstruction went ahead at a breathtaking pace. Just 25 years were needed for Chartres cathedral to rise again, and it has remained substantially unchanged ever since.

The lower half of the facade is all that survives from the 11th-century Romanesque church. (The Romanesque style is evi-

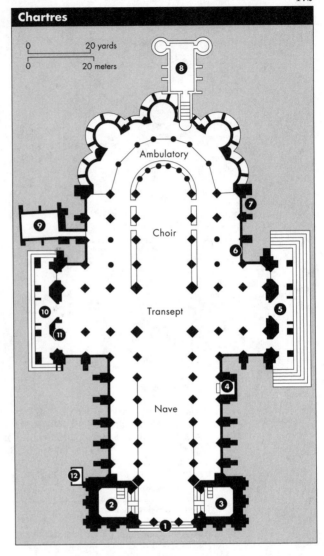

Chartres

0   20 yards
0   20 meters

Ambulatory

Choir

Transept

Nave

dent in the use of round, rather than pointed, arches.) The main
door—the **Portail Royal**—is richly sculpted with scenes from
the Life of Christ. The flanking towers are also Romanesque,
though the upper part of the taller of the two **spires** (380 feet as
against 350 feet) dates from the start of the 16th century, and
its fanciful flamboyance contrasts with the stalwart solemnity
of its Romanesque counterpart. The **rose window** above the
main portal dates from the 13th century. The three windows
below it contain some of the finest examples of 12th-century
stained glass in France.

The interior is somber, and your eyes will need time to get used
to the darkness. Their reward will be a view of the gemlike
richness of the stained glass, with the famous deep "Chartres

So, you're getting away from it all.

Just make sure you can get back.

AT&T Access Numbers
Dial the number of the country you're in to reach AT&T.

*ANDORRA	19◇-0011	GERMANY**	0130-0010	*NETHERLANDS	06◇-022-9111
*AUSTRIA	022-903-011	*GREECE	00-800-1311	*NORWAY	050-12011
*BELGIUM	078-11-0010	*HUNGARY	00◇-800-01111	POLAND¹◆²	0◇010-480-0111
BULGARIA	00-1800-0010	*ICELAND	999-001	PORTUGAL¹	05017-1-288
CROATIA¹◆	99-38-0011	IRELAND	1-800-550-000	ROMANIA	01-800-4288
*CYPRUS	080-90010	ISRAEL	177-100-2727	*RUSSIA¹ (MOSCOW)	155-5042
CZECH REPUBLIC	00-420-00101	*ITALY	172-1011	SLOVAKIA	00-420-00101
*DENMARK	8001-0010	KENYA¹	0800-10	SPAIN	900-99-00-11
*EGYPT¹ (CAIRO)	510-0200	*LIECHTENSTEIN	155-00-11	*SWEDEN	020-795-611
*FINLAND	9800-100-10	LITHUANIA◆	8◇196	*SWITZERLAND	155-00-11
FRANCE	19◇-0011	LUXEMBOURG	0-800-0111	*TURKEY	9◇9-8001-2277
*GAMBIA	00111	*MALTA	0800-890-110	UK	0800-89-0011

Countries in bold face permit country-to-country calling in addition to calls to the U.S. *Public phones require deposit of coin or phone card.
**Western portion. Includes Berlin and Leipzig. ◇Await second dial tone. ¹May not be available from every phone. ◆ Not available from public phones. ¹Dial ''02'' first, outside Cairo. ¹Dial 010-480-0111 from major Warsaw hotels. ©1993 AT&T

Here's a travel tip that will make it easy to call back to the States. Dial the access number for the country you're visiting and connect right to AT&T **USADirect**® Service. It's the quick way to get English-speaking operators and can minimize hotel surcharges.

If all the countries you're visiting aren't listed above, call **1 800 241-5555** before you leave for a free wallet card with all AT&T access numbers. International calling made easy—it's all part of **The i Plan.**℠

THE **i** PLAN™

AT&T

All The Best Trips Start with **Fodor's**

Fodor's Affordables

Titles in the series: Caribbean, Europe, Florida, France, Germany, Great Britain, Italy, London, Paris.

"Travelers with champagne tastes and beer budgets will welcome this series from Fodor's." — *Hartford Courant*

"These books succeed admirably; easy to follow and use, full of cost-related information, practical advice, and recommendations...maps are clear and easy to use." — *Travel Books Worldwide*

Fodor's Bed & Breakfast and Country Inn Guides

Titles in the series: California, Canada, England & Wales, Mid-Atlantic, New England, The Pacific Northwest, The South, The Upper Great Lakes Region, The West Coast.

"In addition to information on each establishment, the books add notes on things to see and do in the vicinity. That alone propels these books to the top of the heap."— *San Diego Union-Tribune*

The Berkeley Guides

Titles in the series: California, Central America, Eastern Europe, France, Germany, Great Britain & Ireland, Mexico, The Pacific Northwest, San Francisco.

The best choice for budget travelers, from the Associated Students at the University of California at Berkeley.

"Berkeley's scribes put the funk back in travel." — *Time*

"Hip, blunt and lively." — *Atlanta Journal Constitution*

"Fresh, funny and funky as well as useful." — *The Boston Globe*

Exploring Guides

Titles in the series: Australia, California, Caribbean, Florida, France, Germany, Great Britain, Ireland, Italy, London, New York City, Paris, Rome, Singapore & Malaysia, Spain, Thailand.

"Authoritatively written and superbly presented, and makes worthy reading before, during or after a trip." — *The Philadelphia Inquirer*

"A handsome new series of guides, complete with lots of color photos, geared to the independent traveler." — *The Boston Globe*

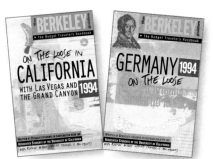

Visit your local bookstore or call 1-800-533-6478 24 hours a day.

Fodor's The name that means smart travel.

blue" predominating. The oldest window, and perhaps the most stunning, is *Notre Dame de la Belle Verrière* (literally, Our Lady of the Beautiful Window), in the south choir. It is well worth taking a pair of binoculars to pick out the details. If you wish to know more about stained-glass techniques and the motifs used, visit the small exhibit in the gallery opposite the north porch. The vast black-and-white medieval pattern on the floor of the nave is the only one of its kind to have survived from the Middle Ages. The faithful were expected to travel along its entire length (some 300 yards) on their knees.

Guided tours of the crypt start from the Maison de la Crypte opposite the south porch. The Romanesque and Gothic chapels running around the crypt have recently been stripped of the 19th-century paintings that used to disfigure them. You will also be shown a 4th-century Gallo-Roman wall and some 12th-century wall paintings. *Admission: 10 frs adults, 7 frs children and students. Guided tours of crypt: Easter–Oct. daily 11, 2:15, 3:30, 4:30, 5:15; Nov.–Easter daily 11, 4.*

Just behind the cathedral stands the **Musée des Beaux-Arts,** a handsome 18th-century building that used to serve as the bishop's palace. Its varied collection includes Renaissance enamels, a portrait of Erasmus by Holbein, tapestries, armor, and some fine, mainly French paintings of the 17th, 18th, and 19th centuries. There is also a room devoted to the forceful 20th-century works of Maurice de Vlaminck, who lived in the region. *29 cloître Notre Dame. Admission: 10 frs (20 frs for special exhibitions). Open Apr.–Oct. Wed.–Mon. 10–6, Nov.–Mar. 10–noon and 2–5, closed Tues.*

The museum gardens overlook the old streets that tumble down to the river Eure. Take rue Chantault down to the river, cross over, and head right, along rue de la Tannerie (which becomes rue de la Foulerie) as far as rue du Pont St-Hilaire. From here, there is a lovely view of the roofs of old Chartres nestling beneath the cathedral. Then cross the bridge and head up to the Gothic **Eglise St-Pierre,** whose own magnificent windows date back to the early 14th century. There is yet more stained glass (17th century) to admire at the **Eglise St-Aignan** nearby, just off rue St-Pierre.

Wander among the steep, narrow streets, with the spires of the cathedral as your guide. Near the station is the striking monument to Jean Moulin, martyred World War II Resistance hero and onetime prefect of Chartres.

The river Eure snakes northeast from Chartres to the town of **Maintenon,** whose Renaissance **château** once belonged to Louis XIV's mistress and morganatic spouse, Madame de Maintenon. Her private apartments are open to visitors. The square, 12th-century keep is the sole vestige of a fortress that once occupied this site. The formal gardens stretch behind the château to the ivy-covered arches of the ruined **aqueduct**—one of the Sun King's most outrageous projects. His aim: to provide the ornamental ponds in the gardens of Versailles (30 miles away) with water from the Eure. In 1684, some 30,000 men were signed up to construct a three-tier, 3-mile aqueduct as part of this project. Many died of fever before the enterprise was called off in 1689. *Admission: 28 frs adults, 20 frs children. Open Apr.–Oct. Wed.–Sat. 2–6, Sun. 10–noon and 2–6, Nov.–Mar. weekends 2–5. Closed Jan.*

Rambouillet, surrounded by a huge forest, was once the residence of kings and dukes; today it is the occasional home of the French president. When he's not entertaining visiting dignitaries here, the **château** and its extensive **grounds** (lake, islands, and flower beds) are open to the public. Most of the buildings date from the early 18th century, but the brawny **Tour François I,** named for the king who breathed his last here in 1547, was part of the 14th-century fortified castle that first stood on this site. *Admission: 24 frs adults, 23 frs senior citizens. Open Wed.–Mon. 10–noon and 2–6 (5 in winter).*

Dining

Le Buisson Ardent. This wood-beamed restaurant offers attentive service, fixed-price menus, imaginative food, and a view of Chartres cathedral. Try the chicken ravioli with leeks or the rolled beef with spinach. *10 rue au Lait, tel. 16/37–34–04–66. Reservations advised. Dress: casual. AE, DC, V. Closed Sun. evening. Inexpensive–Moderate.*

Les Epars. Here's sturdy, no-nonsense French fare for hearty appetites and tight budgets. Lunch or dinner won't cost much more than 100 francs. *11 pl. des Epars, tel. 16/37–21–23–72. Dress: casual. V. Closed Sun. evening and Mon. Inexpensive.*

Fontainebleau

Fontainebleau, with its historic château, is a favorite place for excursions, especially since a lush forest is close by.

Like Chambord in the Loire Valley or Compiègne to the north of Paris, Fontainebleau earned royal esteem as a hunting base. As at Versailles, a hunting lodge once stood on the site of the current château, along with a chapel built in 1169 and consecrated by exiled (later murdered and canonized) English priest Thomas à Becket. The palace you see today was begun under the flamboyant Renaissance king, François I, the French contemporary of England's Henry VIII. The king hired Italian artists Il Rosso (a pupil of Michelangelo) and Primaticcio to embellish his château. In fact they did much more: By introducing the pagan allegories and elegant lines of Mannerism to France, they revolutionized French decorative art. Their extraordinary frescoes and stuccowork can be admired in the Galerie François I and the glorious Salle de Bal, which was completed under Henri II, François's successor.

Although Sun King Louis XIV's architectural fancy was concentrated on Versailles, he commissioned Mansart to design new pavilions and had André Le Nôtre replant the gardens at Fontainebleau, where he and his court returned faithfully each autumn for the hunting season. However, it was Napoléon who made a Versailles, as it were, out of Fontainebleau, by spending lavishly to restore it to its former glory. He held Pope Pius VII prisoner here in 1812, signed the second church-state concordat here in 1813, and, in the cobbled Cour des Adieux, bade farewell to his Old Guard in 1814 as he began his brief exile on the Mediterranean island of Elba.

Another courtyard—the Cour de la Fontaine—was commissioned by Napoléon in 1812 and adjoins the Etang (or pond) des Carpes. Ancient carp are alleged to swim here, although Allied

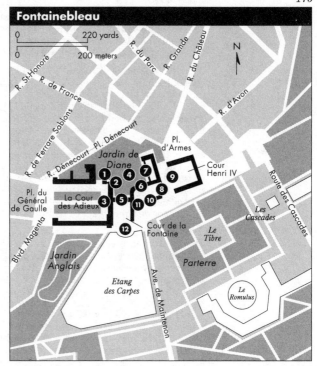

soldiers drained the pond in 1915 and ate all the fish, and, in the event they missed some, Hitler's hordes did likewise in 1940.

Getting There

Fontainebleau is about 50 minutes from the Gare de Lyon; take a bus to complete the trip from the station to the château.

Guided Tours

Paris Vision and **Cityrama** offer half-day trips to Fontainebleau *(see* Guided Tours in Chartres, *above,* for addresses). Cost: 280 frs. Departures 1:30 Wed. and Sun.

Tourist Information

Office du Tourisme, 31 pl. Napoléon-Bonaparte, Fontaine-bleau, tel. 16/64–22–25–68.

Exploring

The **château of Fontainebleau** dates from the 16th century, although additions were made by various royal incumbents over the next 300 years. The famous **horseshoe staircase** that dominates the Cour du Cheval Blanc (which later came to be called the Cour des Adieux, or Courtyard of Farewell) was built by Androuet du Cerceau for Louis XIII (1610–1643). The **Porte**

Dauphine is the most beautiful of the various gateways that connect the complex of buildings; its name commemorates the fact that the Dauphin—the heir to the throne, later Louis XIII—was christened under its archway in 1606.

Napoléon's apartments occupied the first floor. You can see a lock of his hair, his Légion d'Honneur medal, his imperial uniform, the hat he wore on his return from Elba in 1815, and one bed in which he definitely did sleep (almost every town in France boasts a bed in which the emperor supposedly spent a night). There is also a throne room—Napoléon spurned the one at Versailles, a palace he disliked, and established his imperial seat in the former King's Bedchamber, a room with a suitably majestic decor—and the **Queen's Boudoir,** known as the room of the six Maries (occupants included ill-fated Marie Antoinette and Napoléon's second wife, Marie-Louise). Highlights of other salons include 17th-century tapestries, marble reliefs by Jacquet de Grenoble, and paintings and frescoes by the versatile Primaticcio.

The jewel of the interior, though, is the ceremonial ballroom, or **Salle de Bal,** nearly 100 feet long and dazzlingly decorated with 16th-century frescoes and gilding. It is luxuriantly wood-paneled, and a gleaming parquetry floor reflects the patterns in the ceiling. Like the château as a whole, the room exudes a sense of elegance and style—but on a more intimate, human scale than at Versailles: This is Renaissance, not Baroque. *Admission: 30 frs adults, 19 frs ages 18–25, senior citizens, and on Sun. Open Wed.–Mon. 9:30–12:30 and 2–5; gardens open 9–dusk (admission free).*

Dining

Chez Arrighi. Dishes have a pleasing Corsican accent and are plentifully apportioned. Look for sautéed rabbit, sheep's cheese tart, and beef stew. Good value prix-fixe meals (110 and 139 francs) are served at lunch and dinner. *53 rue de France, tel. 64–22–29–43. Reservations advised. Dress: casual. MC, V. Inexpensive.*

Versailles

Paris in the 17th century was a rowdy, rabble-ridden city. Louis XIV hated it and set about in search of a new power base. He settled on Versailles, 15 miles west of Paris, where his father had a small château/hunting lodge.

Today, the château of Versailles seems monstrously big, but it wasn't large enough for the army of 20,000 noblemen, servants, and hangers-on who moved in with Louis. A new city—a new capital, in fact—had to be constructed from scratch to accommodate them. Vast mansions had to be built, along with broad avenues—all in an extravagant Baroque style.

It was hardly surprising that Louis XIV's successors rapidly felt uncomfortable with their architectural inheritance. Indeed, as the 18th century wore on, and the taste for intimate, private apartments expanded at the expense of the public, would-be heroic lifestyles of 17th-century monarchs, subsequent rulers built themselves small retreats on the grounds,

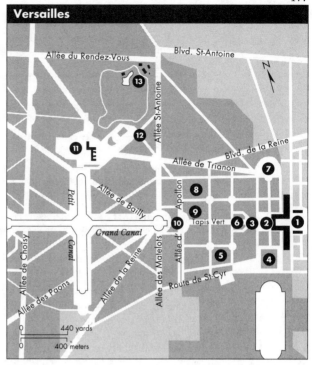

where they could escape the overpowering formality of court life. The two most famous of these structures are the **Petit Trianon,** built by Louis XV and a model of classical harmony and proportion; and the simple, "rustic" **Hameau,** or hamlet, that Marie Antoinette built so that she could play at being a simple shepherdess.

The contrast between the majestic and the domesticated is an important part of Versailles's appeal, but pomp and bombast dominate the mood here, and you won't need reminding that you're in the world's grandest palace—or one of France's most popular tourist attractions. The park outside is the ideal place to get your breath back. Le Nôtre's gardens represent formal landscaping at its most rigid and sophisticated.

Getting There

There are three train routes from Paris to Versailles (20–30 min). The RER-C to Versailles Rive-Gauche takes you closest to the château (just 600 yards from it via avenue de Sceaux). The other trains run from Gare St-Lazare to Versailles Rive-Droite (⅔ mile via rue Foch and avenue de St-Cloud), and from Gare Montparnasse to Versailles-Chantiers (¾ mile via rue des Etats Généraux and avenue de Paris).

Guided Tours

Paris Vision and **Cityrama** *(see* Guided Tours in Chartres, *above,* for addresses) offer half- and full-day guided bus tours of Versailles.

Tourist Information

Office de Tourisme, 7 rue des Réservoirs, Versailles 78000, tel. 39–50–36–22.

Exploring

The **château** was built under court architects Le Vau and Mansart between 1662 and 1690; entrance is through the gilt-and-iron gates from the huge place d'Armes. In the center of the building, across the sprawling cobbled forecourt, are the rooms that belonged to the king and queen. The two wings were occupied by the royal children and princes; attendants were housed in the attics.

The highlight of the tour, for many, is the **Galerie des Glaces** (Hall of Mirrors), now fully restored to its original dazzle. It was here that Bismarck proclaimed the unified German Empire in 1871, and here that the controversial Treaty of Versailles, asserting Germany's responsibility for World War I, was signed in 1919.

The royal bedchambers are formal; the **petits appartements,** where royal family and friends lived, are more on a human scale. The intimate **Opéra Royal,** the first oval hall in France, was designed for Louis XV. Touch the "marble" loges—they're actually painted wood. The chapel, built by Mansart, is a study in white-and-gold solemnity. *Admission to château: 31 frs; Sun. 15 frs. Open Tues.–Sun. 9–7 (5:30 in winter); Galerie des Glaces open 9:45–5; Opéra Royal open 9:45–3:30 (tours every 15 min). Closed Mon.*

The 250-acre **grounds** include woods, lawns, flower beds, statues, lakes, and fountains. They are at their best in the fall. The fountains play on several Sundays in summer, making a fabulous spectacle. *The grounds are free and open daily.*

At one end of the Petit Canal, about a mile from the château, stands the **Grand Trianon,** built by Mansart in the 1680s. This pink-marble pleasure palace is now used to entertain visiting heads of state; at other times it is open to the public. *Admission: Grand Trianon: 17 frs; Petit Trianon: 12 frs. Open Oct.–Apr. Tues.–Fri. 10–12:30 and 2–5:30, weekends 10–5:30; May–Sept. Tues.–Sun. 11–6:30.*

The **Petit Trianon,** close by, is a sumptuously furnished neoclassical mansion erected in 1768 by architect Gabriel. Louis XV had a superb botanical garden planted here; some of the trees from that era survive today. Louis XVI presented the Petit Trianon to Marie Antoinette, who spent lavish sums creating an idealized world, the charming *hameau* (hamlet, a handful of thatched-roof cottages) with watermill, lake, and pigeon loft— outrageously pretty and too good to be true. *Hours same as for Grand Trianon.*

The town of Versailles tends to be underestimated. Visitors are usually exhausted from exploring the palace and park, but the town's broad, leafy boulevards are also agreeable places to stroll. The **Cathédrale St-Louis** is an austere edifice built from 1743 to 1754 by Mansart's grand-nephew, and it contains fine paintings and an organ loft. The **Eglise Notre Dame** is a sturdy Baroque monument, built from 1684 to 1686 by the elder Mansart as the parish church for the Sun King's new town, for which Louis XIV deigned to lay the foundation stone. The collection of the **Musée Lambinet,** housed nearby in an imposing 18th-century mansion, is wide-ranging, with a maze of cozy, finely furnished rooms full of paintings, weapons, fans, and porcelain. *54 blvd. de la Reine. Admission: 10 frs. Open Tues.– Sun. 2–6; closed Mon.*

Dining

Quai No. 1. Barometers, sails, and model boats contribute to the nautical decor at this small, charming fish and seafood restaurant. Home-smoked salmon is a specialty here, though any dish on the two set menus will prove to be a good value. *1 av. de St-Cloud, tel. 39–50–42–26. Reservations advised. Dress: casual. MC, V. Closed Sun. evening and Mon. Moderate.*

La Grande Sirène. The addition of an appealing 148-franc lunch menu (wine included) served every day but Sunday makes this pretty spot near the château a popular noontime choice. Zesty simmered snails and well-prepared fish are good choices here. *25 rue du Maréchal-Foch, tel. 39–53–08–08. Reservations advised. Dress: casual. AE, MC, V. Moderate.*

Conversion Tables

Distance

Kilometers/Miles To change kilometers to miles, multiply kilometers by .621.
To change miles to kilometers, multiply miles by 1.61.

Km to Mi	Mi to Km
1 = .62	1 = 1.6
2 = 1.2	2 = 3.2
3 = 1.9	3 = 4.8
4 = 2.5	4 = 6.4
5 = 3.1	5 = 8.1
6 = 3.7	6 = 9.7
7 = 4.3	7 = 11.3
8 = 5.0	8 = 12.9
9 = 5.6	9 = 14.5

Meters/Feet To change meters to feet, multiply meters by 3.28.
To change feet to meters, multiply feet by .305.

Meters to Feet	Feet to Meters
1 = 3.3	1 = .31
2 = 6.6	2 = .61
3 = 9.8	3 = .92
4 = 13.1	4 = 1.2
5 = 16.4	5 = 1.5
6 = 19.7	6 = 1.8
7 = 23.0	7 = 2.1
8 = 26.2	8 = 2.4
9 = 29.5	9 = 2.7

Weight

Kilograms/Pounds To change kilograms to pounds, multiply kilos by 2.20.
To change pounds to kilograms, multiply pounds by .453.

Kilo to Pound	Pound to Kilo
1 = 2.2	1 = .45
2 = 4.4	2 = .91
3 = 6.6	3 = 1.4
4 = 8.8	4 = 1.8
5 = 11.0	5 = 2.3

6 = 13.2	6 = 2.7
7 = 15.4	7 = 3.2
8 = 17.6	8 = 3.6
9 = 19.8	9 = 4.1

Grams/Ounces To change grams to ounces, multiply grams by .035.
To change ounces to grams, multiply ounces by 28.4.

Grams to Ounces	Ounces to Grams
1 = .04	1 = 28
2 = .07	2 = 57
3 = .11	3 = 85
4 = .14	4 = 114
5 = .18	5 = 142
6 = .21	6 = 170
7 = .25	7 = 199
8 = .28	8 = 227
9 = .32	9 = 256

Liquid Volume

Liters/U.S. Gallons To change liters to U.S. gallons, multiply liters by .264.
To change U.S. gallons to liters, multiply gallons by 3.79.

Liters to U.S. Gallons	U.S. Gallons to Liters
1 = .26	1 = 3.8
2 = .53	2 = 7.6
3 = .79	3 = 11.4
4 = 1.1	4 = 15.1
5 = 1.3	5 = 18.9
6 = 1.6	6 = 22.7
7 = 1.8	7 = 26.5
8 = 2.1	8 = 30.3
9 = 2.4	9 = 34.1

Clothing Sizes

Men To change American suit sizes to French suit sizes, add 10 to
Suits the American suit size.
To change French suit sizes to American suit sizes, subtract 10
from the French suit size.

U.S.	36	38	40	42	44	46	48
French	46	48	50	52	54	56	58

Shirts To change American shirt sizes to French shirt sizes, multiply
the American shirt size by 2 and add 8.

To change French shirt sizes to American shirt sizes, subtract 8 from the French shirt size and divide by 2.

U.S.	14	14½	15	15½	16	16½	17	17½
French	36	37	38	39	40	41	42	43

Shoes French shoe sizes vary in their relation to American shoe sizes.

U.S.	6½	7	8	9	10	10½	11
French	39	40	41	42	43	44	45

Women
Dresses and Coats To change U.S. dress/coat sizes to French dress/coat sizes, add 28 to the U.S. dress/coat size.
To change French dress/coat sizes to U.S. dress/coat sizes, subtract 28 from the French dress/coat size.

U.S.	4	6	8	10	12	14	16
French	32	34	36	38	40	42	44

Blouses and Sweaters To change U.S. blouse/sweater sizes to French blouse/sweater sizes, add 8 to the U.S. blouse/sweater size.
To change French blouse/sweater sizes to U.S. blouse/sweater sizes, subtract 8 from the French blouse/sweater size.

U.S.	30	32	34	36	38	40	42
French	38	40	42	44	46	48	50

Shoes To change U.S. shoe sizes to French shoe sizes, add 32 to the U.S. shoe size.
To change French shoe sizes to U.S. shoe sizes, subtract 32 from the French shoe size.

U.S.	4	5	6	7	8	9	10
French	36	37	38	39	40	41	42

French Vocabulary

Words and Phrases

	English	French	Pronunciation
Basics	Yes/no	Oui/non	wee/no
	Please	S'il vous plaît	seel voo play
	Thank you	Merci	mare-**see**
	You're welcome	De rien	deh ree-**en**
	That's all right	Il n'y a pas de quoi	eel nee ah pah de kwa
	Excuse me, sorry	Pardon	pahr-**doan**
	Sorry!	Désolé(e)	day-zoh-**lay**
	Good morning/ afternoon	Bonjour	bone-**joor**
	Good evening	Bonsoir	bone-**swar**
	Goodbye	Au revoir	o ruh-**vwar**
	Mr. (Sir)	Monsieur	mih-see-**oor**
	Mrs. (Ma'am)	Madame	ma-**dam**
	Miss	Mademoiselle	mad-mwa-**zel**
	Pleased to meet you	Enchanté(e)	on-shahn-**tay**
	How are you?	Comment allez-vous?	ko-mon-tahl-ay-**voo**
	Very well, thanks	Très bien, merci	tray bee-**en,** mare-**see**
	And you?	Et vous?	ay voo?
Numbers	one	un	un
	two	deux	deu
	three	trois	twa
	four	quatre	**cat**-ruh
	five	cinq	sank
	six	six	seess
	seven	sept	set
	eight	huit	wheat
	nine	neuf	nuf
	ten	dix	deess
	eleven	onze	owns
	twelve	douze	dooz
	thirteen	treize	trays
	fourteen	quatorze	ka-torz
	fifteen	quinze	cans
	sixteen	seize	sez
	seventeen	dix-sept	deess-**set**
	eighteen	dix-huit	deess-**wheat**
	nineteen	dix-neuf	deess-**nuf**
	twenty	vingt	vant
	twenty-one	vingt-et-un	vant-ay-**un**
	thirty	trente	trahnt
	forty	quarante	**ka**-rahnt
	fifty	cinquante	**sang**-kahnt
	sixty	soixante	**swa**-sahnt
	seventy	soixante-dix	swa-sahnt-**deess**
	eighty	quatre-vingts	cat-ruh-**vant**
	ninety	quatre-vingt-dix	cat-ruh-vant-**deess**

	one-hundred	cent	sahnt
	one-thousand	mille	meel

Colors	black	noir	nwar
	blue	bleu	blu
	brown	brun	brun
	green	vert	vair
	orange	orange	o-**ranj**
	pink	rose	rose
	red	rouge	rouge
	violet	violette	vee-o-**let**
	white	blanc	blahnk
	yellow	jaune	jone

Days of the Week	Sunday	dimanche	dee-**mahnsh**
	Monday	lundi	lan-**dee**
	Tuesday	mardi	mar-**dee**
	Wednesday	mercredi	mare-kruh-**dee**
	Thursday	jeudi	juh-**dee**
	Friday	vendredi	van-dra-**dee**
	Saturday	samedi	sam-**dee**

Months	January	janvier	jan-**vyay**
	February	février	feh-vree-**ay**
	March	mars	maars
	April	avril	a-**vreel**
	May	mai	meh
	June	juin	jwan
	July	juillet	jwee-**ay**
	August	août	oot
	September	septembre	sep-**tahm**-bruh
	October	octobre	ok-**toe**-bruh
	November	novembre	no-**vahm**-bruh
	December	décembre	day-**sahm**-bruh

Useful Phrases	Do you speak English?	Parlez-vous anglais?	par-lay vooz ahng-**glay**
	I don't speak French	Je ne parle pas français	jeh nuh parl pah fraun-**say**
	I don't understand	Je ne comprends pas	jeh nuh kohm-prahn **pah**
	I understand	Je comprends	jeh kohm-**prahn**
	I don't know	Je ne sais pas	jeh nuh say **pah**
	I'm American/ British	Je suis américain/ anglais	jeh sweez a-may-ree-**can**/ahng-**glay**
	What's your name?	Comment vous appelez-vous?	ko-mahn voo za-pel-ay-**voo**
	My name is . . .	Je m'appelle . . .	jeh ma-**pel** . . .
	What time is it?	Quelle heure est-il?	kel ur et-**il**
	How?	Comment?	ko-**mahn**
	When?	Quand?	kahn
	Yesterday	Hier	yair
	Today	Aujourd'hui	o-zhoor-**dwee**

Tomorrow	Demain	deh-**man**
This morning/ afternoon	Ce matin/cet après-midi	seh ma-**tanh**/set ah-pray-mee-**dee**
Tonight	Ce soir	seh **swar**
What?	Quoi?	kwa
What is it?	Qu'est-ce que c'est?	kess-kuh-**say**
Why?	Pourquoi?	poor-**kwa**
Who?	Qui?	kee
Where is . . .	Où est . . .	oo ay
the train station?	la gare?	la gar
the subway station?	la station de métro?	la sta-syon deh may-**tro**
the bus stop?	l'arrêt de bus?	la-ray deh **booss**
the terminal (airport)?	l'aérogare?	lay-ro-**gar**
the post office?	la poste?	la post
the bank?	la banque?	la bahnk
the . . . hotel?	l'hôtel . . .?	low-**tel**
the store?	le magasin?	luh ma-ga-**zan**
the cashier?	la caisse?	la **kess**
the . . . museum?	le musée . . .?	leh mew-**zay**
the hospital?	l'hôpital?	low-pee-**tal**
the elevator?	l'ascenseur?	la-sahn-**seur**
the telephone?	le téléphone?	leh te-le-**phone**
Where are the restrooms?	Où sont les toilettes?	oo son lay twah-**let**
Here/there	Ici/là	ee-**see**/la
Left/right	A gauche/à droite	a goash/a drwat
Straight ahead	Tout droit	too drwa
Is it near/far?	C'est près/loin?	say pray/lwan
I'd like . . .	Je voudrais . . .	jeh voo-**dray**
a room	une chambre	ewn **shahm**-bra
the key	la clé	la clay
a newspaper	un journal	un joor-**nahl**
a stamp	un timbre	un **tam**-bruh
I'd like to buy . . .	Je voudrais acheter . . .	jeh voo-**dray** ash-**tay**
a cigar	un cigare	un see-**gar**
cigarettes	des cigarettes	day see-ga-**ret**
matches	des allumettes	days a-loo-**met**
dictionary	un dictionnaire	un deek-see-oh-**nare**
soap	du savon	dew sa-vone
city plan	un plan de ville	un plahn de la **veel**
road map	une carte routière	ewn cart roo-tee-**air**
magazine	une revue	ewn reh-**view**
envelopes	des enveloppes	dayz ahn-veh-**lope**
writing paper	du papier à lettres	dew pa-pee-ay a **let**-ruh

airmail writing paper	du papier avion	dew pa-pee-ay a-vee-**own**
postcard	une carte postale	ewn cart post-**al**
How much is it?	C'est combien?	say comb-bee-**en**
It's expensive/ cheap	C'est cher/pas cher	say sher/pa sher
A little/a lot	Un peu/beaucoup	un puh/bo-**koo**
More/less	Plus/moins	ploo/mwa
Enough/too (much)	Assez/trop	a-**say**/tro
I am ill/sick	Je suis malade	jeh swee ma-**lahd**
Call a doctor	Appelez un médecin	a-pe-lay un med-**san**
Help!	Au secours!	o say-**koor**
Stop!	Arrêtez!	a-reh-**tay**
Fire!	Au feu!	o fuw
Caution!/Look out!	Attention!	a-tahn-see-**own**

Dining Out

A bottle of . . .	une bouteille de . . .	ewn boo-**tay** deh
A cup of . . .	une tasse de . . .	ewn tass deh
A glass of . . .	un verre de . . .	un vair deh
Ashtray	un cendrier	un sahn-dree-**ay**
Bill/check	l'addition	la-dee-see-**own**
Bread	du pain	dew pan
Breakfast	le petit-déjeuner	leh pet-**ee** day-zhu-**nay**
Butter	du beurre	dew bur
Cheers!	A votre santé!	ah vo-truh sahn-**tay**
Cocktail/aperitif	un apéritif	un ah-pay-ree-**teef**
Dinner	le dîner	leh dee-**nay**
Dish of the day	le plat du jour	leh pla do **zhoor**
Enjoy!	Bon appétit!	bone a-pay-**tee**
Fixed-price menu	le menu	leh may-**new**
Fork	une fourchette	ewn four-**shet**
I am diabetic	Je suis diabétique	jeh swee-dee-ah-bay-**teek**
I am on a diet	Je suis au régime	jeh sweez o ray-**jeem**
I am vegetarian	Je suis végétarien(ne)	jeh swee vay-jay-ta-ree-**en**
I cannot eat . . .	Je ne peux pas manger de . . .	jeh nuh puh pah mahn-**jay** deh
I'd like to order	Je voudrais commander	jeh voo-**dray** ko-mahn-**day**

I'd like . . .	Je voudrais . . .	jeh voo-**dray**
I'm hungry/thirsty	J'ai faim/soif	jay fam/swahf
Is service/the tip included?	Est-ce que le service est compris?	ess keh leh sair-veess ay comb-**pree**
It's good/bad	C'est bon/mauvais	say bon/mo-**vay**
It's hot/cold	C'est chaud/froid	say sho/frwah
Knife	un couteau	un koo-**toe**
Lunch	le déjeuner	leh day-juh-**nay**
Menu	la carte	la cart
Napkin	une serviette	ewn sair-vee-**et**
Pepper	du poivre	dew **pwah**-vruh
Plate	une assiette	ewn a-see-**et**
Please give me . . .	Donnez-moi . . .	doe-nay-**mwah**
Salt	du sel	dew sell
Spoon	une cuillère	ewn kwee-**air**
Sugar	du sucre	dew **sook**-ruh
Waiter!/Waitress!	Monsieur!/ Mademoiselle!	mih-see-**oor**/ mad-mwah-**zel**
Wine list	la carte des vins	la cart day **van**

Menu Guide

English	French
Set menu	Menu à prix fixe
Dish of the day	Plat du jour
Choice of vegetable accompaniment	Garniture au choix
Made to order	Sur commande
Extra charge	Supplément/En sus
When available	Selon arrivage

Breakfast

Jam	Confiture
Honey	Miel
Boiled egg	Oeuf à la coque
Bacon and eggs	Oeufs au bacon
Ham and eggs	Oeufs au jambon
Fried eggs	Oeufs sur le plat
Scrambled eggs	Oeufs brouillés
(Plain) omelet	Omelette (nature)
Rolls	Petits pains

Starters

Anchovies	Anchois
Chitterling sausage	Andouille(tte)
Assorted cold cuts	Assiette anglaise
Assorted pork products	Assiette de charcuterie
Mixed raw vegetable salad	Crudités
Snails	Escargots
Assorted appetizers	Hors-d'oeuvres variés
Ham (Bayonne)	Jambon (de Bayonne)
Cured pig's knuckle	Jambonneau
Bologna sausage	Mortadelle
Deviled eggs	Oeufs à la diable
Liver purée blended with other meat	Pâté
Light dumplings (fish, fowl, or meat)	Quenelles
Dried sausage	Saucisson
Pâté sliced and served from an earthenware pot	Terrine
Cured dried beef	Viande séchée

Salads

Diced vegetable salad	Salade russe
Endive salad	Salade d'endives
Green salad	Salade verte
Mixed salad	Salade panachée
Riviera combination salad	Salade niçoise
Tuna salad	Salade de thon

Soups

Cold leek and potato cream soup	Vichyssoise
Cream of . . .	Crême de . . .
Cream of . . .	Velouté de . . .

Hearty soup	Soupe
day's soup	*du jour*
French onion soup	*à l'oignon*
Provençal vegetable soup	*au pistou*
Light soup	Potage
shredded vegetables	*julienne*
potato	*parmentier*
Fish and seafood stew	Bouillabaisse
Seafood stew (chowder)	Bisque
Stew of meat and vegetables	Pot-au-feu

Fish and Seafood

Angler	Lotte de mer
Bass	Bar
Burbot	Lotte
Carp	Carpe
Catfish	Loup
Clams	Palourdes
Cod	Morue
Creamed salt cod	Brandade de morue
Fresh cod	Cabillaud
Crab	Crabe
Crayfish	Ecrevisses
Eel	Anguille
Fish stew from Marseilles	Bourride
Fish stew in wine	Matelote
Frogs' legs	Cuisses de grenouilles
Herring	Harengs
Lobster	Homard
Spiny lobster	Langouste
Mackerel	Maquereau
Mussels	Moules
Octopus	Poulpes
Oysters	Huîtres
Perch	Perche
Pike	Brochet
Prawns	Ecrevisses
Dublin bay prawns (scampi)	Langoustines
Red mullet	Rouget
Salmon	Saumon
Scallops in creamy sauce	Coquille St-Jacques
Sea bream	Daurade
Shrimp	Crevettes
Skate	Raie
Smelt	Eperlans
Sole	Sole
Squid	Calmar
Trout	Truite
Tuna	Thon
Whiting	Merlan
Fish used in bouillabaisse	Rascasse

Meat

Beef	Boeuf
Brains	Cervelle
Chops	Côtelettes
Cutlet	Escalope
Fillet steak	Filet

Double fillet steak	Chateaubriand
Kabob	Brochette
Kidneys	Rognons
Lamb	Agneau
Leg	Gigot
Liver	Foie
Loin strip steak	Contre-filet
Meatballs	Boulettes de viande
Pig's feet	Pieds de cochon
Pork	Porc
Rib	Côte
Rib or rib-eye steak	Entrecôte
Saddle	Selle
Sausages	Saucisses
Sausages and cured pork served with sauerkraut	Choucroute garnie
Shoulder	Epaule
Steak (always beef)	Steak/steack
Stew	Ragoût
T-bone steak	Côte de boeuf
Tenderloin steak	Médaillon
Tenderloin of T-bone steak	Tournedos
Tongue	Langue
Veal	Veau
Veal sweetbreads	Ris de veau
Casserole of white beans and meat	Cassoulet toulousain

Methods of Preparation

Very rare	Bleu
Rare	Saignant
Medium	A point
Well-done	Bien cuit
Baked	Au four
Boiled	Bouilli
Braised	Braisé
Fried	Frit
Grilled	Grillé
Roast	Rôti
Sautéed	Sauté
Stewed	A l'étouffée

Game and Poultry

Chicken	Poulet
Chicken breast	Suprême de volaille
Chicken stewed in red wine	Coq au vin
Chicken stewed with vegetables	Poule au pot
Spring chicken	Poussin
Duck/duckling	Canard/caneton
Fattened pullet	Poularde
Fowl	Volaille
Guinea fowl/young guinea fowl	Pintade/pintadeau
Goose	Oie
Partridge/young partridge	Perdrix/perdreau
Pheasant	Faisan
Pigeon/squab	Pigeon/pigeonneau
Quail	Caille

Rabbit	Lapin
Thrush	Grive
Turkey/young turkey	Dinde/dindonneau
Venison (red/roe)	Cerf/chevreuil
Wild boar/young wild boar	Sanglier/marcassin
Wild hare	Lièvre

Vegetables

Artichoke	Artichaut
Asparagus	Asperge
Broad beans	Fèves
Brussels sprouts	Choux de Bruxelles
Cabbage (red)	Chou (rouge)
Carrots	Carottes
Cauliflower	Chou-fleur
Chicory	Chicorée
Eggplant	Aubergine
Endive	Endive
Leeks	Poireaux
Lentils	Lentilles
Lettuce	Laitue
Mushrooms	Champignons
Onions	Oignons
Peas	Petits pois
Peppers	Poivrons
Potato	Pomme de terre
Radishes	Radis
Spinach	Epinard
Tomatoes	Tomates
Watercress	Cresson
Zucchini	Courgette
White kidney/French beans	Haricots blancs/verts

Potatoes, Rice, and Noodles

Noodles	Nouilles
Pasta	Pâtes
Potatoes	Pommes (de terre)
matchsticks	*allumettes*
mashed and deep-fried	*dauphine*
mashed with butter and egg yolks	*duchesse*
in their jackets	*en robe des champs*
french fries	*frites*
mashed	*mousseline*
boiled/steamed	*nature/vapeur*
Rice	Riz
boiled in bouillon with onions	*pilaf*

Sauces and Preparations

Brown butter, parsley, lemon juice	Meunière
Curry	Indienne
Egg yolks, butter, vinegar	Hollandaise
Hot pepper	Diable
Mayonnaise flavored with mustard and herbs	Tartare
Mushrooms	Forestière
Mushrooms, red wine, shallots, beef marrow	Bordelaise

Onions, tomatoes, garlic	Provençale
Pepper sauce	Poivrade
Red wine, herbs	Bourguignon
Vinegar, egg yolks, white wine, shallots, tarragon	Béarnaise
Vinegar dressing	Vinaigrette
White sauce	Béchamel
White wine, mussel broth, egg yolks	Marinière
Wine, mushrooms, onions, shallots	Chasseur
With goose or duck liver purée and truffles	Périgueux
With Madeira wine	Madère

Fruits and Nuts

Almonds	Amandes
Apple	Pomme
Apricot	Abricot
Banana	Banane
Blackberries	Mûres
Blackcurrants	Cassis
Blueberries	Myrtilles
Cherries	Cerises
Chestnuts	Marrons
Coconut	Noix de coco
Dates	Dattes
Dried fruit	Fruits secs
Figs	Figues
Grapefruit	Pamplemousse
Grapes green/blue	Raisins blancs/noirs
Hazelnuts	Noisettes
Lemon	Citron
Lime	Citron vert
Melon	Melon
Nectarine	Brugnon
Orange	Orange
Peach	Pêche
Peanuts	Cacahouètes
Pear	Poire
Pineapple	Ananas
Plums	Prunes
Prunes	Pruneaux
Raisins	Raisins secs
Raspberries	Framboises
Red currants	Groseilles
Strawberries	Fraises
Tangerine	Mandarine
Walnuts	Noix
Watermelon	Pastèque

Desserts

Apple pie	Tarte aux pommes
Caramel pudding	Crème caramel
Chocolate cake	Gâteau au chocolat
Chocolate pudding	Mousse au chocolat
Custard	Flan
Ice cream	Glace
Ice-cream cake	Vacherin glacé

Layer cake	Tourte
Sundae	Coupe (glacée)
Water ice	Sorbet
Whipped cream	Crème Chantilly
Thin pancakes simmered in orange juice and flambéed with orange liqueur	Crêpe suzette

Alcoholic Drinks

Straight	Sec
On the rocks	Avec des glaçons
With water	A l'eau
Apple brandy	Calvados
Beer	Bière
Light/dark	*Blonde/brune*
Brandy	Eau–de–vie
Cocktails	Apéritifs
Chilled white wine mixed with blackcurrant syrup	*Kir/blanc-cassis*
Cherry brandy	Kirsch
Cordial	Liqueur
Pear brandy	Poire William
Port	Porto
Wine	Vin
dry	*sec*
very dry	*brut*
light	*léger*
sweet	*doux*
red	*rouge*
rosé	*rosé*
sparkling	*mousseux*
white	*blanc*

Nonalcoholic Drinks

Coffee	Café
black	*noir*
cream	*crème*
with milk	*au lait*
caffein-free	*décaféiné*
espresso	*express*
Ginger ale	Limonade gazeuse
Herb tea	Tisane
Hot chocolate	Chocolat chaud
Lemonade	Limonade
Milk	Lait
Mineral water	Eau minérale
carbonated	*gazeuse*
still	*non gazeuse*
. . . juice (see fruit)	Jus de . . .
Tea	Thé
with milk/lemon	*crème/citron*
iced tea	*glacé*
Tonic water	Schweppes

Index

Personal Itinerary

Departure *Date*

Time

Transportation

Arrival *Date*   *Time*

Departure *Date*   *Time*

Transportation

Accommodations

Arrival *Date*   *Time*

Departure *Date*   *Time*

Transportation

Accommodations

Arrival *Date*   *Time*

Departure *Date*   *Time*

Transportation

Accommodations

Fodor's Travel Guides

Available at bookstores everywhere, or call 1–800–533–6478, 24 hours a day.

U.S. Guides

Alaska	Las Vegas, Reno, Tahoe	Philadelphia & the Pennsylvania Dutch Country	The Upper Great Lakes Region
Arizona	Los Angeles	The Rockies	USA
Boston	Maine, Vermont, New Hampshire	San Diego	Vacations in New York State
California	Maui	San Francisco	Vacations on the Jersey Shore
Cape Cod, Martha's Vineyard, Nantucket	Miami & the Keys	Santa Fe, Taos, Albuquerque	Virginia & Maryland
The Carolinas & the Georgia Coast	New England	Seattle & Vancouver	Waikiki
Chicago	New Orleans	The South	Walt Disney World and the Orlando Area
Colorado	New York City	The U.S. & British Virgin Islands	Washington, D.C.
Florida	Pacific North Coast		
Hawaii			

Foreign Guides

Acapulco, Ixtapa, Zihuatanejo	The Czech Republic & Slovakia	Japan	Provence & the Riviera
Australia & New Zealand	Eastern Europe	Kenya & Tanzania	Rome
Austria	Egypt	Korea	Russia & the Baltic Countries
The Bahamas	Euro Disney	London	Scandinavia
Baja & Mexico's Pacific Coast Resorts	Europe	Madrid & Barcelona	Scotland
Barbados	Europe's Great Cities	Mexico	Singapore
Berlin	Florence & Tuscany	Montreal & Quebec City	South America
Bermuda	France	Morocco	Southeast Asia
Brazil	Germany	Moscow & St. Petersburg	Spain
Brittany & Normandy	Great Britain	The Netherlands, Belgium & Luxembourg	Sweden
Budapest	Greece	New Zealand	Switzerland
Canada	The Himalayan Countries	Norway	Thailand
Cancun, Cozumel, Yucatan Peninsula	Hong Kong	Nova Scotia, Prince Edward Island & New Brunswick	Tokyo
Caribbean	India	Paris	Toronto
China	Ireland	Portugal	Turkey
Costa Rica, Belize, Guatemala	Israel		Vienna & the Danube Valley
	Italy		Yugoslavia

WHEREVER YOU TRAVEL, *H*ELP IS NEVER FAR AWAY.

From planning your trip to replacing
lost Cards, American Express® Travel Service
Offices* are always there to help.

PARIS

11 Rue Scribe
1-47-777-707

38 Avenue de Wagram
1-42-275-880

5 Rue de Chaillot
1-47-237-215

155 Avenue Victor Hugo
1-47-274-319

83 Bis, Rue de Courcelles
1-47-660-300

Euro Disney®
Disneyland Hotel
Marne la Vallée
1-60-456-520

American Express Travel Service Offices are found in
central locations throughout Paris.

INTRODUCING

Fodor's
WORLDVIEW
TRAVEL UPDATE

**AT LAST, YOUR OWN PERSONALIZED
LIST OF WHAT'S GOING ON IN THE
CITIES YOU'RE VISITING.**

**KEYED TO THE DAYS WHEN YOU'RE
THERE, CUSTOMIZED FOR YOUR
INTERESTS, AND SENT TO YOU
BEFORE YOU LEAVE HOME.**

**EXCLUSIVE FOR PURCHASERS OF
FODOR'S GUIDES...**

Fodor's WORLDVIEW
TRAVEL UPDATE

Introducing a revolutionary way to get customized, time-sensitive travel information just before your trip.

Now you can obtain detailed information about what's going on in each city you'll be visiting <u>before</u> you leave home—up-to-the-minute, objective information about the events and activities that interest you most.

This is a special offer for purchasers of Fodor's guides – a customized Travel Update to fit your specific interests and your itinerary.

Travel Updates contain the kind of time-sensitive insider information you can get only from local contacts – or from city magazines and newspapers once you arrive. But now you can have the same information before you leave for your trip.

The choice is yours: current art exhibits, theater, music festivals and special concerts, sporting events, antiques and flower shows, shopping, fitness, and more.

The information comes from hundreds of correspondents and thousands of sources worldwide. Updated continuously, it's like having your own personal concierge or friend in the city.

You specify the cities and when you'll be there. We'll do the rest — personalizing the information for you the way no guidebook can.

It's the perfect extension to your Fodor's guide and the best way to make the most of your valuable travel time.

Your Itinerary:
Customized reports available for 160 destinations

to
99(
Regen
The ar
in this
domain o
tion as Joe
worthwhile.
the performan
Tickets are usua
venue. Alternat
mances are cancell
given. For more info
Open-Air Theatre, Inne
NW1 4NP Open Air T
Tel: 935-5756. Ends: 9-11.
International Air Tattoo
Held biennially, the world
military air display i
demostra-
tions, milit
band

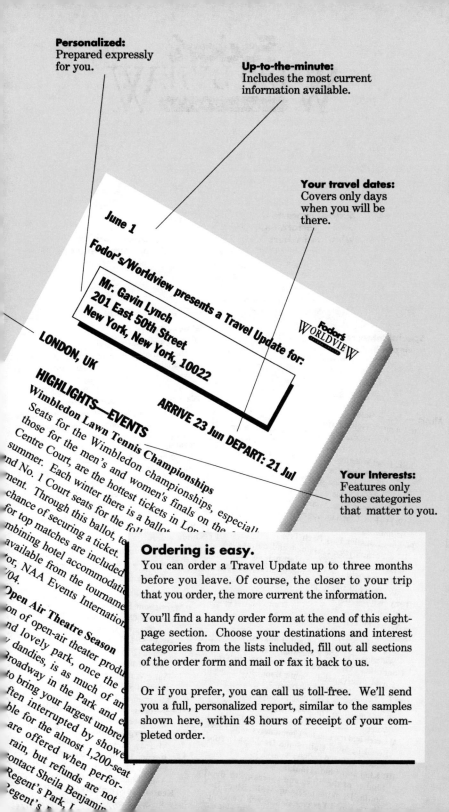

Personalized:
Prepared expressly
for you.

Up-to-the-minute:
Includes the most current
information available.

Your travel dates:
Covers only days
when you will be
there.

June 1

Fodor's/Worldview presents a Travel Update for:

Mr. Gavin Lynch
201 East 50th Street
New York, New York, 10022

Fodor's
WORLDVIEW

LONDON, UK

ARRIVE 23 Jun DEPART: 21 Jul

HIGHLIGHTS—EVENTS

Wimbledon Lawn Tennis Championships

Seats for the Wimbledon championships, especiall
those for the men's and women's finals on the
Centre Court, are the hottest tickets in Lon
summer. Each winter there is a ballo
nd No. 1 Court seats for the foll
ment. Through this ballot, te
chance of securing a ticket.
for top matches are included
mbining hotel accommodati
available from the tourname
or, NAA Events Internation
/04.

Open Air Theatre Season
on of open-air theater produ
nd lovely park, once the
y dandies, is as much of an
roadway in the Park and e
to bring your largest umbre
ften interrupted by showe
ble for the almost 1,200-seat
are offered when perfor-
rain, but refunds are not
ontact Sheila Benjamin
Regent's Park, I
egent's

Your Interests:
Features only
those categories
that matter to you.

Ordering is easy.

You can order a Travel Update up to three months
before you leave. Of course, the closer to your trip
that you order, the more current the information.

You'll find a handy order form at the end of this eight-
page section. Choose your destinations and interest
categories from the lists included, fill out all sections
of the order form and mail or fax it back to us.

Or if you prefer, you can call us toll-free. We'll send
you a full, personalized report, similar to the samples
shown here, within 48 hours of receipt of your completed order.

**Special interest,
in-depth listings**

**Special concerts—
who's performing
what and where**

**One-of-a-kind,
one-time-only events**

Music — Jazz & Blues

Tito Puente's Golden Men of Latin Jazz
The father of mambo and Cuban rumba king comes to town. Royal Festival Hall. South Bank. SE1. Tube: Waterloo. Tel: 928 8800. 8pm. 7/15.

Georgie Fame and The New York Band
Riding a popular tide with his latest album, the smoky-voiced Fame and his keyboard are on a tour yet again. The Grand. Clapham Junction. SW11. BR: Clapham Junction. Tel: 738 9000. 7:30pm. 7/07.

Jacques Loussier Play Bach Trio
The French jazz classicist and colleagues. Kenwood Lakeside. Hampstead Lane. Kenwood. NW3. Tube: Golders Green, then bus 210. Tel: 413 1443. 7pm. 7/10.

Tony Bennett and Ronnie Scott
Royal Festival Hall. South Bank. SE1. Tube: Waterloo. Tel: 928 8800. 8pm. 7/11.

Santana
Royal Festival Hall. South Bank. SE1. Tube: Waterloo. Tel: 928 8800. 8pm. 7/12.

Count Basie Orchestra and Nancy Wilson Trio
Royal Festival Hall. South Bank. SE1. Tube: Waterloo. Tel: 928 8800. 8pm. 7/14.

King Pleasure and the Biscuit Boys
Royal Festival Hall. South Bank. SE1. Tube: Waterloo. Tel: 928 8800. 6:30 and 9pm. 7/16.

Al Green and the London Community Gospel Choir
Royal Festival Hall. South Bank. SE1. Tube: Waterloo. Tel: 928 8800. 8pm. 7/13.

BB King and Linda Hopkins
Mother of the blues and successor to Bessie Smith, Hopkins meets up with "Blues Boy" King. Royal Festival Hall. South Bank. SE1. 6:30 and 9pm

Children — Events

Angel Canal Festival
The festivities include a children's funfair, entertainers, a boat rally and displays on the water. Regent's Canal. Islington. N1. Tube: Angel. Tel: 267 9100. 11:30am-5:30pm. 7/04.

Blackheath Summer Kite Festival
Stunt kite displays with parachuting teddy bears and trade stands. Free admission. SE3. BR: Blackheath. 10am. 6/27.

Megabugs
Children will delight in this infestation of giant robotic insects, including a praying mantic 60 times life size. Mon-Sat 10am-6pm; Sun 11am-6pm. Admission 4.50 pounds. Natural History Museum, Cromwell Road. SW7. Tube: South Kensington. Tel: 938 9123. Ends 10/01.

Childminders
This establishment employs only women, providing nurses and qualified nannies to

Music — Classical

Marylebone Sinfonia
Kenneth Gowen conducts music by Puccini and Rossini. Queen Elizabeth Hall. South Bank. SE1. Tube: Waterloo. Tel: 928 8800. 7:45pm. 7/16.

London Philharmonic
Franz Welser-Moest and George Benjamin conduct selections by Alexander Goehr, Messiaen, and some of Benjamin's own compositions. Queen Elizabeth Hall. South Bank. SE1. Tube: Waterloo. Tel: 928 8800. 8pm.

London Pro Arte Orchestra and Forest Choir
Murray Stewart conducts selections by Rossini, Haydn and Jonathan Willcocks. Queen Elizabeth Hall. South Bank. SE1. Tube: Waterloo. Tel: 928 8800. 7:45pm. 7/17.

Kensington Symphony Orchestra
Russell Keable conducts Dvorak's Dream

Here's what you get . . .

Detailed information about what's going on — precisely when you'll be there.

Show openings during your visit

Reviews by local critics

Exhibitions & Shows—Antique & Flower

Westminster Antiques Fair

Over 50 stands with pre-1830 furniture and other Victorian and earlier items. Thu-Fri 11am-8pm; Sat-Sun 11am-6pm. Admission 4 pounds, children free. Old Royal Horticultural Hall. Vincent Square. SW1. Tel: 0444/48 25 14. 6-24 thru 6/27.

Royal Horticultural Society Flower Show

The show includes displays of carnations, summer fruit and vegetables. Tue 11am-7pm; Wed 10am-5pm. Admission Tue 4 pounds, Wed 2 pounds. Royal Horticultural Halls. Greycoat Street and Vincent Square. SW1. Tube: Victoria. 7/20 thru 7/21.

...mpton Court Palace International Flower Show

Major international garden and flower show ...king place in conjunction with the British

Theater — Musical

Sunset Boulevard

In June, the four Andrew Lloyd Webber musicals which dominated London's stages in the 1980s (Cats, Starlight Express, Phantom of the Opera and Aspects of Love) are joined by the composer's latest work, a show rumored to have his best music to date. The 1950 Billy Wilder film about a helpless young writer who is drawn into the world of a possessive, aging silent screen star offers rich opportunities for Webber's evolving style. Soaring, aching melodies, lush technical effects and psychological thrills are all expected. Patti Lupone stars. Mon-Sat at 8pm; matinee Thu-Sat at 3pm. In-person sales only at the box office; credit card bookings, Tel: 344 0055. Admission 15-32.50 pounds. Adelphi Theatre. The Strand. WC2. Tube: Charing Cross. Tel: 836 7611. Starts: 6/21

Leonardo A Portrait of Love

A new musical about the great Renaissance arti... and inventor comes in for a London premier... tested by a brief run at Oxford's Old Fire Stati... ...autumn. The work explores the relations... ...Vinci and the woman '...

Spectator Sports — Other Sports

Greyhound Racing: Wembley Stadium

This dog track offers good views of greyhound racing held on Mon, Wed and Fri. No credit cards. Stadium Way. Wembley. HA9. Tube: Wembley Park. Tel: 902 8833.

Benson & Hedges Cricket Cup Final

Lord's Cricket Ground. St. John's Wood Road. NW8. Tube: St. John's Wood. Tel: 289 1611. 11am. 7/10.

Business-Fax & Overnight Mail

Post Office, Trafalgar Square Branch

Offers a network of fax services, the Intelpost system, throughout the country and abroad. Mon-Sat 8am-8pm, Sun 9am-5pm. William IV Street. WC2. Tube: Charing Cross. Tel: 930 95...

Alberquerque • Atlanta • Atlantic City • Ne...
Baltimore • Boston • Chicago • Cincinnati
Cleveland • Dallas/Ft.Worth • Denver • De...
• Houston • Kansas City • Las Vegas • Los
Angeles • Memphis • Miami • Milwaukee •
New Orleans • New York City • Orlando •
Springs • Philadelphia • Phoenix • Pittsbur...
Portland • Salt Lake • San Antonio • San Di...
San Franc... • Seattle • St Louis • Tamp...
Oslo • Wash... • Island •
Hawaii • Kauai • Maui • Abacos • Bimini •
Ex... • Countryside • Hamilton • ...lar...
Antigua & B... • ...vis • Torto...
...Gorda • Barbados • Dominica • Gren...
...cia • St. Vincent • Trinidad &Tobago
...ymans • Puerto Plata • Santo Doming...
Aruba • Bonaire • Curacao • St. Ma...
...ec City • Monterrey • Montreal • Ottawa • Toron...
Vancouver • Guadeloupe • Martiniqu...
...nelemy • St. Martin • Kingston • Ixta...
...o Bay • Negril • Ocho Rios • Ponce •
...n • Grand Turk • Providenciales • S...
St. John • St. Thomas • Acapulco •
& Isla Mujeres • Cozumel • Guadal...
...a • Los Cabos • Manzinillo • Mazatl...
City • Monterrey • Oaxaca • Puerto
...do • Puerto Vallarta • Veracruz • Ix...
...dam • Athens • Barcelona • B...

Fodor's WORLDVIEW TRAVEL UPDATE

Interest Categories

For <u>your</u> personalized Travel Update, choose the categories you're most interested in from this list. Every Travel Update automatically provides you with *Event Highlights* – the best of what's happening during the dates of your trip.

1.	**Business Services**	Fax & Overnight Mail, Computer Rentals, Photocopying, Secretarial , Messenger, Translation Services

Dining

2.	**All Day Dining**	Breakfast & Brunch, Cafes & Tea Rooms, Late-Night Dining
3.	**Local Cuisine**	In Every Price Range—from Budget Restaurants to the Special Splurge
4.	**European Cuisine**	Continental, French, Italian
5.	**Asian Cuisine**	Chinese, Far Eastern, Japanese, Indian
6.	**Americas Cuisine**	American, Mexican & Latin
7.	**Nightlife**	Bars, Dance Clubs, Comedy Clubs, Pubs & Beer Halls
8.	**Entertainment**	Theater—Drama, Musicals, Dance, Ticket Agencies
9.	**Music**	Classical, Traditional & Ethnic, Jazz & Blues, Pop, Rock
10.	**Children's Activities**	Events, Attractions
11.	**Tours**	Local Tours, Day Trips, Overnight Excursions, Cruises
12.	**Exhibitions, Festivals & Shows**	Antiques & Flower, History & Cultural, Art Exhibitions, Fairs & Craft Shows, Music & Art Festivals
13.	**Shopping**	Districts & Malls, Markets, Regional Specialities
14.	**Fitness**	Bicycling, Health Clubs, Hiking, Jogging
15.	**Recreational Sports**	Boating/Sailing, Fishing, Ice Skating, Skiing, Snorkeling/Scuba, Swimming
16.	**Spectator Sports**	Auto Racing, Baseball, Basketball, Football, Horse Racing, Ice Hockey, Soccer

Please note that interest category content will vary by season, destination, and length of stay.

Destinations

The Fodor's/Worldview Travel Update covers more than 160 destinations worldwide. Choose the destinations that match your itinerary from this list. (Choose
bulleted destinations only.)

**United States
(Mainland)**
- Albuquerque
- Atlanta
- Atlantic City
- Baltimore
- Boston
- Chicago
- Cincinnati
- Cleveland
- Dallas/Ft.
  Worth
- Denver
- Detroit
- Houston
- Kansas City
- Las Vegas
- Los Angeles
- Memphis
- Miami
- Milwaukee
- Minneapolis/
  St. Paul
- New Orleans
- New York City
- Orlando
- Palm Springs
- Philadelphia
- Phoenix
- Pittsburgh
- Portland
- St. Louis
- Salt Lake City
- San Antonio
- San Diego
- San Francisco
- Seattle
- Tampa
- Washington,
  DC

Alaska
- Anchorage/Fair-
  banks/Juneau

Hawaii
- Honolulu
- Island of Hawaii
- Kauai
- Maui

Canada
- Quebec City

- Montreal
- Ottawa
- Toronto
- Vancouver

Bahamas
- Abacos
- Eleuthera/
  Harbour Island
- Exumas
- Freeport
- Nassau &
  Paradise Island

Bermuda
- Bermuda
  Countryside
- Hamilton

**British
Leeward
Islands**
- Anguilla
- Antigua &
  Barbuda
- Montserrat
- St. Kitts &
  Nevis

**British Virgin
Islands**
- Tortola &
  Virgin Gorda

**British
Windward
Islands**
- Barbados
- Dominica
- Grenada
- St. Lucia
- St. Vincent
- Trinidad &
  Tobago

Cayman Islands
- The Caymans

**Dominican
Republic**
- Puerto Plata
- Santo Domingo

**Dutch Leeward
Islands**
- Aruba
- Bonaire
- Curacao

**Dutch Windward
Islands**
- St. Maarten

**French West
Indies**
- Guadeloupe
- Martinique
- St. Barthelemy
- St. Martin

Jamaica
- Kingston
- Montego Bay
- Negril
- Ocho Rios

Puerto Rico
- Ponce
- San Juan

Turks & Caicos
- Grand Turk
- Providenciales

**U.S. Virgin
Islands**
- St. Croix
- St. John
- St. Thomas

Mexico
- Acapulco
- Cancun &
  Isla Mujeres
- Cozumel
- Guadalajara
- Ixtapa &
  Zihuatanejo
- Los Cabos
- Manzanillo
- Mazatlan
- Mexico City
- Monterrey
- Oaxaca
- Puerto
  Escondido
- Puerto Vallarta
- Veracruz

Europe
- Amsterdam
- Athens
- Barcelona
- Berlin
- Brussels
- Budapest
- Copenhagen

- Dublin
- Edinburgh
- Florence
- Frankfurt
- French Riviera
- Geneva
- Glasgow
- Interlaken
- Istanbul
- Lausanne
- Lisbon
- London
- Madrid
- Milan
- Moscow
- Munich
- Oslo
- Paris
- Prague
- Provence
- Rome
- Salzburg
- St. Petersburg
- Stockholm
- Venice
- Vienna
- Zurich

**Pacific Rim
Australia &
New Zealand**
- Auckland
- Melbourne
- Sydney

China
- Beijing
- Guangzhou
- Shanghai

Japan
- Kyoto
- Nagoya
- Osaka
- Tokyo
- Yokohama

Other
- Bangkok
- Hong Kong &
  Macau
- Manila
- Seoul
- Singapore
- Taipei

Fodor's WORLDVIEW
Order Form

THIS TRAVEL UPDATE IS FOR (Please print):

Name _____

Address _____

City	State	ZIP

Country	Tel # ( ) -

Title of this Fodor's guide: _____

Store and location where guide was purchased: _____

INDICATE YOUR DESTINATIONS/DATES: Write in below the destinations you want to order. Then fill in your arrival and departure dates for each destination.

		Month	Day		Month	Day
(Sample) LONDON	From:	6 /	21	To:	6 /	30
1	From:	/		To:	/	
2	From:	/		To:	/	
3	From:	/		To:	/	

You can order up to three destinations per Travel Update. Only destinations listed on the previous page are applicable. Maximum amount of time covered by a Travel Update cannot exceed 30 days.

CHOOSE YOUR INTERESTS: Select up to eight categories from the list of interest categories shown on the previous page and circle the numbers below:

1 2 3 4 5 6 7 8 9 10 11 12 13 14 15 16

CHOOSE HOW YOU WANT YOUR TRAVEL UPDATE DELIVERED (Check one):

❏ Please mail my Travel Update to the address above **OR**

❏ Fax it to me at **Fax #** ( ) - _____

DELIVERY CHARGE (Check one)

	Within U.S. & Canada	Outside U.S. & Canada
First Class Mail	❏ $2.50	❏ $5.00
Fax	❏ $5.00	❏ $10.00
Priority Delivery	❏ $15.00	❏ $27.00

All orders will be sent within 48 hours of receipt of a completed order form.

ADD UP YOUR ORDER HERE. *SPECIAL OFFER FOR FODOR'S PURCHASERS ONLY!*

	Suggested Retail Price	Your Price	This Order
First destination ordered	$13.95	$ 7.95	$ 7.95
Second destination (if applicable)	$ 9.95	$ 4.95	+
Third destination (if applicable)	$ 9.95	$ 4.95	+
Plus delivery charge from above			+
		TOTAL:	$

METHOD OF PAYMENT (Check one): ❏ AmEx ❏ MC ❏ Visa ❏ Discover
❏ Personal Check ❏ Money Order

Make check or money order payable to: Fodor's Worldview Travel Update

Credit Card # _____ **Expiration Date:** _____

Authorized Signature _____

SEND THIS COMPLETED FORM TO:
Fodor's Worldview Travel Update, 114 Sansome Street, Suite 700, San Francisco, CA 94104

OR CALL OR FAX US 24-HOURS A DAY
Telephone **1-800-799-9609** • Fax **1-800-799-9619** (From within the U.S. & Canada)

(Outside the U.S. & Canada: Telephone 415-616-9988 • Fax 415-616-9989)

(Please have this guide in front of you when you call so we can verify purchase.)

Offer valid until 12/31/94.